AF716499

Matthew Hoe is a solicitor and advocate, and director of dispute resolution at national firm Taylor Rose TTKW. He has specialised in legal costs for almost 17 years. He has acted in some of the major costs cases of the last decade, including most recently cases such as *Bamrah v Gempride* on misconduct in assessment proceedings, *Hislop v Perde* on late Part 36 acceptance in fixed costs cases, *Cham v Aldred* on counsel's fees in fixed costs cases and *Adelekun v Ho* on contracting out of fixed costs. Outside of work, Matthew watches far too much YouTube and enjoys fixing broken electronics and general tinkering with computers. He lives with his family near Peterborough.

A Practical Guide to Costs in Personal Injury Claims

2nd edition

A Practical Guide to Costs in Personal Injury Claims

2nd edition

Matthew Hoe

MA Cantab

Solicitor Advocate (Higher Rights Civil Proceedings)

Law Brief Publishing

© Matthew Hoe

All rights reserved. No part of this publication may be reproduced, stored in a retrieval system, or transmitted, in any form or by any means, electronic, mechanical, photocopying, recording or otherwise, without the prior permission of the publisher.

Excerpts from judgments and statutes are Crown copyright. Any Crown Copyright material is reproduced with the permission of the Controller of OPSI and the Queen's Printer for Scotland. Some quotations may be licensed under the terms of the Open Government Licence (http://www.nationalarchives.gov.uk/doc/open-government-licence/version/3).

Cover image © iStockphoto.com/Ruslan Danyliuk

The information in this book was believed to be correct at the time of writing and is up-to-date to 7th August 2020. All content is for information purposes only and is not intended as legal advice. No liability is accepted by either the publisher or author for any errors or omissions (whether negligent or not) that it may contain. Professional advice should always be obtained before applying any information to particular circumstances.

Published 2020 by
Law Brief Publishing
30 The Parks
Minehead
Somerset
TA24 8BT

www.lawbriefpublishing.com

Paperback: ISBN 978-1-913715-37-3

PREFACE

Before the first edition, my publisher asked me why I would want to write a book. My glib answer was 'so people stop asking me questions'. It got a chuckle – apparently it's the opposite of why lawyers usually write books – but I genuinely wanted to gather all the reference material into one place. This is meant to be a 'light' book compared to the handful of others on the market, so the focus became commonplace costs issues in personal injury claims. Solicitors, insurers – you shouldn't need to instruct a costs draftsman or negotiator, at least not for fixed costs cases. Help is at hand.

This book is written for anyone who wants to deal with costs without calling on expert help. I had in mind solicitors and the junior members of their in-house teams, insurers and their claims handlers, barristers, astute litigants in person and, dare I say it, judges. Costs are not as simple as they might be, and even with the expansion of fixed costs there is an array of possibilities.

This book is intended to be a practical guide to costs law and procedure that offers advice for common situations. It may reveal some 'trade secrets': arguments that a party may prefer the opponent overlooks. However, that equal footing may foster earlier settlements and save costs in the long run.

The book cites some binding senior courts cases. It often cites County Court decisions as well, not to suggest that they are binding, but because there is no higher authority and the decision seems to be sensible, (probably) right and helpful.

Finally, despite the lofty aims, this book cannot be the complete answer in itself. It's a supplement to reading and applying the rules. It's also not a book about the procedure of making claims, and it assumes some knowledge of that process – especially in terminology.

This book excludes the law and practice surroundings CFAs, success fees and ATEs. The law that built up in that area is substantial, but it is all now in run-off following the reforms under the Legal Aid, Sentencing and Punishment of Offenders Act 2012. Other books on costs dedicated many pages to that area, and leaving it out makes this book more manageable in size and focussed on the present law.

Inevitably the book does not deal with all remaining costs issues either. This second edition does now touch on costs budgeting, which just as at the time of the first edition is undergoing limited reform. But it is not a manual on how to draft a costs budget or a bill of costs.

This second edition has less cause to speculate about the correct approach because many more of the major points have now been decided. Costs litigation has calmed down. I felt it was possible to make this second edition more complete, and ultimately more helpful. The material has been substantially reorganised compared to the first edition, with the hope of making the relevant guidance easier to find.

Of course, it may just be the calm before the storm. Further reform is expected, beginning next year. The Government purportedly remains committing to expanding the fixed costs regime, but there is no set timetable. The expansion will bring new fixed costs scheme, and perhaps new problems. And perhaps a third edition.

Matthew Hoe
July 2020

ACKNOWLEDGEMENTS

I would not have been able to write this book without colleagues and clients who have brought to me and let me run with the cases I have learned from. Thank you. Thanks also to the barristers I work with, especially for telling me gently when I am wrong.

I am grateful to my publishers, Tim and Garry, for supporting this second edition. It has been a privilege to put it together and see it in print, and looking so good owing to their design work.

Thank you to Afton and Mallory who have supported me at home, Afton by making me get on with it, and Mallory for bringing the sunshine when I was stuck inside and for being such a good little sleeper when I was writing into the night.

I belatedly thank my Dad, now dearly departed, who tried valiantly to proof-read the first edition without understanding any of it.

CONTENTS

CHAPTER ONE
FIXED COSTS SCHEMES

Introduction to fixed costs

There are different types of fixed costs in the CPR.

There are *fixed costs*, where the amount is fixed for all claims falling within the category. There may be different tiers of fixed costs depending on the amount of damages or the stage reached in the case, but there is no maths involved. Small claims costs, portal costs and fast track trial costs are examples.

There are *fixed recoverable costs*, which are calculated with a formula based on damages. Predictable costs and CPR 45 Section IIIA costs are examples.

There are *capped costs*, where there is a prescribed upper limit. Costs of a provisional assessment are an example.

In personal injury claims, the applicable costs are unknown at the outset of the claim. Fixed costs or fixed recoverable costs may apply depending on what happens in the claim and it becomes clear by the conclusion of the claim.

It can be helpful to think of Part 45 as providing a fixed costs *regime* for these claims, comprising of several different schemes (which have been called 'regimes' in themselves, but this book does not do so). This chapter looks at the regime as a whole.

The intention of the fixed costs regime

In *Nizami v Butt* [2006] 1 WLR 3307, Simon J (as he then was) said at [23]:

> *It seems to me clear that the intention underlying CPR rr 45.7-45.14 was to provide an agreed scheme of recovery which was certain and*

> *easily calculated. This was done by providing fixed levels of remuneration which might over-reward in some cases and under-reward in others, but which were regarded as fair when taken as a whole.*

He was speaking about predictable costs, using the rule numberings at that time. What he said is also true of portal costs and Section IIIA costs which have arrived since.

Coulson LJ said in *Hislop v Perde* [2019] 1 WLR 201 at [50]:

> *The whole point of the regime is to ensure that both sides begin and end the proceedings with the expectation that fixed costs is all that will be recoverable. The regime provides certainty. It also ensures that, in low value claims, the costs which are incurred are proportionate. In addition, whatever the perceived injustice in any given case, the "swings and roundabouts" identified by Briggs LJ in* Sharp's *case [2017] 4 WLR 98 will still apply.*

'Certainty' is a policy reason for fixed costs; certainty is preferred to leaving scope for argument about costs. Costs has been criticised as a satellite industry and previously took up considerable court time. Fixing costs saves costly arguments about costs. 'Proportionality' is elusive, noticed mainly when it is absent. Fixed costs are not disproportionate. Fixed recoverable costs are by calculation proportionate to the damages.

'Swings and roundabouts' had already become the catchphrase of fixed costs law. The phrase recurs across the key judgments. *What you lose on the swings you make up on the roundabouts*. It is shorthand for *Nizami*'s fuller explanation of over-rewarding and under-rewarding. It is often the answer to any party who argues that a fixed recoverable costs result is not fair (no pun intended) in particular (but presumably not exceptional) circumstances.

<u>Getting the right fixed costs</u>

The first step is to decide which fixed costs scheme applies, if any. That is harder than it may sound. There is no one scheme for each claim type. The facts of the case decide which scheme applies and thus one needs some knowledge of the claim.

Usually, the successful claimant will seek to work out which scheme applies as a matter of procedural law and will present a claim for costs accordingly. The flow chart in the next section should assist.

The defendant will then vet the claim and decide whether to agree that scheme applies or to argue that as a matter of reasonableness or by one of the other means that the law allows, a less generous fixed costs scheme should be applied.

The different schemes

Predictable costs under CPR 45 Section II apply to RTA claims which do not belong in the RTA Protocol or exit it where the CNF pre-dates 31 July 2013, and which settle under the Personal Injury Pre-Action Protocol for damages between £1,000 and £10,000. This is the oldest scheme, beginning in 2003.

Portal costs in CPR 45 Section III apply to RTA, EL, PL and ELD claims which settle under the relevant Protocol. This scheme began in 2010. They are also known as Protocol costs or, more colloquially, as 'MOJ Costs' – because the scheme was brought in as a result of stakeholders talks facilitated by the Ministry.

Section IIIA costs apply to claims which start under the RTA Protocol after 31 July 2013 or the EL/PL Protocol but exit that Protocol before settlement (except for EL Disease claims), and also to claims under the Pre-Action Protocol for Resolution of Package Travel Claims. This scheme began in 2013. They are also known as 'Ex-Protocol costs'.

Small claims fixed costs apply to Part 7 claims allocated to that track. They have been in the CPR since the beginning. The amounts are in CPR 45 Section I. Claims with a value below the small claims threshold which settle after exiting or which never even start under the RTA or EL/PL Protocol and which are not allocated to the small claims track may be argued to be subject to small claims costs per CPR 46.13(3).

Fixed fast track trial costs apply to costs of the trial advocacy and attendance in claims allocated to the fast track which are not otherwise subject to any fixed costs.

'Apply' is used in a loose sense in those descriptions; a right to costs is not usually automatic.

Fixed costs flow chart – which scheme applies

The flowchart will be right in about 99% of claims, but there will always be aberrations.

In order to work out conclusively which fixed costs scheme applies you will need to know: the type of claim, the accident date, any CNF date, the amount of damages and whether Part 7 proceedings were started.

There are all sorts of complications that may alter the result. It is important to know whether a claim should have started under one or other of the RTA, EL/PL or Package Travel Protocols. The amount of damages can affect things. All those complications are covered in subsequent sections.

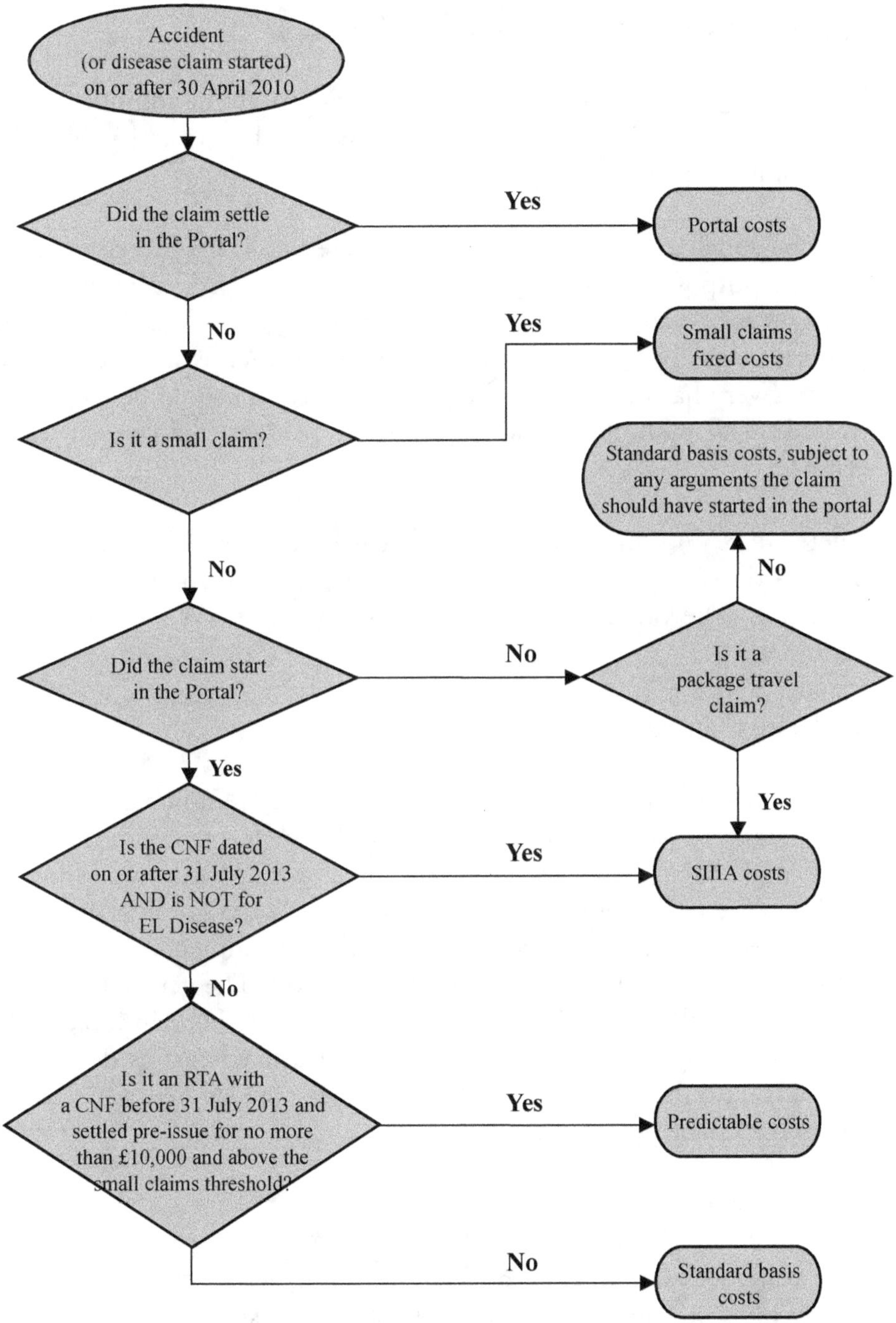
Accident
(or disease claim started)
on or after 30 April 2010
Did the claim settle
in the Portal?
Yes
Portal costs
No
Yes
Small claims
fixed costs
Is it a small claim?
Standard basis costs, subject to
any arguments the claim
should have started in the portal
No
No
No
Did the claim start
in the Portal?
Is it a
package travel
claim?
Yes
Yes
Is the CNF dated
on or after 31 July 2013
AND is NOT for
EL Disease?
Yes
SIIIA costs
No
Is it an RTA with
a CNF before 31 July 2013 and
settled pre-issue for no more
than £10,000 and above the
small claims threshold?
Yes
Predictable costs
No
Standard basis
costs

Adjustments which apply to all fixed costs schemes

VAT on fixed costs and fixed recoverable costs

VAT on costs is recoverable from the paying party in addition, where applicable. The rules for portal costs, post portal costs and predictable costs all make provision for it.

In a personal injury claim the claimant, even if VAT registered for business purposes, is unlikely to be able to recover VAT as input tax on damages for personal injury. If there is a subrogated claim for business losses it might be argued that a proportion of VAT is not recoverable, but it is very hard to decide what that proportion should be so VAT is treated as all or nothing and is ordinarily paid on the costs in those claims.

There is no VAT in small claims. That is by concession from HMRC, but the decisive point is that there is no provision for it in CPR 45 Section I. The other fixed costs rules state where VAT is payable in addition.

VAT rate changes

PD44 2.8 sets out a presumption that where the VAT rate changes, the receiving party will take advantage of a right to elect to claim the lower VAT rate. PD44 2.9 says that bills must be divided into different sections where different VAT rates apply. Fixed costs fall into the 'lump sum' exception also described by PD44 2.9. It is impractical to attempt splitting fixed costs between different VAT rates. The general approach is 'as the axe falls'. The VAT rate applied is the VAT rate in force at the time the damages claim settled. VAT is not a fixed cost as defined by the CPR, and therefore must be for assessment (where needed), and the test of reasonableness will apply.

London weighting

Everything costs more in London, including legal services. Lawyers' hourly rates in London are higher. To achieve a similar effect for fixed costs under CPR 45 Section III and fixed recoverable costs under CPR

45 Sections II and IIIA, the costs are uprated by 12.5%. It is called 'London weighting' in the CPR.

To qualify for it, the solicitor must practise in London, and the client must live or work in London – such that it would be reasonable to instruct a London lawyer.

London is defined by PD45 2.6 as 'the area served by':

(within London) the County Court hearing centres at	• Barnet • Brentford • Central London • Clerkenwell and Shoreditch • Edmonton • Ilford • Mayors and City of London • Romford • Wandsworth • West London (now Hammersmith) • Willesden
(outside London) the County Court hearing centres at	• Bromley • Croydon • Dartford • Gravesend • Uxbridge

Bow, Lambeth, West London (which became Hammersmith) and Woolwich have fallen off the list as those hearing centres have closed.

Applying London weighting requires a map. Find the locations of the solicitor's office and where the claimant lives or works, and check if the nearest County Court hearing centre is one on the list. Other hearing centres in the London area are at:

- Guildford
- Kingston Upon Thames
- Slough
- Staines
- Watford

If one of those is the nearest hearing centre, London weighting won't apply.

A useful but not completely accurate guide is whether the claimant and solicitor are within the M25. It is not quite accurate as some areas to the western edge are not covered, and some areas across the eastern loop are. Online maps can be invaluable here.

A solicitor's firm might argue that it can have the 12.5% when it has a London office, even though the work on the claim was done in a regional office. The defendant is likely to say that the solicitor doing the work must practise in London to qualify for the 12.5%. There are no cases on the point, but a purposive approach is likely to favour the latter.

The trick known as 'post-boxing', where a solicitor's postal address is a London PO Box to give the impression that he practises in London when in fact he does not, is both a sharp practice and insufficient to create a right to the 12.5%. Thankfully it is very rarely encountered.

The workings of each fixed costs scheme

Small claims fixed commencement costs

The small claims track is the normal track for a claim worth no more than £10,000 in which the personal injury head of claim is worth no more than £1,000.

Fixed commencement costs apply to claims allocated to the small claims track. They may also apply if they are stated on the claim form and the claim is settled promptly, within 14 days of service. 'Commencement' means the commencement of Part 7 proceedings. These fixed costs are not payable if there are no proceedings. The fixed commencement costs notionally cover the work by a legal representative. They are very low. The amounts are set out in Table 1 of Part 45:

Fixed costs on commencement of a claim for the recovery of money or goods			
Relevant band	Where the claim form is served by the court or by any method other than personal service by the claimant	Where – • the claim form is served personally by the claimant; and • there is only one defendant	Where there is more than one defendant, for each additional defendant personally served at separate addresses by the claimant
Where – • the value of the claim exceeds £25 but does not exceed £500	£50	£60	£15
Where – • the value of the claim exceeds £500 but does not exceed £1,000	£70	£80	£15
Where – • the value of the claim exceeds £1,000 but does not exceed £5,000; or • the only claim is for delivery of goods and no value is specified or stated on the claim form	£80	£90	£15
Where – • the value of the claim exceeds £5,000	£100	£110	£15

Source: CPR 45 Table 1

By concession of HMRC, no VAT applies to small claims fixed costs. The sums in Table 1 are all that are payable for the legal representative's work. There is no provision that VAT applies in addition.

Additional costs are allowed in limited circumstances. An additional amount up to £260 (per PD27 7.2) is payable for legal advice and assistance in proceedings which include a claim for an injunction or an order for specific performance: CPR 27.14(2)(b).

If there are no proceedings, there are no fixed commencement costs. The legal representative would recover nothing for his work. If he was to be paid at all, the fees would be paid by the client. In reality, the client will be paying the solicitor for his time even where fixed commencement costs are recovered. The modest damages likely in a small claim may not cover the solicitor's costs. These provisions generally discourage litigants from instructing solicitors in small claims and solicitors from taking on small claims.

Applicability of small claims fixed costs

Small claims costs apply as a matter of procedural law to claims that have been allocated to the small claims track. They also extend to appeals on the small claims track: *Akhtar v Boland* [2014] EWCA Civ 943.

If the fixed commencement costs are stated in a claim form and the claim is paid within 14 days of service of the particulars of claim on the defendant, the defendant is liable only for the fixed commencement costs unless the court orders otherwise: CPR 45.3.

They do not apply automatically to other claims that settle before allocation. However, CPR 46.13(3) allows the court to limit costs to small claims costs in the course of an assessment on the standard basis (i.e. the court cannot do it when assessing costs on the indemnity basis) if that was the track to which the claim would have been allocated.

That rule in part codifies *O'Beirne v Hudson* [2010] 1 WLR 1717, which said that the court should give 'anxious scrutiny' to see whether costs were reasonably and necessarily incurred and whether it is reasonable for the paying party to pay more than would have been recoverable in a claim which would have been allocated to the small claims track. That 'anxious scrutiny' test proved desperately hard to apply in practice, with district judges unsure what qualities they were looking for in the costs and reluctant to disallow costs that would normally be allowed on the standard basis. CPR 46.13(3) is considerably simpler. If the court is satisfied that the claim would have been allocated to the small claims track, it can simply allow small claims costs without further ado.

It may not be obvious that the claim would have been allocated to the small claims track. At one end of the scale is a claim which obviously belonged in the small claims track. *Voice and Script International Ltd v Alghafar* [2003] EWCA Civ 736 is an example. Owing to claiming some items twice and currency errors, the value of the claim was artificially elevated. Once the duplication and conversion problem were eliminated, the value of the claim was below the small claims threshold. At the other end of the scale is the claim in which the defendant gets a good settlement, at a value below the small claims threshold. An example is *Randhawa v Hogan* (Senior Costs Judge Hurst, SCCO, 14 May 2012, unreported). The claimant presented a claim for vehicle hire charges above the small claims limit. He had an invoice for the sum, but after negotiations the sum agreed was less than the small claims threshold. The Senior Costs Judge did not find there had been exaggeration of the claim, and would not limit costs. Most claims lie between those extremes. Defendants considering running a CPR 46.13(3) point should look for a strong argument on the facts that the true value of the claim did not exceed the small claims threshold.

<u>Reallocation of small claims</u>

CPR 46.13(2) provides that where a claim has been allocated to one track and is then reallocated to another track, any special rules for costs applying to the first track apply down to the date of reallocation, and any special rules for the new track apply from the date of reallocation. CPR 27.15 duplicates that specifically for claims reallocated from the small claims track.

PD46 8.1 requires the court to decide whether either party must pay small claims fixed costs immediately when reallocating from that track. It is a strange provision because it also requires a summary assessment. The fixed costs will not require summary assessment, but perhaps some disbursements or any additional costs for unreasonable behaviour might (see 'The powers to allow more than small claims costs' in Chapter Three).

The court has the power to make a different order for costs on reallocation, as set out in the rule. For instance, if the claim is reallocated from the small claims track, the court may say small claims fixed costs will not apply to the period before reallocation. However, the court must make the order there and then. A party cannot return to the issue much later, for instance when it knows it has the costs of the case, and try to get a different order for the costs prior to reallocation: *Tibbles v SIG plc* [2012] 1 WLR 2591.

Bundling small claims

Where several claimants have claims arising from the same cause of action, they may include their claims in the same claim form. By that way, two or more small claims may be bundled together, or a small claim may be bundled with a fast track claim.

CPR 26.8(3) requires the court to consider each claimant's claim separately when considering financial value for allocation purposes. If bundled small claims are allocated to the fast track and the defendant would want to argue for small claims costs, it may be easier to achieve the result if the defendant successfully applies for reallocation rather than leaving the issue until the end.

If a small claim is bundled with a fast track claim, and the proceedings are allocated to the fast track, the claimant may argue that small claims fixed commencement costs do not apply. For the reasons given in Chapter 2, the mere fact of allocation cannot preclude a costs argument. But an underlying presumption of small claims costs is that a legal representative should not be required. It is a rule of procedure that co-claimants must have the same legal representative: *Lewis v Daily Telegraph (No. 2)* [1964] 2 QB 601. Therefore costs will inevitably be incurred. So while the defendant can argue for limitation to small claims costs, he may not succeed. Much may turn on how much in costs the small claim added. To avoid those arguments, defendants may be better served by reaching an agreement to exclude small claims from the proceedings and abide by the outcome of the fast track claim.

Predictable costs

These are fixed recoverable costs. There is just one formula but it is more simply expressed by putting it two ways:

- If the damages are no more than £5,000, costs are £800 plus 20% of the damages.
- If the damages are more than £5,000 but no more than £10,000, costs are £1,800 plus 15% of the balance of the damages in excess of £5,000.

This is the oldest scheme, bar small claims costs. It is helpful to review this scheme before others because the operation of Section II and the cases about it are instructive about the operation and interpretation of the fixed costs schemes that followed it. McCombe LJ said in *Cham* at [72]:

> *It seems to me that in matters affecting the proper construction and meaning of the CPR (as of any other enactment), it is impossible to approach the matter in discrete compartments. It is necessary to construe any such instrument as a whole. I do not think that comparisons between the wording of the various Sections of Part 45 of the Rules will always be avoidable. Nor do I think that such comparisons are unhelpful. It is necessary that the CPR and, even more so, particular Parts of them are approached and interpreted as a coherent whole. The fixed costs rules should not be allowed to hold within their various Sections different meanings for essentially similar words.*

Qualifying for predictable costs

The qualifying criteria are stated in CPR 45.9 and are broken down below. As so many RTA claims now start under the RTA Protocol and attract portal costs or Section IIIA costs, very few cases now fall under predictable costs.

Cham v Aldred [2020] 1 WLR 1276 identified at [17] that RTA claims by **protected parties** would fall under predictable costs. They will also apply also to claims started under the RTA Protocol **before 31 July 2013** which have exited, subject to the other conditions in CPR 45.9 being satisfied, or to other claims excluded from the RTA Protocol. Possibilities include claims in which the **portal's special definition of RTA is not satisfied** (see Chapter Two), claims against **non-road users**, claims involving a **foreign registered defendant vehicle** (as long as the accident happened in England & Wales), claims in which either party is a **personal representative** of a person involved in the accident, or claims in which the claimant is **bankrupt**. Still, that is a small fraction of claims.

In contrast to qualifying for Section IIIA costs (see below), the qualifying criteria for predictable costs in CPR 45 Section II which are set out in CPR 45.9 are much more complicated.

Predictable costs do not apply where portal costs or Section IIIA costs apply, or the claimant is a litigant in person: CPR 45.9(3).

Predictable costs are the costs to be allowed in costs-only proceedings under CPR 46.14 or approval proceedings under CPR 20.10(2): CPR 45.9(1). That requirement for a specific type of proceedings clashes with the understanding that predictable costs are for unlitigated cases. It can be explained. The substantive claim has finished before there are costs-only or approval proceedings, and in that sense the damages claim itself was unlitigated. Further, defendants do not usually require claimants to start the costs-only proceedings. That would just add extra costs. Instead, knowing the predictable costs will apply if proceedings are started, defendants pay them anyway. Approval proceedings on the other hand must be started, but again the expectation of what will be payable allows parties to agree the costs in advance of the approval hearing.

However, that expectation of what would be payable in costs-only proceedings does not mean that the defendant will always pay predictable costs. In the hey-day of predictable costs, claimants would often present a claim for predictable costs on the basis that the subsequent criteria in CPR 45.9(2) were fulfilled, forgetting the criteria in CPR 45.9(1). Assuming that it is not a claim requiring approval proceedings, it must be a claim in which costs-only proceedings are available. Pursuant to CPR 46.14(1)(a), costs-only proceedings are available only where 'the parties to a dispute have reached an agreement on all issues (including which party is to pay the costs) which is made or confirmed in writing'. An agreement confirmed by exchange of correspondence (see the general guidance in *Thomas v Home Office* [2007] 1 WLR 230 at [25]-[26]) or a Part 36 offer and acceptance (a Part 36 acceptance where there is no proceedings does not create a 'deemed order' for costs on the standard basis: CPR 44.9(2), codifying *Solomon v Cromwell* [2012] 1 WLR 1048 at [16]) would suffice. If the defendant has refused to pay costs, then costs-only proceedings are not available and predictable costs will not apply. Circumstances in which the defendant might reasonably do that are where the claim was for 'bent metal' only, i.e. vehicle damage, and the defendant's insurer is not persuaded the claim needed lawyers to become involved.

CPR 45.9(2) sets out the fact specific criteria. First, the claim must have arisen from a road traffic accident that occurred on or after 6 October 2003. Road traffic accident has a specific definition for the Section at CPR 45.9(4):

> *'road traffic accident' means an accident resulting in bodily injury to any person or damage to property caused by, or arising out of, the use of a motor vehicle on a road or other public place in England and Wales.*

The claimant does not have to be the one injured; it can be any person. The property does not need to be the claimant's; it can be anyone's. (For more on this definition, see the sections 'Differing definitions of RTA' and 'Use of a vehicle' in Chapter Two.)

Second under CPR 45.9(2), the agreed damages must include damages in respect of personal injury or damage to property (or both). So although the definition of road traffic accident is broader, the second criterion makes it personal to the claimant. His claim must include his own personal injury or damaged property.

The definition of road traffic accident and that criterion mean that claims which do not include personal injury or damage to property are outside the scope of predictable costs. Claims for hire charges only are an example. Although they arise from damage to a vehicle rendering it unroadworthy, they are consequential losses rather than actual damage to property. If there is an agreement to pay costs in such a claim, it is likely to be as a small claim or on the standard basis instead. If there are other damages in addition to those for personal injury and damage to property, the claim can still fall within predictable costs and, subject to other factors covered in the next section, costs would be calculated on the grand total of damages.

Third under CPR 45.9(2), the total value of the agreed damages must not exceed £10,000. 'Agreed damages' here is generally held to be the net amount – the amount the claimant receives in hand – because of the explanation in the PD45 2.3: 'Fixed recoverable costs are to be calculated by reference to the amount of agreed damages which are payable to the receiving party. In calculating the amount of these damages… (c) where the parties have agreed an element of contributory negligence, the amount of damages attributed to that negligence must be deducted'.

PD45 2.2 deserves an honourable mention. It is sometimes read to mean that that £10,000 refers to the gross amount of the claim, because of a confusing reference to calculating the value of the claim for allocation purposes. 'The Section does not apply to disputes where the total agreed value of the damages is within the small claims limit or exceeds £10,000. Rule 26.8(2) sets out how the financial value of a claim is assessed for the purposes of allocation to track.' Value for allocation under CPR 26.8 is the gross not net value of the claim. However, the practice direction refers also to the small claims limit, and it seems the signpost is there for that purpose. It does not create two conflicting and unnecessarily confusing definitions of 'agreed damages' for the purposes of predictable costs. PD45 2.2 appears to be imperfectly worded and it also possibly conflicts with CPR 45.9(2)(d), the upcoming fourth criterion.

Fourth and finally, if a claim had been issued for the amount of the agreed damages, the small claims track would not have been the normal track for the claim. Broadly speaking, small claims are excluded. However, that is not quite what the rule says. (See the sections below 'Predictable costs and small claims' and 'Split liability and the small claims threshold'.)

Despite their narrow residual applicability, predictable costs should not be forgotten. Occasionally a claim will arise that does not seem to fit in the RTA or EL/PL Protocols. For instance, the claim in *Prescott v Trustees of the Pencarrow 2012 Maintenance Fund* (District Judge Richards, County Court at Plymouth, 12 June 2017, unreported). The claimant's car collided with a tree that fell on the road. The claim did not fall under the RTA Protocol as it excludes claims against non-road users. It did not fall under the EL/PL Protocol because it was a road traffic accident. The judge applied a purposive constructive to allow fixed costs, but on the face of the judgment predictable costs would have applied and would have given a substantially similar result.

<u>Predictable costs and MIB claims</u>

PD45 2.4 provides '*The Section* [Section II] *applies to cases which fall within the scope of the Uninsured Drivers Agreement dated 13 August 1999. The section does not apply to cases which fall within the scope of the Untraced Drivers Agreement dated 14 February 2003.*' Both agreements have been superseded (we now have the Uninsured Drivers' Agreement of 3 July 2015 and the Untraced Drivers' Agreement of 28 February 2017) but the practice direction has not been updated. But the position will remain the same; uninsured claims fall within scope, but untraced claims do not. There is no way to make predictable costs apply to untraced claims because CPR 45.9(1) explains that predictable costs apply in two types of proceedings, and there is no way to legitimately bring such proceedings in untraced claims.

<u>What damages should be included in the fixed recoverable costs calculation?</u>

Predictable costs in CPR 45.11 and Section IIIA costs in Part 45 Tables 6B, 6C and 6D set out simple formulas for the costs based on the amount of damages.

PD45 2.3 assists in defining damages for the purposes of predictable costs. 'Damages' includes general damages, special damages and interest, interim and final payments. It is the amount net of a deduction for contributory negligence. Any payment made under statute to a third party does not count (that practice direction is directed primarily at CRU charges).

There is no mirror provision for Section IIIA costs. That appears to be a drafting omission. It would be reasonable for parties and the court to adopt the same approach as for predictable costs.

The rules do not specify whether the solicitor has to have acted for the claimant in recovery of a particular head of loss for it to be included in the damages for the formula. That may be an issue where an insurer or hire care company recovers directly from the defendant's insurer. On the one hand, as the formula is by nature rough and ready, does it really matter? But on the other, as the costs are proportionately higher where damages are higher, is it right that a solicitor gets paid according to heads of loss that he did nothing to recover? Those questions have never been authoritatively answered but there are two helpful County Court circuit level decisions.

Swatton v Smithurst (Oxford County Court, 3 February 2005, unreported) favours limiting the heads of loss. HHJ Harris QC finished up with a memorable phrase:

> *The total value of the agreed damages with which the solicitors were concerned in the instant case was £1850, and it is on that figure that the costs entitlement should be paid. If this conclusion is correct it can be foreseen that some solicitors may endeavour to give themselves entitlement to greater levels of costs by modifying the terms of their retainers and by addressing themselves directly to car hire providers or insurers. This is one of the considerations behind Mr Bacon's "necessary and reasonable" test. I would only observe that of this happens the Court should be astute to the reality and not the form, and should be ready to intervene if it appears that costs are being claimed by masking the work of others behind a misleading solicitor's carapace.*

Judge Harris' last sentence is directed at some dishonesty on the part of the solicitor in passing off the work of non-employees as his own. It is not directed against the practice of the solicitor taking on the work. Predictable costs did have the effect of encouraging solicitors to get involved in the recovery of sums formerly recovered by insurers and credit hirers using in house teams. In some such claims there was no personal injury, and some liability insurers refused to agree to pay costs at all, with considerable success.

Byrne v Richwood (Liverpool County Court, 25 January 2008, unreported) considered the work taken on by the solicitor. The defendant argued that some heads of loss which the solicitor had recovered should be excluded from the predictable costs calculation because someone other than the solicitor, such as an insurer or credit hire company, could have recovered them. HHJ Stewart QC (as he then was) decided that there was nothing in the rules supporting that approach. The rules simply referred to 'damages'. It did not exclude damages that someone else could have recovered.

The general approach is to calculate costs by including in the damages any sum recovered by the solicitor and leaving out any not recovered by the solicitor. Attempts to claim predictable costs by including damages recovered on behalf of the claimant by others generally do not arise for the simple reason that if the solicitor was not involved, he does not know about the damages to include in his calculation.

The same approach should apply to Section IIIA costs.

Predictable costs and small claims

CPR 45.9(2)(d) provides that Section II applies where '*if a claim had been issued for the amount of the agreed damages, the small claims track would not have been the normal track for that claim.*' That is an obscure requirement.

Predictable costs apply in costs-only proceedings and approval proceedings, per CPR 45.9(1). Part 7 claims are out of scope. 'If a claim had been issued' refers to a notional Part 7 claim. To paraphrase, the rule is asking whether the amount of damages received in hand by the claimant means the normal track for the claim would be the small claims track, i.e. if it includes personal injury is that element less than £1,000, and generally is the value of the claim below £10,000.

Claims subject to the small claims exclusion are likely instead to be captured by CPR 46.13(3).

Split liability and the small claims threshold

Where the deduction from damages for contributory negligence or where a settlement after 'split liability' results in a net damages settlement below the small claims threshold it seems that predictable costs will no longer apply. The small claims threshold for a personal injury claim is presently £1,000.

For predictable costs, CPR 45.9(2)(d) provides: '*The Section applies where... if a claim had been issued for the amount of the agreed damages, the small claims track would not have been the normal track for that claim.*' That rule is not the most clearly drafted. It is asking whether the normal track for Part 7 proceedings for the amount of the damages that were paid in the end would be the small claims track. A definition of 'amount of agreed damages' must be supplied. There used to be a 'signpost' – a note in the CPR – to CPR 26.6 which explains the normal track for each claim, but that disappeared when the rules were renumbered on 1 April 2013 as a result of implementing the Jackson reforms. PD45 2.2 and 2.3 seem to provide the definition, but do not use those exact words. PD45 2.2 covers where Section II applies and 2.3 deals with what is included in damages for the purposes of the formula. It would make little sense if what constituted 'damages' for the purpose of working out whether the Section II applied differed from 'damages' for calculating the costs. So they are generally construed identically, and 2.3 excludes any amount for contributory negligence. That has led to decisions such as *Parveen v Farooq* (HHJ Stewart QC, Liverpool County Court, 30 June 2009, unreported) and *Lisbie v SKS Scaffolding* [2011] EWHC 90203 (Costs) which restrict a claimant's costs to small claims costs where the net damages are below the small claims limit.

The effect is that a claim for a sum exceeding the small claims threshold, say general damages of £1,500, would be excluded from predictable costs by this small claims exclusion if it settled on a 50/50 basis and the claimant received £750 in hand.

While it is easier to see why the Section does not apply where net damages are below the small claims threshold, it is harder to see why a leap should be made to applying small claims costs. Why would standard basis costs not apply? Some assistance may be derived from the reasoning of Patten LJ in *Dockerill v Tullett* [2012] 1 WLR 2092 at [45]. He was talking about children with small claims when construing the rule, but the principle could be extended to net settlements:

> *to apply a normal multi-track assessment of costs in all such cases seems to me to run contrary to the purpose of [CPR r 45.9(2)(d)] which must, in my view, have been intended to allow the court to apply a less generous regime to approval applications based on small claims. The predictive costs regime could have been applied to all cases involving claims of less than £10,000 but it was not.*

Thus a 'less generous' regime such as small claims costs may be reasonably applied.

Predictable costs and children

Predictable costs can apply to children's claims: CPR 21.10(3) and CPR 45.9(1)(b).

Part 21 sets out the procedure to obtain the court's approval of a settlement. While CPR 45 Section II applies in approval proceedings, it does make approval proceedings mandatory. Predictable costs also applied where the parties agreed to conclude by way of parental indemnity. It is not set out in the CPR, and instead is a contractual remedy. The parent or litigation friend confirms he or she will indemnify the defendant against a subsequent claim by the child for mis-settlement. Parental indemnity may be attractive to the solicitor in predictable costs cases and also Section IIIA costs cases, as neither scheme allows additional fixed costs for dealing with the approval. Still, parental indemnity appears usually in very low value claims, below the small claims threshold, where the amount of any indemnity if it ever arose would be very modest. Approval hearings are overwhelmingly more common.

There are two key principles for children's claims under predictable costs, both of which come from *Dockerill v Tullett* [2012] 1 WLR 2092.

First, there is no special rule for children's small claims that they are not subject to small claims costs, so CPR 45.9(2)(d) can exclude children's small claims from fixed recoverable costs. Their costs should be allowed on a less generous basis, perhaps with reference to the *O'Beirne* anxious scrutiny approach, but with reasonable allowance for the costs of obtaining court approval where sought. The court recognised that its decision might discourage solicitors from taking on children's small claims, but that did not affect the conclusion.

Second, coming from the case of *Tubridy v Sarwar* reported with *Dockerill*, counsel's fees are recoverable for providing advice but not usually for attending the approval hearing as well. CPR 45.9(2)(b) provides that counsel's fees may be allowed '*where they are necessarily incurred by reason of one or more of the claimants being a child or protected party as defined in Part 21*'. The test of necessity is a high threshold. Patten LJ said at [53]-[56]:

> *53. It seems to me that the wording of CPR 45.10 contemplates that the fees of counsel will only be recoverable if they had to be incurred because of the special status of the claimant. 'Necessarily' imports a causal link of this kind which is not established merely by general considerations such as that counsel may be more competent or better equipped to deal with a hearing than a local agent appointed on an ad hoc basis. The rule is looking to identify some factor attributable to the claimant being a child or protected person as defined in CPR 21 which requires counsel to be instructed and which by process of elimination would not exist in a case where the claimant was a competent adult.*
>
> *54. The costs of instructing counsel to provide the opinion required under 21 PD 5.2 and 6.4 will ordinarily satisfy this test because they are a specific requirement of Part 21.10 proceedings. But for counsel's fees for attending a hearing to be recoverable there must, I think, be*

> *some complexity in the case which justified their being instructed to appear on the approval hearing. It is not enough to say that counsel would help to remove the stress of the occasion. That is a problem in every case. It is not unique to claimants under CPR 21.10.*
>
> *55. Judge Hornby thought that children and protected parties merited the services of counsel in all cases but that, I think, puts the matter too widely. If the use of counsel in all Part 21.10 cases had been considered appropriate by the Rules Committee then one would have expected to see that reflected in CPR 45.10(2)(c) or in the provisions of the Practice Direction to CPR 21. As it is, a much stricter test has to be satisfied.*
>
> *56. Many of these cases (and this one seems to be no exception) do not involve difficult issues and can be dealt with shortly on the basis of the written advice on the merits. In such cases the convenience of having counsel attend the hearing has, I think, to be borne by the solicitors as part of their costs just as they would have had to meet the costs of instructing a local agent.*

This principle is often misremembered as meaning counsel's fees are not recoverable in any fixed costs case for attending an approval hearing. That is not true; in some circumstances they may be allowed, and in other circumstances they are not recoverable because the relevant rules make no provision at all (but that is an entirely separate concern). This *Tubridy* principle applies only to predictable costs claims.

Predictable costs apply also to protected parties, and the principles would be the same.

<u>Predictable costs for multiple parties</u>

PD45 2.7 provides: '*Where two or more potential claimants instruct the same legal representative, the provisions of the section apply in respect of each claimant.*'

Thus it would be wrong to aggregate the damages of all claimants and calculate one set of fixed costs on the grand total. At very least the solicitors would lose at least one of the £800 base fees. Instead, predictable costs should be calculated per claimant.

The practice direction typically comes into play in children's claims, where two or more children's claims are included in the same claim form for approval.

Portal costs

This is a fixed costs scheme. It was introduced on 30 April 2010 for RTAs on or after that date with a value up to £10,000 excluding vehicle related damages. On 30 April 2013, the fixed costs were reduced for claims with CNFs on or after that date. On 31 July 2013, the scheme was expanded horizontally to cover EL, PL and EL Disease claims and vertically to damages of £25,000.

For a while it was a muddle, but it became simpler as time passed by as claims subject to the older, higher costs got settled.

The costs are payable in instalments for each of the three stages of the Protocol (but most settle at stage 2).

Fixed costs in relation to the RTA Protocol			
Where the value of the claim for damages is not more than £10,000		**Where the value of the claim for damages is more than £10,000, *but not more than £25,000***	
Stage 1 fixed costs	£200*	Stage 1 fixed costs	£200
Stage 2 fixed costs	£300**	Stage 2 fixed costs	£600
Stage 3 - Type A fixed costs	£250	Stage 3 - Type A fixed costs	£250
Stage 3 - Type B fixed costs	£250	Stage 3 - Type B fixed costs	£250
Stage 3 - Type C fixed costs	£150	Stage 3 - Type C fixed costs	£150

* £400 if CNF before 30 April 2013
** £800 if CNF before 30 April 2013

Source: CPR 45 Table 6

Fixed costs in relation to the EL/PL Protocol			
Where the value of the claim for damages is not more than £10,000		**Where the value of the claim for damages is more than £10,000,** ***but not more than £25,000***	
Stage 1 fixed costs	£300	Stage 1 fixed costs	£300
Stage 2 fixed costs	£600	Stage 2 fixed costs	£1300
Stage 3 - Type A fixed costs	£250	Stage 3 - Type A fixed costs	£250
Stage 3 - Type B fixed costs	£250	Stage 3 - Type B fixed costs	£250
Stage 3 - Type C fixed costs	£150	Stage 3 - Type C fixed costs	£150

Source: CPR 45 Table 6A

At the time of writing, the Civil Procedure Rules Committee have identified the italicised words '*but not more that £25,000*' as a drafting error and they are due to be deleted from the CPR in October 2020.

Scope of the Protocols

Protocol fixed costs and Section IIIA costs apply only to claims beginning in the RTA or EL/PL Protocol, or in the case of Section IIIA costs only, the Package Travel Protocol. Many claims are outside the scope of the Protocols to start with. This is not a book about making Protocol claims, but these exclusions are relevant to the scope of fixed costs and costs arguments about whether claims should have been started under the Protocols (see Chapter Three).

General exclusions:

- A claim that **does not involve personal injury** – PI includes physical or mental impairment (Both protocols para 4.1(2));
- **Small claims** (Both protocols para 4.1(4));
- Claims with a likely **value over £25,000** (Both protocols para 4.1(3));
- Claims by **litigants in person** (RTA Protocol para 4.6, EL/PL Protocol 4.4);

- Where claimant or defendant is a **PR of a deceased person** (presumably a deceased person who would otherwise be party to the claim) (RTA Protocol para 4.5(3), EL/PL Protocol 4.3(1));
- Where the claimant or defendant is a **protected party** (RTA Protocol para 4.5(4), EL/PL Protocol 4.3(2));
- Where the claimant is **bankrupt** (RTA Protocol para 4.5(5), EL/PL Protocol 4.3(7));
- Accidents or breaches of duty occurring outside of England & Wales (RTA Protocol para 1.1(16), EL/PL Protocol 4.3(7)).

Additional exclusions from RTA Protocol:

- Injuries caused by a breach by the defendant of the statutory provisions in the **Health & Safety at Work etc Act 1974**: e.g. excludes accidents caused by hazardous substances, lifting at work, manual handling, protective equipment, work equipment, work at height etc (RTA Protocol para 1.1(16));
- Where the defendant is **not a road user** (e.g. farmer who allows animals to escape onto a road, causing an accident) (RTA Protocol para 4.5(1));
- Claims under **MIB Untraced** Drivers' Agreement (RTA Protocol para 4.5(2));
- Where the defendant's **vehicle is registered outside UK** (RTA Protocol para 4.5(6)).

Additional exclusions from EL/PL Protocol and Package Travel Protocol:

- In **PL** claims, where the **defendant is an individual** as opposed to a business or an officer of a business (EL/PL Protocol 4.3(3));
- Where the defendant is **insolvent** and there is **no identifiable insurer** (EL/PL Protocol 4.3(5));
- **Disease** claims where there are **co-defendants** (EL/PL Protocol 4.3(6));
- Claims for damages for **harm, abuse or neglect** of children and vulnerable adults (EL/PL Protocol 4.3(8));
- **Clinical negligence** claims (EL/PL Protocol 4.3(9));
- **Mesothelioma** claims (EL/PL Protocol 4.3(10));

- Claims covered by the RTA Protocol (EL/PL Protocol 4.3(11)).

Paragraphs 6.13 and 6.14 of the RTA Protocol sets out the modified steps applicable '*Where no insurer is identified and the claim falls to be dealt with by the MIB*', showing that uninsured claims are within scope of the Protocol. Untraced claims are not; see paragraph 4.5(2). Costs for uninsured claims are covered briefly at the end of this chapter.

Portal costs and litigants in person

Where the claimant is a litigant in person, the claim should be started under the relevant Protocol but the fixed costs for the RTA and EL/PL Protocols do not apply (paras 4.6 and 4.4 respectively). That applies only to the fixed profit costs; it seems the provisions on disbursements in CPR 45 Section III would still apply. It is not clear how a litigant in person would know or be able to access the claims portal, but that is beyond the scope of this book.

Capture Date for Protocols

The EL/PL Protocol applies to accidents on or after 31 July 2013 or in disease claims where there was no letter of claim before 31 July 2013. Therefore only EL/PL accidents after that date attract fixed costs.

The RTA Protocol, in its current form, applies where the CNF is sent on or after 31 July 2013. Thus the accident itself could be before 31 July 2013, in contrast with the EL/PL Protocol. The reason for the difference is that RTA claims were already being started under the former version of the RTA Protocol and this provision provided continuity while making clear which version of the Protocol applied. The date of the CNF is relevant for Section IIIA costs as set out below.

Protocol upper limit

In the RTA Protocol, paragraph 1.2(1) provides:

> *(1) The 'Protocol upper limit' is—*
> *(a) £25,000 where the accident occurred on or after 31 July 2013; or*

> *(b) £10,000 where the accident occurred on or after 30 April 2010 and before 31 July 2013,*
>
> *on a full liability basis including pecuniary losses but excluding interest.*

The elaborate definition is required because the RTA Protocol increased in scope on 31 July 2013. No such elaboration is required in the EL/PL Protocol, the scope of which has not changed since its inception. Paragraph 4.1(3) of the Protocol defines the upper limit as £25,000 on a full liability basis including pecuniary losses but excluding interest. Paragraph 4.1(4) of the Package Travel Protocol is in identical terms.

Claims in excess of the upper limit are excluded.

For RTA claims, while the CNF may have fallen to be sent on or after 31 July 2013, if the accident was before that date and the claim's value exceeded £10,000, that claim will not belong in the Protocol. An easy mistake would be to think that the Protocol captures all RTA claims started on or after 31 July 2013 with a value up to £25,000.

Vehicle related damages in RTA claims

The definition of the upper limit often gives the mistaken impression that the Protocol is simply for the fast track. Not so. Under paragraph 4.1(3) of the RTA Protocol, a claim falls within scope of the Protocol if 'the claimant values the claim at no more than the Protocol upper limit'. Paragraph 4.4 says 'A claim may include vehicle related damages but these are excluded for the purposes of valuing the claim under paragraph 4.1.' Vehicle related damages are defined under paragraph 1.1:

> *(18) 'vehicle related damages' means damages for—*
> *(a) the pre-accident value of the vehicle;*
> *(b) vehicle repair;*
> *(c) vehicle insurance excess; and*
> *(d) vehicle hire.*

Once those are included in addition, a claim under the Protocol could have a total value in excess of £25,000. The Court of Appeal recognised in *Qader v Esure* [2017] 1 WLR 1924 at [17] that a claim with a value exceeding £25,000 might belong in the RTA Protocol on this basis. *Raja v Day & MIB* (HHJ Gregory, County Court at Liverpool, 2 March 2015, unreported) was an instance where the court had overlooked the effect of vehicle related damages at first instance and corrected on appeal the mistaken finding that the claim was in excess of the upper limit and sure to exit the RTA Protocol.

Portal costs in detail

Stage 1 costs

Stage 1 fixed costs are payable at the start of Stage 2. There are ten days to make payment from receipt of the Stage 2 Settlement Pack via the portal: paragraph 6.18 of the RTA Protocol and paragraph 6.16 of the EL/PL Protocol.

That assumes that liability was admitted and the claim proceeds to Stage 2. If liability was denied or in an RTA claim contributory negligence other than the failure to wear a seatbelt in the case of a vehicle occupant was alleged, the claim will never make it to Stage 2 and the costs will not be paid.

In RTA claims, the fees for a fixed cost medical report and any medical records must be paid also. The RTA Protocol uses a portmanteau term for the stage 1 fixed costs and those medical fees: 'Stage 1 Fixed Recoverable Costs'. That is an unusual usage of 'recoverable', because there is no formula involved in those costs.

There is a proviso that the invoices for the medical fees must have been included with the Settlement Pack. It may have been the intention that if those invoices were missing, the Stage 1 fixed costs would still be payable; but on the way paragraph 6.18 is worded it appears arguable that none of the Stage 1 Fixed Recoverable Costs would be payable at that time.

The only exception is where the claimant is a child. The rationale is that the child's settlement requires approval, so nothing is paid until that approval is given.

If Stage 1 costs or Stage 1 Fixed Recoverable Costs are not paid by the time they should be, the claimant has 10 days from the date when they should have been paid to give written notice that the claim will not continue under the Protocol: 6.19 of the RTA Protocol and 6.17 of the EL/PL Protocol. There is a limited window of opportunity because the claimant cannot keep the threat of an exit hanging over the defendant as the claim proceeds under Stage 2 or Stage 3. That might have a blackmailing effect. There needs to be certainty about whether or not the claim is continuing under the Protocol.

If the defendant fails to make payment and the claimant lets the claim continue under the Protocol, the defendant does not avoid paying the Stage 1 costs. There are provisions for settlement at Stage 2 or going on to Stage 3 for unpaid Stage 1 costs to be paid: paragraphs 7.47 and 7.70 of the RTA Protocol and 7.44 and 7.53 of the EL/PL Protocol.

The former version of the RTA Protocol required Stage 1 fixed costs to be paid at the end of Stage 1. There were an alarming number of claims in which Stage 1 costs were paid and a Stage 2 Settlement pack never followed, and consequential concerns about dishonest or duplicative claims. It was coined the '£400 Club'. Nevertheless, in *JC&A Solicitors v Iqbal* [2017] EWCA Civ 355, the Court of Appeal held that there was no obligation to repay Stage 1 fixed costs in claims which did not progress to Stage 2. The court had no evidence of the £400 Club, but it would not have changed the outcome.

If Stage 1 costs are paid and the claim goes on to exit the Protocol, the court must take into account the fixed costs paid by the defendant when making any order as to costs: CPR 45.28. In *JC&A v Iqbal* at [27], Briggs LJ (as he then was) held that the predecessor version of that rule did not treat the Stage 1 fixed costs as a mere payment on account of costs, but instead was intended to prevent double recovery in respect of the work covered by the payment. That is a fine distinction; in practice, the payments will be treated identically to a payment on account and will be taken off the total costs to leave the balance payable. In light of what Briggs LJ said, there might also be an argument that the rule would prevent a standard basis recovery of costs for the work covered by Stage 1 in excess of the Stage 1 fixed costs, but there are as yet no cases on the point.

Stage 2 costs

Stage 2 costs are payable at the end of Stage 2, which is reached when the claim settles or when it is proceeding to Stage 3.

An offer to settle made under the RTA or EL/PL Protocol automatically includes an offer to pay the costs of the claim (paragraphs 7.44 and 7.41 respectively). Thus on acceptance, there is an agreement to pay costs. Those automatic terms are inserted by the Protocols because the common law does not recognise an automatic right to costs just because a claim is won. The provisions save arguments about whether the defendant has to pay costs.

There is an exception if the claimant is a child. The claim has to proceed to Stage 3 for approval, and costs are not payable until the court's approval is given.

Where the claim has settled, paragraph 7.47 of the RTA Protocol or paragraph 7.44 of the EL/PL Protocol applies. Both paragraphs are headed 'Settlement'. Regarding costs, they require payment of any unpaid Stage 1 costs, the Stage 2 costs, relevant disbursements and if applicable a success fee, all within 10 days of the settlement.

Unlike Stage 1, there is no provision for exiting the Protocol if that deadline is missed. The reason is straightforward: the claim has settled, so it cannot exit the Protocol. Failure to comply with post-settlement obligations may require a polite reminder or ultimately enforcement action from the claimant. However, it does not mean it is reasonable for the claimant to declare unilaterally that the claim has 'exited' the Protocol and demand the greater post-portal costs. See *Coggon v Irvine* (Regional Costs Judge Jenkinson, County Court at Birkenhead, 17 October 2014, unreported).

Where the claim is proceeding to Stage 3, paragraph 7.70 of the RTA Protocol and paragraph 7.53 of the EL/PL Protocol require the defendant to pay the same costs save for any success fee (the claim not yet having been won) within 15 days of receiving the Court Proceedings Pack. There is an exception; if the defendant does not have a CRU certificate that remains in force for at least 10 days, the defendant must request one as soon as possible, inform the claimant and pay the costs within 30 days of receiving the Court Proceedings Pack.

If the defendant fails in either of those things, the claimant may give notice to the defendant that the claim will no longer continue under the Protocol. Unlike Stage 1, there is no time limit for that notice: see paragraphs 7.75 and 7.58 of the Protocols respectively. So the claimant has a choice; but an astute claimant will surely exit in order to claim greater costs.

If Stage 1 and/or Stage 2 costs are paid and the claim exits the Protocol at Stage 3, the court must take into account the fixed costs paid by the defendant when making any order as to costs: CPR 45.28. See the last paragraph under 'Stage 1 costs' above.

Stage 3 costs

Stage 3 costs are split into three types. Type A fixed costs are the legal representative's costs, and cover the paperwork done by the solicitor. Type B fixed costs are the advocate's costs for attending a Stage 3 hearing. Type C fixed costs are for the cost of advice, whether given by counsel or solicitor, on the amount of damages where the claimant is a child.

If the claimant is a child and seeks approval at Stage 3, the claimant gets Types A, B and C (CPR 45.21 and 45.22). Those rules also deal with multiple approval hearings.

Otherwise, the winner at Stage 3 gets the Stage 3 costs.

If the claimant beats the defendant's Protocol offer, the claimant gets Stage 3 fixed costs as appropriate: no hearing – Type A only; at a hearing – Types A and B; at a hearing and the claimant is a child – Types A, B and C (CPR 45.20).

If the claimant does not beat the defendant's Protocol offer, the claimant pays the defendant's Type A and B fixed costs if the claim was determined at a Stage 3 hearing, or just the Type A fixed costs if the claim was determined on the papers (CPR 45.26).

Fixed late settlement costs

If the claim settles after the Court Proceedings Pack has been sent by the claimant but before proceedings are started, CPR 45.23A says the claimant gets Stage 3 Type A fixed costs. They are called 'Fixed Late Settlement Costs' by the Protocols. That rule insertion reversed the position under several first instance decisions which held that no Stage 3 costs were payable if the Part 8 proceedings had not been started. However, if the claimant sent the Court Proceedings Pack before the total consideration period under Stage 2 of the Protocol had expired, the defendant may still object. In *Korczynski v Garbrah* (County Court at Birkenhead, 22 April 2016, unreported), Regional Costs Judge Baldwin disallowed the fixed late settlement costs when the claimant has sent the Court Proceedings Pack just after the end of the end of the initial consideration period. In *Laycock v Scott* (County Court at Liverpool, 23 October 2017, unreported), Regional Costs Judge Baldwin this time allowed the fixed late settlement costs, finding that the total consideration period had expired even though the defendant contended the Stage 2 Settlement Pack was incomplete and the total consideration period never started running. The defendant may need to exit the claim from the Protocol in order to give pursue that sort of objection or obtain information it considers is missing; the defendant may decide it is disproportionate.

Portal costs and children

The RTA and EL/PL Protocols require that all children's claims (protected parties' claims are excluded from the Protocols) go to court for approval at a Stage 3 Hearing (called a 'settlement hearing'). Part 21 sets out the procedure to obtain the court's approval of a settlement.

The costs of attending the approval hearing and producing advice on the settlement are part of the fixed costs: Stage 3 Type B and Type C fixed costs, of £250 and £150 respectively. Junior counsel will usually deal with those aspects, but his or her fee is not charged as a disbursement.

Additional fixed costs

CPR 45 Section III makes provision for additional fixed costs in rare circumstances. CPR 45.27 deals with adjournment of a stage 3 hearing or a child settlement hearing, and provides that the court may order payment of Stage 3 Type B fixed costs and any court fee. The rule appears to cater both for adjournments coming about at the hearing and adjournments by application in advance. An application on the papers would apparently attract double the fixed costs allowed for an interim application under CPR 45.29H (see below).

The court may also allow a sum equivalent to Stage 3 Type C fixed costs for additional advice in claims worth more than £10,000. That provision is dealt with fully in the Chapter Five on disbursements.

Portal costs and small claims

If a claim settles under the RTA or EL/PL Protocol, portal costs are payable by automatic effect of CPR 45 Section III. Defendants who consider that the claim is likely to be a small claim should exit the claim from the portal before settlement if they wish to pay small claims costs rather than portal costs.

The claimant can keep any Stage 1 and Stage 2 fixed costs paid before the claim exited the RTA or EL/PL Protocol where certain conditions are satisfied. They are set out in CPR 27.14(2)(h):

- the claim was within scope of the relevant Protocol (this would appear to exclude claims started wrongly or mistakenly under either Protocol); and
- the claimant reasonably believed that the claim was valued at more than the small claims track limit in accordance with paragraph 4.1(4) of the relevant Protocol.

If those conditions are met and the defendant admitted liability under the Protocol but did not pay the Stage 1 costs and, where the claim did not exit before they became payable, the Stage 2 costs, the defendant still has to pay them.

These provisions are very difficult in practice. It is a matter for evidence whether the claimant had a reasonable belief in the value of his claim exceeding the small claims threshold. In order to avoid paying or to obtain credit for or a refund of those costs, the defendant would need to show that the claimant cannot reasonably have believed the value of the claim exceeded the small claims threshold. That may be possible based on the medical evidence, or any statement of the nature and duration of injuries. In some cases, the legal knowledge of the solicitor will need to be imputed to the claimant, on the basis the solicitor would or should have given advice. A belief would arguably be unreasonable if it was not an informed belief.

If the defendant successfully argues that the portal fixed costs are not payable, any payments that have been made will be taken into account when making any order as to costs under CPR 45.28. Once disbursements are accounted for, the claimant may need to make a full or partial refund of any costs paid. Interest is unlikely to apply to the refund: not least because the sums would fall below the £5,000 threshold in the County Court (Interest on Judgment Debts) Order 1991.

Portal costs for multiple claimants

Where a solicitor acts for related claimants, e.g. a driver and a passenger, the rules are silent on whether portal costs apply per claimant or for the total damages. Two or more claimants' damages may add up to more than £10,000 and entitle the solicitor to the higher band of fixed costs; but not as much as the fixed costs would be for the claimants separately. There is an argument that running claims in parallel has costs savings.

However, a consistent interpretation of Part 45 suggests that the position for predictable costs should be followed, where PD45 2.7 spells out that costs will be allowed per claimant. This is not without contention, but most of that contention arises in connection with this issue in Section IIIA claims, as set out below.

Starting a claim under the wrong Protocol

In rare circumstances it might arise that a claim is started under the wrong protocol. The series of exclusions means there is very limited scope for that to happen and it is difficult to think of accident circumstances where there might be confusion. Hypothetically a claim may fall within the RTA Protocol's definition of RTA, but be started under the EL/PL Protocol as a PL claim. There are accidents which have been presented as PL claims where the court held that they were RTAs within the fixed costs definitions: see *Green v KIS Coaches* (Plymouth County Court, 2008, unreported). Using the EL/PL Protocol rather than the RTA Protocol may be an issue because the costs are greater under the EL/PL Protocol – and also after exiting it into Section IIIA (see below). The point that costs should be limited to RTA portal costs could only be taken if the claim exits the Protocol and Part 7 proceedings were started, meaning CPR 45.24 was available (see the guidance below on the power to limit to portal costs).

In practice this hypothetical problem may be unheard of because insurers have different portal IDs for different risk categories. Submission of an EL/PL claim to an RTA insurer would be difficult; even if a CNF is sent, the insurer would be likely to ask for a fresh CNF under the RTA Protocol.

Changing solicitors

In fixed costs cases, if a new firm takes over that firm will collect all of the fixed costs. Whether the former solicitor gets some of the fixed costs is something to be resolved between the solicitors and the client, and does not involve the paying party.

Under the RTA and EL/PL Protocols, if the claimant changes solicitor (or appears to change solicitor to the defendant) and Stage 1 fixed costs were paid to the former solicitor, the successor solicitor cannot insist a duplicate payment is made to it. Again that is something for the solicitors to sort out between themselves. See the notes from the Claims Portal Behaviour Committee cited in Chapter Three, 'Circumstances that engage CPR 45.24'.

Death of the claimant

His Honour Judge Gargan considered unusual circumstances in which a claimant unfortunately died for reasons unconnected with the accident after he had started a claim under the RTA Protocol. His personal representatives went on to recover damages.

Claims by personal representatives are outside the scope of the Protocol: paragraph 4.5(3). The claim did not continue under the Protocol. Judge Gargan held that the Protocol claim had ended rather than exited and that the claim by the personal representatives was a 'fresh claim'. He allowed portal costs down to the death of the claimant, and costs assessed on the standard basis thereafter.

The decisions that the claim could not continue under the Protocol and could not exit into Section IIIA appear doubtful. The personal representatives pursued the same claim. The judge appeared persuaded by arguments that whether the claimant died before or after starting a Protocol claim should not affect the costs recoverable. But 'swings and roundabouts' is surely the answer. It is an interesting point, but not worth another death to clarify further.

Section IIIA costs

These are fixed recoverable costs. The scheme came into force at the same time as the expansion of portal costs on 31 July 2013. It was extended to Package Travel Protocol claims on 7 May 2018 (by letter of claim date).

There are simple formulae for the costs based on the damages, where the formula is selected according to the stage at which settlement was reached plus, for pre-issue settlements, the amount of damages.

Although the structure is the same, there are different sets of formulae for RTA, EL and PL claims. Package Travel claims adopt the EL formulae.

Fixed costs where a claim no longer continues under the RTA Protocol			
A. If Parties reach a settlement prior to the claimant issuing proceedings under Part 7			
Agreed damages	At least £1,000, but not more than £5,000	More than £5,000, but not more than £10,000	More than £10,000, but not more than £25,000
Fixed costs	The greater of— (a) £550; or (b) the total of— (i) £100; and (ii) 20% of the damages	The total of— (a) £1,100; and (b) 15% of damages over £5,000	The total of— (a) £1,930; and (b) 10% of damages over £10,000
B. If proceedings are issued under Part 7, but the case settles before trial			
Stage at which case is settled	On or after the date of issue, but prior to the date of allocation under Part 26	On or after the date of allocation under Part 26, but prior to the date of listing	On or after the date of listing but prior the date of trial
Fixed costs	The total of— (a) £1,160; and (b) 20% of the damages	The total of— (a) £1,880; and (b) 20% of the damages	The total of— (a) £2,655; and (b) 20% of the damages
C. If the claim is disposed of at trial			
Fixed costs	The total of— (a) £2,655; and (b) 20% of the damages agreed or awarded; and (c) the relevant trial advocacy fee		

Source: CPR 45 Table 6B

Fixed costs where a claim no longer continues under the EL/PL Protocol – employers' liability claims & Package Travel Protocol claims			
A. If Parties reach a settlement prior to the claimant issuing proceedings under Part 7			
Agreed damages	At least £1,000, but not more than £5,000	More than £5,000, but not more than £10,000	More than £10,000, but not more than £25,000
Fixed costs	The total of— (a) £950; and (b) 17.5% of the damages	The total of— (a) £1,855; and (b) 12.5% of damages over £5,000	The total of— (a) £2,500; and (b) 10% of damages over £10,000
B. If proceedings are issued under Part 7, but the case settles before trial			
Stage at which case is settled	On or after the date of issue, but prior to the date of allocation under Part 26	On or after the date of allocation under Part 26, but prior to the date of listing	On or after the date of listing but prior the date of trial
Fixed costs	The total of— (a) £2,630; and (b) 20% of the damages	The total of— (a) £3,350; and (b) 25% of the damages	The total of— (a) £4,280; and (b) 30% of the damages
C. If the claim is disposed of at trial			
Fixed costs	The total of— (a) £4,280; (b) 30% of the damages agreed or awarded; and (c) the relevant trial advocacy fee		

Source: CPR 45 Table 6C

Fixed costs where a claim no longer continues under the EL/PL Protocol – public liability claims			
A. If Parties reach a settlement prior to the claimant issuing proceedings under Part 7			
Agreed damages	At least £1,000, but not more than £5,000	More than £5,000, but not more than £10,000	More than £10,000, but not more than £25,000
Fixed costs	The total of— (a) £950; and (b) 17.5% of the damages	The total of— (a) £1,855; and (b) 10% of damages over £5,000	The total of— (a) £2,370; and (b) 10% of damages over £10,000
B. If proceedings are issued under Part 7, but the case settles before trial			
Stage at which case is settled	On or after the date of issue, but prior to the date of allocation under Part 26	On or after the date of allocation under Part 26, but prior to the date of listing	On or after the date of listing but prior the date of trial
Fixed costs damages	The total of— (a) £2,450; and (b) 17.5% of the damages	The total of— (a) £3,065; and (b) 22.5% of the damages	The total of— (a) £3,790; and (b) 27.5% of the damages
C. If the claim is disposed of at trial			
Fixed costs	The total of— (a) £3,790; (b) 27.5% of the damages agreed or awarded; and (c) the relevant trial advocacy fee		

The trial advocacy fees are the same for all claims. Each Table shares an identical Part D:

D. Trial advocacy fees				
Damages agreed or awarded	Not more than £3,000	More than £3,000, but not more than £10,000	More than £10,000, but not more than £15,000	More than £15,000
Trial advocacy fee	£500	£710	£1,070	£1,705

Source: CPR 45 Table 6D

Qualifying for Section IIIA costs

There are two basic criteria under CPR 45.29A(1) for getting Section IIIA costs in an RTA, EL or PL claim. The claim must have (a) started under the RTA or EL/PL Protocol and (b) exited that Protocol or the Stage 3 procedure in PD8B. Completely separately, a claim might fulfil the criterion of being under the Package Travel Claims Protocol in order to attract Section IIIA costs in a package travel claim. A further implied criterion is that the claim must fit somewhere within Table 6B, 6C or 6D. If there are no fixed recoverable costs specified, the Section cannot apply.

A possible example of that, perhaps one that was not intended, is a claim that exits the Stage 3 procedure under PD8B and continues as a Part 7 claim. Part B in each table, and the definitions in CPR 45.29C(4) and 45.29D(4) refer to proceedings being 'issued' under Part 7. That has not happened in a PD8B claim. The proceedings were issued under Part 8, and the court has used the power in CPR 8.1(3) to direct that the claim continues as if the claimant had not used the Part 8 procedure. In order to claim greater costs, a claimant may say such a claim was not issued under Part 7. A defendant may seek to apply Section IIIA by saying the proceedings are to be treated as if issued under Part 7 and that is enough. There have not yet been any cases on the point, probably because there are relatively few Stage 3 claims and most are concluded at Stage 3. Further, this problem would not arise if the claim proceeded to trial. Part C in the relevant table would apply, which requires only that the claim went to trial and is not concerned with how proceedings were started.

The only express exclusion is in CPR 45.29A(2): the Section does not apply to a **disease** claim which is started under the EL/PL Protocol.

Section IIIA and MIB claims

As uninsured claims can start in the RTA Protocol, Section IIIA costs will apply to them also. The Section will not apply to uninsured claims.

Section IIIA and litigants in person

There appears to be no provision excluding litigants in person from Section IIIA costs, which is inconsistent with the position when the claim settles under the Protocol: portal costs are expressly excluded. The court would have to decide whether CPR 45 Section IIIA or CPR 46.5 (see Chapter Five – Recoverable Costs) prevailed.

What damages should be included in the fixed recoverable costs calculation?

See this heading under Predictable Costs above for guidance.

Section IIIA and track allocation

Section IIIA does not apply only to fast track claims. It will apply to some claims for which the normal track may be the small claims track or the multi-track.

Anecdotal evidence suggests claims that do not belong in the Protocols often start under them. There may be various reasons. There may be uncertainty about the value of the claim at the outset. A particular firm may zealously follow the procedure of starting claims under the Protocols. Some claimants may be angling for a prompt admission of liability. Either way, once a claim starts under the Protocol and then exits it could be in scope of Section IIIA.

Section IIIA and small claims

Small claims are excluded from the RTA and EL/PL Protocols. Thus a small claim exiting a Protocol into the scope of Section IIIA should be rare.

But say a claim did exit the Protocols because its value dropped below the small claims limit. If unlitigated, it would not fall under Part A of Tables 6B, 6C and 6D because they provide costs formulae only for claims with a value of at least £1,000. But if litigated the claim could fall under the first column of fixed costs in Part B of the Tables. There is no reference to a minimum damages value in Part B. That would result in costs of £1,160 plus 20% of damages in an RTA claim. However, if the court somehow made an order for assessment, CPR 46.13(3) would allow the court to limit the costs to fixed commencement costs for a small claim.

Once a claim is allocated to the small claims track, the further columns in Part B should not apply as instead the claim would be subject to the specific rules for small claims in CPR 27.14. There is nevertheless tension between CPR 27.14 and Section IIIA, which both apply on the face of the rules. In *Singh v Ajaz* (County Court at Bristol, 27 September 2016, unreported), HHJ Denyer QC came to the opposite conclusion. He held that Section IIIA applied to these claims, taking cues from dicta in *Phillips v Willis* [2016] 3 Costs LR 473. Jackson LJ said at [4]:

> *Cases which dropped out of the earlier version* [of the RTA Protocol] *fell under the general provisions of the small claims track or the multi-track or fast track. Cases which dropped out of the later version fell into a newly created fixed costs regime.*

There are three reason why *Singh v Ajaz* is doubtful. First, Jackson LJ was not addressing this point and his dicta was proven unreliable by the *Qader* case below concerning the multi-track. Second, HHJ Denyer did not apply the rule of interpretation that general rules give way to specific rules: see *Solomon v Cromwell* [2012] 1 WLR 1048. Arguably the small claims rules are more specific for small claims. Third, he did not account for CPR 27.14(2)(h), which provide that Protocol Stage 1 and Stage 2 fixed costs, as applicable, may still be payable where the claimant can show he had a reasonable belief that the claim's value would exceed the small claims threshold. That provision would be redundant if ex-Protocol small claims fell under Section IIIA rather than CPR 27.14.

Split liability and the small claims threshold

Part 45 Tables 6B, 6C and 6D do not provide a formula where damages are less than £1,000 and no Part 7 proceedings have been started. If 'damages' for Section IIIA is the net sum, as argued above, then it will not apply to pre-issue net settlements under £1,000. The result might be the same as for predictable costs in light of *Dockerill* (see above under the same sub-heading). However, if Part 7 proceedings are started then the tables no longer categorise by the amount of damages, and small claims net settlements may fall within the Section as explained above.

<u>Section IIIA and the multi-track</u>

Qader v Esure [2017] 1 WLR 1924 held that claims allocated to the multi-track are excluded from Section IIIA. It resulted in amendment to CPR 45.29B and 45.29D, so that they provide:

> *Subject to rules 45.29F, 45.29G, 45.29H and 45.29J, and for as long as the case is not allocated to the multi-track, in a claim started under the* [relevant] *Protocol... the only costs allowed are...*

The choice of words introduces a perhaps unnecessary temporal element. 'For as long as' could have instead been 'if'. The result in *Qader* is understood to have been Section IIIA was disapplied for all of the costs; but the wording suggests that Section IIIA applies up to the time of allocation. The wording may have in mind re-allocation. Newey LJ observed in *Ho v Adelekun* [2019] Costs LR 1963 at [33]:

> *Mr Mallalieu also relied on the fact that CPR 45.29B provides for the fixed costs regime to apply "for as long as the case is not allocated to the multi-track" and suggested that, in consequence, the regime would automatically cease to apply from the start on re-allocation. This, however, is very far from obvious. The more natural interpretation of CPR 45.29B might be thought to be that, where a case is transferred from the fast track to the multi-track, the fixed costs regime ceases to apply prospectively, not in relation to past costs, incurred when the case was in the fast track.*

CPR 46.13(2) provides that where a claim has been allocated to one track and is then reallocated to another track, any special rules for costs applying to the first track apply down to the date of reallocation, and any special rules for the new track apply from the date of reallocation.

Multi-track value claims that settle before allocation are subject to Section IIIA. Briggs LJ said in *Qader* at [55]:

> *I do not consider that the Rule Committee would have carried back to a pre-allocation stage a policy to disapply fixed costs, merely because a claim properly started in the Protocols had grown in value beyond £25,000, or had become the subject of a pleaded defence of fraud or dishonesty. As I have said, it by no means follows that every such case would be inappropriate for management and determination in the fast track. To require the parties to guess, or the court to decide, whether a case which settled prior to allocation (to which therefore part A or the first column of part B of Table 6B would apply) was or was not subject to fixed costs would introduce a damaging and unnecessary degree of uncertainty into a scheme which depends upon its predictability for its contribution towards the proportionate, speedy and effective disposal of civil proceedings.*

That conclusion is unpopular with claimants. Other novel arguments seeking to escape fixed costs are taken in multi-track value claims (e.g. unwitting contracting out in *Ho v Adelekun*, in which damages were £30,000). The Civil Procedure Rules Committee has rejected arguments to reverse paragraph 55 by rule amendment: see the 15 May 2020 minutes at https://www.gov.uk/government/organisations/civil-procedure-rules-committee/about#minutes (accessed 26 July 2020).

<u>Section IIIA and abuse of process</u>

If the damages are expected to be very high, a wily claimant may see benefit in starting a multi-track claim under the Protocol and then removing it. A £1M claim would lead to very high costs under the Section IIIA formulae. Unsurprisingly, defendants argue that bringing such claims under the Protocol is an abuse of process. In *Cable v Liverpool Victoria* [2020] EWCA Civ 1015, the Court of Appeal identified three abuses of process in a high value claim stayed under PD8B:

> *a) At the point when the appellant's solicitors issued the claim under Part 8, they knew (or ought to have known) that this was not a Part 8 claim. They should have issued a claim under Part 7;*

> *b) The appellant's solicitors sought a stay so as to comply with Stage 2 of the RTA Protocol when they knew (or ought to have known) that the RTA Protocol was inapplicable to this claim;*
>
> *c) The appellant's solicitors did not intend to and did not in fact use the stay of proceedings for the purposes for which it was sought and granted.*

Coulson LJ said at [70]:

> *I consider that a) and c) were abuses of the court proceedings themselves, whilst b) is better categorised as an abuse of the RTA Protocol process.*

The strike out of the claim was not upheld but the claimant was ordered to pay the defendant's costs down to the hearing before the district judge on the indemnity basis, and was deprived of interest on special damages. The claim was transferred to Part 7. That claimant would not get costs, and the claim may arguably not even fall within Section IIIA having been transferred to rather than started under Part 7 (see 'Qualifying for Section IIIA costs' above).

Section IIIA costs for other possible outcomes in litigation

Section IIIA covers the whole duration of a claim, including litigation all the way to trial. The aim is that the scheme is a complete costs solution, so that any party's costs are fixed in the event of obtaining a costs order. There are some exceptions, but in addition to the claimant's costs at the conclusion of the claim the scheme does cover the following:

- Defendant's costs
- Counterclaims
- Interim applications

Defendant's costs under Section IIIA

Section IIIA caps (not fixes) the defendant's recoverable costs. When the defendant wins outright, CPR 45.29F applies. When a claimant accepts a defendant's Part 36 offer out of time, CPR 36.20 applies. When the defendant wins at trial on a Part 36 offer, CPR 36.21 applies.

When the defendant wins outright, the defendant's costs are capped at the amount of fixed recoverable costs that the claimant would have recovered had the claimant won. As the amount of fixed recoverable costs is calculated from the damages, a notional figure for damages is required. CPR 45.29F(4) defines that as the amount sought in the claim form (or failing that, the upper limit in the claim form, and if that is blank too, £25,000) less any amount not in dispute, any vehicle related damages where the claim started under the RTA Protocol, interest and costs. Contributory negligence is to be ignored. VAT, disbursements under CPR 45.29I and London weighting where appropriate are in addition.

The court would assess the defendant's costs on the standard basis, applying the cap. However, the cap is lifted if a QOCS exception applies (see Chapter Nine): CPR 45.29F(10).

Under Part 36, the principles are similar. There is a cap; and VAT, disbursements and London weighting are in addition. The cap is the difference between the amount of fixed recoverable costs applicable on the date the claim settled and the amount that applied at the expiry of the relevant period of the defendant's offer. The offer might be an offer made under the RTA or EL/PL Protocol or an offer made after the claim exited.

The claimant gets the amount applicable at the end of the relevant period; the defendant can recover costs up to the cap. The longer ago the offer was made, the higher that cap is likely to be. In many cases, it may be nil. The claim would have to have progressed to a later stage under Table 6B, 6C or 6D after the expiry of the offer's relevant period in order for there to be any difference in the figures.

A claimant could therefore accept a defendant's Part 36 offer after the expiry of its relevant period and as long as the case had not progressed to the next stage under the relevant Table, the costs allowed would be the same.

The rule incentivises defendants to make good Part 36 offers as soon as possible. No other type of offer will have these costs consequences.

CPR 36.20(4)(b) and (5)(b) and CPR 36.21(2)(b) and (3)(b) provide that the claimant is liable for the defendant's costs after the expiry of the defendant's offer's relevant period. The inflexible wording – 'is liable' – means that there is an automatic right.

The rules leave some scope for argument about the cap on the defendant's costs, but it is very narrow. CPR 36.20(12) and CPR 36.21(9) impose the limit on defendant's costs where the court makes an order for the defendant's costs. A defendant might argue that he should be allowed uncapped costs under the automatic right and it is only when the court makes an order that the cap will apply. A claimant might argue that the liability to pay the defendant's costs should or could be reduced to an order, and once the court does that the cap will apply; and in expectation that the court will do that the cap should be applied in any event.

The rules make provision at CPR 36.20(11) for situations where the parties cannot agree the liability for costs. There might be a dispute about whether a particular defendant's offer should have costs consequences. The court can then make an order. The rules do not specify how the matter should be brought before the court but affected parties have generally made an application on notice under Part 23.

Counterclaim costs under Section IIIA

CPR 45.29G deals with the costs of successful counterclaims by defendants. It applies only in RTA claims.

Where the counterclaim includes personal injury and it succeeds, the counterclaimant gets the same costs any other successful claimant would be allowed under Section IIIA. Where the counterclaim does not include personal injury, the counterclaimant gets the same fixed costs allowed on an interim application.

Interim applications under Section IIIA

Section IIIA sets fixed costs (not fixed recoverable costs, like the rest of the Section) for interim applications at CPR 45.29H.

Where the court makes an order for the costs of an interim application in favour of either party, the amount of costs will be half of the Type A and Type B costs from Table 6 in Part 45 if it is an RTA claim or Table 6A if it is an EL or PL claim. On present figures there is no difference; half the sum for both types is £250. VAT and disbursements under CPR 45.29I (likely only to be the court fee, but may include a telephone conference fee – although telephone conference fees are not listed as a recoverable disbursement so there may be some argument as set out in the disbursements section) are in addition, as is London weighting where appropriate.

Because Type B fixed costs are the advocate's costs, it appears that half of the Type B costs should be allowed only where there is a hearing. Some interim applications will be dealt with on paper. The rule refers to the 'applicable Type A and Type B costs in Table 6 or 6A'. It is arguable whether 'applicable' refers to the Types or the Tables of costs. It was read as Types in *Davis v Asda Stores*, a decision on appeal by HHJ Denyer (County Court at Bristol, 9 June 2015, unreported). Thus an interim application dealt with on paper or by consent would attract fixed costs of £125 plus VAT and court fee (no other disbursements being likely), and London weighting if relevant.

The rule implies or expects that an interim application should involve half of the work of a Stage 3 hearing for a claim under the RTA or EL/PL Protocols. That may be true of a simple application, but some are more complicated and will not be based on precedents. The fixed costs may be very low compared to the work required and a party might consider carefully whether it is truly necessary to make the application.

Interim applications plainly include such things as applications to vary directions or extend time.

'Interim' in the CPR generally means 'not final'; therefore an application for any remedy that is not final would arguably fall under the definition. Examples are applications for summary judgment or strike out. An application for an order that was 'final', for instance an order for the costs of the claim in principle (as opposed to an application to decide the amount of costs), would not fall within scope of CPR 45.29H. An application under CPR 36.20(11) may be an example. In such cases, it is arguable that no additional costs would be payable, as the work would fall within the limitation on costs in CPR 45.29B for RTA claims or CPR 45.29D for EL/PL claims.

The Court of Appeal decided a contentious point in *Sharp v Leeds City Council* [2017] 4 WLR 98: whether CPR 45.29H applies to pre-action applications for disclosure. Briggs LJ (as he then was) held at [35]:

> *it seems to me entirely apposite for a PAD application to fall within the description of interim applications in rule 45.29H, as being "an interim application ... in a case to which this section applies". The "case" in which the application is made is, in my view, the claim for damages for personal injury, during and in the pursuit of which the PAD application is made. It is plainly an application for an interim remedy within the meaning of Part 25, and it is in my view "interim" in the fullest sense, because it follows the institution of the "claim" by the uploading of a CNF on the Portal, even though no proceedings under Part 7 have yet been issued, and precedes the resolution of the claim by settlement or final judgment.*

It follows also then that an application made after damages have been settled would not fall under CPR 45.29H, even if it were for an interim remedy. Thus an application concerning the amount of costs to be allowed after damages were settled was not subject to CPR 45.29H: per Carr J (as she then was) in *Parsa v D S Smith plc* [2019] Costs LR 331 at [35]-[38].

Disposal hearings under Section IIIA

In *Bird v Acorn Group plc* [2017] 1 WLR 1915, the Court of Appeal held that a public liability claim in which a disposal hearing had been listed by the time of settlement fell under the third column in Part B of

Table 6D; i.e. the maximum amount of fixed recoverable costs before trial applied. The formula in that column applies '*On or after the date of listing but prior the date of trial*'. CPR 45.29E(4)(a) clarifies that it is listing for trial. A disposal hearing fulfilled the definition of 'trial' in CPR 45.29E(4)(c): 'the final contested hearing'. The same principles apply to Tables 6B and 6C.

This is a generous outcome as the work to prepare for a short disposal hearing cannot be squarely equated with the work that goes into a fast track trial. The formulae in Section IIIA were derived from the costs of actual claims, and in that dataset disposal hearings were not equated with trials. But as ever, the justification must be 'swings and roundabouts'.

The judgment confirms that the columns need not be triggered in succession, so that as well as listing a disposal hearing, simultaneous allocation and listing of a trial in the same order would also skip over the second column, straight from the first column to the third column. The court also held that there could be no 'backtracking'. Once a claim reached the third column, it would not back track to the second column if it was not concluded at a disposal hearing and was allocated instead, and then went on to settle. Work correlating to the third column had been done.

Section IIIA and court door settlements

Coulson J (as he then was) held in *Mendes v Hochtief (UK) Construction Ltd* [2016] 3 Costs LO 429 that Part C of the relevant Table and thus the trial advocacy costs under Part D were recoverable when a claim settled on the day of trial but before the trial started, i.e. there was a 'court door settlement'.

Section IIIA costs and children

Section IIIA makes no special provision at all for dealing with children's claims, so the claimant's solicitor will not recover greater costs than in any other claim even though there may be some extra, albeit straightforward, work for obtaining the court's approval when following the procedure under Part 21.

That said, nothing in Section IIIA strictly requires an approval hearing, so there is the option of parental indemnity. See the section 'Predictable costs and children'. As no extra costs are payable for the steps involved in obtaining the court's approval in Section IIIA cases, parental indemnity would make the fixed costs more profitable. However, solicitors act in the best interests of their clients and to leave a litigation friend with a risk of liability is undesirable. Parental indemnity is infrequently encountered in Section IIIA cases.

Otherwise, if damages are provisionally agreed before Part 7 proceedings are issued then a Part 8 claim for approval will be started. The claimant's costs will be the appropriate sum under Part A of the relevant table in Section IIIA. The court fees for the proceedings will be recoverable, but there is no provision for any other sums being payable, for instance for counsel's advice on the settlement sum or for attending the approval hearing. Counsel's fees will not normally be recoverable under the provision in CPR 45.29I(2)(h) for '*any other disbursement arising due to a particular feature of the dispute*': *Cham v Aldred* [2020] 1 WLR 1276. Coulson LJ said at [35]:

> *The fact that, in a particular case, a claimant is a child, or someone who cannot speak English, or who requires an intermediary, is nothing whatever to do with the dispute itself. Age, linguistic ability and mental wellbeing are all characteristics of the claimant regardless of the dispute. They are not generated by or linked in any way to the dispute itself and cannot therefore be said to be a particular feature of that dispute.*

If the child's claim proceeds to Part 7 and then settles, a claimant may argue that the approval hearing is the 'trial' and attracts the fixed recoverable costs in Part D of the relevant table. The difficulty there is that 'trial' is defined as 'the final contested hearing'. An approval hearing is not contested; it takes place because the parties are provisionally agreed. An approval hearing would also not logically be an interim hearing carrying the additional fixed costs in CPR 45.29H. It seems therefore that no additional costs or disbursements are recoverable in Part 7 children's claims either.

That is not necessarily to say there is a problem. The fixed recoverable costs may be thought adequate to cover the work required on the 'swings and roundabouts' basis.

Section IIIA for multiple claimants

Where two or more claimants' claims with the scope of Section IIIA are brought in the same claim form, Section IIIA costs should be allowed per claimant following the approach for predictable costs per PD45 2.7.

In *Neary v Bedspace* (County Court at Chester, 4 December 2015, unreported), His Honour Judge Pearce came to that conclusion on the reasoning that Tables 6B applied in its heading 'where a claim no longer continues under the RTA Protocol' and claims could not be bundled under the Protocols pre-issue, so the table must apply per claimant.

But there have been differing views about the trial advocacy fee. Judge Pearce allowed two trial advocacy fees; in *Karnicka v Zborek* (County Court at Reading, 13 February 2018, unreported), His Honour Judge Hand QC allowed only one. He drew analogy with fast track trial costs under CPR 45 Section VI where only one trial advocacy fee is allowed even where there are multiple claimants. The point in *Cham* that Part 45 should be construed as 'a coherent whole' cuts both ways when Section II and Section VI take different approaches. However, in a different context, the Court of Appeal in *Bird v Acorn Group* at [22] was not persuaded on the interpretation of Table 6B by a comparison to the position under Section VI. Ultimately it seems doubtful that Parts A, B and C of Table 6B (and by extension, Tables 6C and 6D) should be applied per claimant, but Part D should be applied per trial. That is not a coherent interpretation.

Section IIIA lacunae

Lacunae in Section IIIA have been alleged in various claims, unsuccessfully: e.g. *Hislop v Perde* at [49]. There do whoever seem to be some low-level gaps where the correct approach is not stated by Section IIIA. One of them is addressed in the previous section, concerning multiple claimants. Comparison to the practice direction for Part 45 Section II's predictable costs offers assistance there.

Section IIIA has only one practice direction of its own, dealing with loss of earnings/leave disbursements. Section II has ten practice directions in PD45 paragraph 2. One of those, on London weighting, has been expressly extended to portal costs and Section IIIA costs. The others have not been. Paragraphs 2.8 to 2.10 concerning costs-only proceedings could all sensibly extend to Section IIIA, but in particular paragraph 2.3, which describes what amounts are included in 'agreed damages' for the purposes of the fixed recoverable costs calculation, could help Section IIIA. See 'What damages should be included in the fixed recoverable costs calculation?' above.

Section IIIA and Part 36

Where a Part 36 offer is accepted and the claim has exited the relevant Protocol, CPR 36.20 sets out the costs consequences.

Parties may refer specifically to CPR 36.20 when making Part 36 offers by letter. But the rule appears to apply regardless of express mention. Although the standard Part 36 Offer form N232A refers to consequences under CPR 36.13 if the offer is accepted, CPR 36.13(1) is subject to CPR 36.20; and CPR 36.13(3) says costs will not be on the standard basis where fixed costs apply. Essentially, CPR 36.13 redirects to CPR 36.20 in Section IIIA cases, which then substitutes CPR 36.13.

CPR 36.20 deals with specific circumstances in which a Part 36 offer is accepted. CPR 36.20(1) states the rule applies 'where a claim no longer continues under the RTA or EL/PL Protocol pursuant to rule 45.29A(1)', and then the following subsections deal with costs consequences:

(2) where offer accepted within its relevant period;
(3) where offer for part of the claim is accepted and rest of claim abandoned;
(4) where defendant's offer accepted after its relevant period;
(5) where the defendant's Protocol offer is accepted after the claim has left the Protocol.

The remaining subsections clarify various points:

(6) where the defendant makes an offer before receiving a fixed price medical report;
(7) what is meant by fixed price medical report;
(8) what is meant by Protocol offer;
(9) what is meant by Court Proceedings Pack Form and business day;
(10) that fixed costs are calculated on the amount accepted;
(11) the court's residual jurisdiction to make an order where the parties cannot agree the liability for costs;
(12) the cap on defendant's costs;
(13) the parties' right to disbursements.

CPR 36.20 prescribes the costs entitlement in many scenarios but does not expressly address every scenario. For instance, if a claimant's offer is accepted outside of its relevant period there is no special rule. Claimants sought to argue that indemnity costs should apply after the expiry of the relevant period. In *Hislop v Perde* [2019] 1 WLR 201, the Court of Appeal held that fixed recoverable costs apply down to the date of settlement. In the absence of an exception in CPR 36.20, the basic rule in CPR 45.29B (or 45.29D in and EL, PL or Package Travel claim) continues to mean Section IIIA applies.

That is to be contrasted with the result in *Broadhurst v Tan* [2016] 1 WLR 1928, in which the Court of Appeal held that indemnity costs did apply after the offer's relevant period (and fixed recoverable costs down to that date) if the claimant bettered the offer at trial.

The difference in result between late acceptance and beating an offer at trial is because of the differences in the rules. CPR 36.20 applies to late acceptance, and it *replaces* CPR 36.13 and creates no discretion to depart from fixed recoverable costs. CPR 36.21 applies to trial outcomes, and it *modifies* CPR 36.17 while retaining right to indemnity costs under that rule. The replacement/ modification is evident from the wording of the rules. CPR 36.20: '*This rule applies…*'; CPR 36.21: '*rule 36.17 applies with the following modifications…*'

Hislop is a deeply unpopular decision with claimants, who say that it deprives Part 36 of 'teeth' and leaves them uncompensated for additional costs they were put to after the relevant period. But in answer, defendants would say Part 36 still has consequences at trial. While an aim of Part 36 may be encouraging settlement, in this context priority is given to discouraging trials. Also, if Section IIIA costs represent the reasonable and proportionate costs down to damages settlement, it is hard to see why those costs become too low after an offer happens to be made. The reality is that most Section IIIA disputes boil down to the same point: the claimant contends Section IIIA costs are not enough.

A difference between CPR 36.13 and 36.20 is the absence of a deemed order under the latter. A deemed order is not created for fixed costs. CPR 44.9 creates deemed orders only for costs to be assessed on the standard basis, and consistently with that it does not list CPR 36.20. See Chapter Two on 'assessment' of fixed costs. If there is a dispute about the liability for costs, CPR 36.20(11) leaves the matter to the court. Parties would apply under Part 23.

The interaction between CPR 36.17 and CPR 36.21 which apply when judgment is entered is clearer than the interaction between CPR 36.13 and CPR 36.20 when a Part 36 offer is accepted. CPR 36.21(1) specifically says that rule *modifies* CPR 36.17.

CPR 36.17(3) provides the defendant gets costs from the expiry of the relevant period of the defendant's offer if it is not beaten by the claimant. CPR 36.21(2) modifies that so that the claimant gets costs as appropriate from Table 6B, 6C or 6D in Part 45 to the end of the relevant period, and the defendant gets costs after the relevant period, which are capped at the difference between the claimant's fixed costs and the fixed costs applicable at the date of judgment. CPR 36.20(3) modifies that further for when the claimant does not beat the defendant's Protocol offer; the claimant then gets only Stage 1 and Stage 2 portal costs.

Those are the only modifications to CPR 36.17. Thus, where the claimant beats his own offer, nothing in CPR 36.21 applies, and instead the claimant would be likely, at the court's discretion as to whether it was unjust, to receive the package under CPR 36.17(4): interest on the damages at up to 10% above base rate, costs on the indemnity basis after the expiry of the successful offer's relevant period; interest on the costs at up to 10% above base rate; an additional amount of 10% or as capped against the damages. That was the result in *Broadhurst.* As nothing in CPR 36.17 or 36.21 displaces the basic rule as to costs in CPR 45.29B (or CPR 45.29D as the case may be), then costs down to the expiry of the relevant period are Section IIIA costs.

See also 'Section IIIA, Part 36 and portal costs arguments' in Chapter Three.

Exclusions and exceptions from Section IIIA

There is a closed list of exclusions and exceptions from Section IIIA. That list comprises:

- CPR 45.29F (defendant's costs);
- CPR 45.29G (counter claims);
- CPR 45.29H (interim applications);
- CPR 45.29J (exceptional circumstances);
- claims that have been allocated to multi-track (CPR 45.29B, codifying *Qader v Esure*);
- claims in which a claimant beats his own Part 36 offer at trial (CPR 36.17(4), per *Broadhurst v Tan*);
- where parties expressly agree that Section IIIA does not apply (per *Ho v Adelekun*).

The authorities treat the allowances under Section IIIA differing to Tables 6B, 6C and 6D as 'exclusions', even though they are specified in Section IIIA. The *Ho v Adelekun* exception is one made expressly by the parties rather than the rules.

The list is closed because it is not permissible to recognise implied exceptions to Section IIIA, per Briggs LJ in *Sharp v Leeds City Council* at [14] and [31]:

> *Section IIIA of Part 45 provides almost as comprehensively for fixed recoverable costs in relation to claims which start within one of those Protocols, but no longer continue under them. I say "almost as comprehensively" because there are a small number of limited exclusions and exceptions from the applicability of the fixed costs regime, to some of which I will refer in due course. With one exception, those exclusions were all expressly made.*
>
> *The starting point is that the plain object and intent of the fixed costs regime in relation to claims of this kind is that, from the moment of entry into the Portal pursuant to the EL/PL Protocol (and, for that matter, the RTA Protocol as well) recovery of the costs of pursuing or defending that claim at all subsequent stages is intended to be limited to the fixed rates of recoverable costs, subject only to a very small category of clearly stated exceptions. To recognise implied exceptions in relation to such claim-related activity and expenditure would be destructive of the clear purpose of the fixed costs regime, which is to pursue the elusive objective of proportionality in the conduct of the small or relatively modest types of claim to which that regime currently applies.*

The stray exclusion to which Briggs LJ referred is now the expressly made multi-track exclusion.

Claims started 'mistakenly' under the Protocols

In the section above on the 'Scope of the Protocols', the various exclusions from the Protocols are laid out. Notwithstanding those exclusions, where on or more applies it is still possible to submit a CNF to the claims portal. It does not filter for all of the exclusions. If such a claim goes on to settle under the Protocol, then portal costs will apply. There do not appear to be any cases where there has been an issue in the regard.

It does become an issue when the claim has exited the Protocol. Often the claim will exit the Protocol very early, often with the defendant's first response when it spots the exclusion. On the face of it, such claims are subject to Section IIIA costs. The claim has 'started' under the Protocol (for these purposes, a claim is started when the CNF is uploaded to the claims portal, per *Sharp* at [29]) and has exited, engaging Section IIIA.

However, several County Court judges have found that the claim did not in fact start under the Protocol, despite the actual steps taken, because it is not conceptually possible to start a claim under the Protocol that is outside the scope of the Protocol. That appears to recognise an 'implied exception' to Section IIIA costs that was outlawed by *Sharp*. In contrast, applying the authorities strictly, Master Leonard found Section IIIA costs applied in *Hammond v SIG plc* [2019] EWHC B7 (Costs). The claimant said the claim should not have been in the Protocol owing to its value exceeding the Protocol upper limit and it exited when liability was admitted. This issue may eventually advance to the senior courts for determination. While it is a point of law, there may be an important sympathy factor depending on the facts of the case. Where a claimant has made an innocent mistake spotted quickly by the defendant, the senior courts may recognise an exception; where there is some lingering suspicion that the claimant was trying to take advantage of a swift liability admission under the Protocol, or otherwise abusing the process, the senior courts may be less likely to recognise an exception. Still, it will difficult to say there is an express exception to *Section IIIA*. There may be an exception to the *Protocol*, but if all exceptions to the Protocol were extended to Section IIIA, there would be no claims left for Section IIIA.

Fast track trial costs

Fast track trial costs are set in CPR 45 Section VI. They are fixed rather than capped costs. They are the costs of the advocate (solicitor, counsel or any other person with a right of audience) preparing for and attending the trial.

'Trial' here has its traditional sense of the hearing at the end of the claim. Fast track trial costs do not apply to summary judgment or approval hearings (CPR 45.37(2)) or disposal hearings (PD45 4.3). They would not usually apply to split trials; cases suited to split trials are not suited to the fast track, where the trial should last no more than one day (CPR 26.6(5)(a)).

The claim has to be allocated to the fast track at the time of the trial in order for the costs to apply: PD45 4.2.

A statement of costs for a fast track trial must be filed and served not less than 2 days before the trial: PD44 9.5(4)(a). The fixed costs might be set out in the fixed costs box or the counsel's fee box, depending on the particular advocate attending.

The amount of costs is set out in Part 45 Table 9:

Value of the claim	**Amount of fast track trial costs which the court may award**
No more than £3,000	£485.00
More than £3,000 but not more than £10,000	£690.00
More than £10,000 but not more than £15,000	£1,035.00
For proceedings issued on or after 6th April 2009, more than £15,000	£1,650.00

These costs are slightly less than the advocate's fees allowed under Section IIIA as trial advocacy fees. Sections IIIA and Section VI do not mutually exclude each other, and on the face of the Rules, both Sections could apply in a claim allocated to the fast track. As a matter of common sense, Section IIIA is applied in the cases to which it applies. Fast track trial costs apply to other fast track claims that did not begin under the RTA or EL/PL Protocols or are not within scope of Section IIIA (e.g. EL disease claims).

The remainder of the rules in Section VI deal with the court's limited discretion to award more than fast track trial costs; to apportion the fixed sum where both parties have succeeded to an extent; working out the value of the claim; where the court decided there must be separate trials of specific issues; litigants in person; multiple claimants and defendants.

When a fast track claim settles before trial, CPR 46.12 provides that the advocate's trial preparation costs cannot exceed the fast track trial costs.

MIB Untraced claims

Claims under the Untraced Drivers' Agreement have their own fixed costs which are provided by that agreement, not the CPR.

Part 4 of the Untraced Drivers' Agreement 2017 set out a contribution to cost where a claimant seeks the assistance of a legal representative. The full detail is in that Part, but for reference the costs contribution is:

Amount of the award	**Fee Entitlement**
Not more than £10,000 (but excluding claims within the definition of the small claims track in which case there shall be no costs entitlement)	£450
More than £10,000 but not more than £25,000	£700
More than £25,000 but not more than £50,000	The total of— (a) £700; and (b) 10% of the damages over £25,000
More than £50,000 but not more than £100,000	The total of— (a) £3,200; and (b) 10% of the damages over £50,000
More than £100,000 but not more than £175,000	The total of— (a) £8,200; and (b) 7% of the damages over £100,000
More than £175,000 but not more than £250,000	The total of— (a) £13,450; and (b) 7% of the damages over £175,000
More than £250,000	The total of— (i) £18,700; and (ii) 7% of the damages over £250,000 subject to a maximum £250,000

For accidents before 1 March 2017, the older schedule to the Untraced Drivers' Agreement 2003 set out the MIB's contribution to costs.

Amount of the award	Specified fee
Not exceeding £150,000	15% of the amount of the award, subject to a minimum of £500 and a maximum of £3000
Exceeding £150,000	2% of the amount of the award

The 'amount of the award' means gross compensation, including CRU repayments except those for benefits which cannot be validly offset against the claim and hospital charges.

The MIB will also pay VAT on those costs, and 'reasonable disbursements', which are defined as:

> *(a) reasonable expenditure incurred by or on behalf of the claimant which MIB has specifically authorised in advance (MIB's consent not having been unreasonably withheld) where the evidence resulting from such expenditure has been disclosed to MIB; and*
> *(b) counsel's reasonable fees where reasonably incurred.*

If a claimant is unhappy with what the defendant pays for disbursements, the claimant cannot start proceedings against the MIB as the Agreement does not create the right to do so. Instead, the dispute would be referred to arbitration.

The new scheme is considerably more detailed and thought through than the earlier 2003 scheme, adapting many of the lessons of fixed costs.

CHAPTER TWO
COMPLEX ISSUES IN FIXED COSTS

This chapter considers in more detail some issues that were too expansive for the Chapter One's summary of the fixed costs regime. These issues do not fit under the heading of one costs scheme, as they may span the whole regime.

Can there be an assessment of fixed costs?

The CPR appear to say that fixed costs should not be subject to detailed assessment. That leaves a puzzle: if the court is asked to decide the amount of fixed costs, what process should be followed?

The problem may not be immediately obvious. Part 47 describes the procedure of detailed assessment, and a bill of costs, points of dispute, replies and judicial decision appears an adequate means to resolve disputes. Detailed assessment of fixed costs disputes has proved entirely satisfactory to parties on both sides and the courts for many years, so any contrary intention in the CPR has been slow to catch on. Some of the reported fixed costs cases originally came before the court by detailed assessment.

The CPR do steer away from that however. CPR 44.6 is the main rule here:

> *(1) Where the court orders a party to pay costs to another party (other than fixed costs) it may either –*
>
> *(a) make a summary assessment of the costs; or*
>
> *(b) order detailed assessment of the costs by a costs officer,*
>
> *unless any rule, practice direction or other enactment provides otherwise.*
>
> *(2) A party may recover the fixed costs specified in Part 45 in accordance with that Part.*

Its practice direction at PD44 expands:

> *8.1 …where the court does not order fixed costs (or no fixed costs are provided for) the amount of costs payable will be assessed by the court…*
>
> *8.2 An order for costs will be treated as an order for the amount of costs to be decided by a detailed assessment unless the order otherwise provides.*

Note that it appears to be **fixed costs** and **assessment** that are mutually exclusive, not fixed costs and the standard basis or indemnity basis. Lord Dyson MR said in *Broadhurst v Tan* [2016] 1 WLR 1928 at [30]:

> *The starting point is that fixed costs and assessed costs are conceptually different. Fixed costs are awarded whether or not they were incurred, and whether or not they represent reasonable or proportionate compensation for the effort actually expended. On the other hand, assessed costs reflect the work actually done. The court examines whether the costs were incurred, and then asks whether they were incurred reasonably and (on the standard basis) proportionately. This conceptual difference was accepted in the Solomon case [2012] 1 WLR 1048, para 19.*

Moore-Bick LJ said in *Solomon v Cromwell* at [19]:

> *Although I accept that that regime does involve an assessment of some kind (particularly in relation to disbursements and cases where the court is satisfied that exceptional circumstances exist), I do not think that one can properly regard it as representing an assessment on the standard basis in those cases to which it applies.*

Contracting out of fixed costs for an assessment

Broadhurst gave rise to arguments that any order for assessment displaces fixed costs. Claimants contended the parties had 'contracted out'. Those arguments were dispelled by the Court of Appeal in *Ho v Adelekun* [2019] Costs LR 1963, where the court held that the costs agreement must be construed in all the circumstances and in that case the consent order did not displace fixed costs.

The court urged parties to be clearer in future. Newey LJ said at [37]: '*For the future, a defendant wishing to make a Part 36 offer on the basis that the fixed costs regime will apply would, of course, be well-advised to refer in the offer to CPR 36.20, and not CPR 36.13, and to omit any reference to the costs being "assessed".*' Males LJ added at [43]-[44]:

> *If parties wish to settle on terms that fixed costs will be payable if an offer is accepted, it is easy enough to say so and thereby to avoid any scope for argument... parties who wish to settle on terms that fixed costs will be payable would be well advised to avoid reference to assessment "on the standard basis" in any offer letter or consent order which may be drawn up following acceptance of an offer.*

As an aside, an undesirable consequence if fixed costs do not apply automatically is the creation of scope for argument, and at worst for claimants to hold settlement to ransom for assessed costs by refusing to agree fixed costs terms even where there is no reason why fixed costs should not apply. Conduct issues may arise.

<u>The correct procedure for resolving fixed costs disputes</u>

The underlying presumption of the provisions and decisions is that fixed costs are fixed, and are not capable of dispute. Experience tells us otherwise. It is true that in most cases fixed costs will be agreed so there is only an occasional problem. But all sorts of quantification disputes can arise. For instance: disputes whether certain damages should be included for calculating fixed recoverable costs; which stage under the tables in Section IIIA apply; whether there has been an unreasonable exit from the RTA or EL/PL Protocols; whether there are exceptional circumstances under CPR 45.29J. So there needs to be a mechanism for resolution.

The mechanism appears to be an application rather than an assessment.

A right to assessment of fixed costs will not arise automatically under the rules. Take Part 36. There are no 'deemed orders' for fixed costs upon Part 36 acceptance: *Mughal v Higgs & EUI* (Senior Courts Costs Office, 6 October 2017, unreported) and *Ivanov v Lubbe* (His Honour Judge Lethem, County Court at Central London, 17 January 2020, unreported). *Solomon* confirmed at [16] there was no deemed order in predictable costs cases, because those claim settle before there are proceedings in which an order could be deemed to have been made. In Section IIIA cases, an entitlement under CPR 36.20 is not a source of a right to detailed assessment (those rights are listed in CPR 47.7): *Nema v Kirkland* [2019] EWHC B15 (Costs). Hence Part 36 gives no ready way to commence detailed assessment for the fixed costs entitlement.

Where there is a Part 36 acceptance some provisions point in the direction of an application to resolve disputes about the costs, but they are not entirely clear. CPR 36.14(4)(b) confirms the court's jurisdiction. Where a Part 36 offer is accepted in a Section IIIA claim, CPR 36.20(11) provides: '*Where the parties do not agree the liability for costs, the court must make an order as to costs.*' It depends how far that rule will stretch. It is a re-casting of CPR 36.13(4) for fixed costs, and that rule is concerned only with costs in principle – the 'liability' for costs – not their quantification. Assuming 'liability' here includes not only who pays but also how much, then parties should apply to the court to determine fixed costs.

Likewise for pre-issue settlements, the costs-only procedure provides at CPR 46.14(5):

> *In proceedings to which this rule applies the court may make an order for the payment of costs the amount of which is to be determined by assessment and/or, where appropriate, for the payment of fixed costs.*

PD44 9.4 unhelpfully then refers to only one fixed costs scheme:

> *Unless the court orders otherwise or Section II of Part 45 applies the costs will be treated as being claimed on the standard basis.*

The provision is probably as it is because it takes its lead from the pre-April 2013 wording of the costs-only procedure and the decision in *Solomon v Cromwell* [2012] 1 WLR 1048. Absent their specific namecheck, one would expect that Sections III and IIIA would lead to the court 'ordering otherwise'.

The procedure that might be adopted is hinted by PD44 9.6:

> *A costs judge or a district judge has jurisdiction to hear and decide any issue which may arise in a claim issued under this rule irrespective of the amount of the costs claimed or of the value of the claim to which the agreement to pay costs relates.*

Thus the court may convene a hearing to decide the fixed costs issue.

However, in practice, that rarely happens. Very rarely, if the fixed costs appear undisputed and are claimed (usually they are not claimed if they have been agreed and paid already), the court will make an order for the payment of fixed costs on the papers; but otherwise an order for detailed assessment will be made. That appears to suit most parties. The dispute then typically goes to provisional assessment, which might be preferred to short notice of a short Part 8 hearing, perhaps in a distant court.

The only way an assessment of fixed costs will arise is if the court orders it, either by consent or at a hearing in Part 7 proceedings, or on request in costs-only proceedings. Many courts and parties may not appreciate such an order is against the intention of the CPR, although *Ho v Adelekun* should raise awareness.

Where proceedings have already been started and a settlement is reached, the procedure would be a general application under Part 23. If an application is made in a Section IIIA case, it is not an interim application subject to fixed costs: *Parsa v DS Smith plc* [2019] Costs LR 331 at [35]-[38].

The difficulty is that the rules say nothing about the court's approach to such an application. Presumably the applicant would seek an order for an amount of fixed costs and advance his argument as to why that was the correct amount, and the respondent would reply with an alternative sum and reasons. But it is all rather uncertain and less attractive to parties that the familiar detailed assessment procedure which is, after all, designed for the resolution of costs disputes. Parties might choose to apply for an order for assessment, perhaps by consent.

In a claim where the parties disagree on whether fixed costs apply at all, HHJ Simkiss held on appeal in *Cox v Ronayne* (County Court at

Dartford, 18 July 2017, unreported) at [10] that an assessment or an application were both acceptable:

> *in my judgment, it is open to the party wishing to determine whether the fixed costs regime applies, or some other regime, either to leave it to the receiving party to issue an assessment and then contend that it is inappropriate, or to issue its own application to have the matter determined by the court.*

A possible problem is the divergent approach required for disbursements. The receiving party may have accrued a right to detailed assessment of disbursements; so he might commence detailed assessment for disbursements if they are in dispute but may need also to make a separate application to resolve a dispute about fixed costs. Fixed costs disputes often get drawn into a detailed assessment that way, because it is easier to deal with everything in one place.

It is not clear whether an application or an assessment would be cheaper. Assessment would be by way of provisional assessment, where costs are capped at £1,500 plus VAT and court fees. A hearing should cost less, but these disputes have a way of escalating and generating greater costs.

The problem of the uncertain means of resolving fixed costs disputes was recognised by Sir Rupert Jackson in his *Review of Civil Litigation Costs: Supplemental Report – Fixed Recoverable Costs* in July 2017:

> *Assessment of costs. In most cases, the assessment of recoverable costs should be a straightforward exercise, not requiring judicial input. In so far as there is any dispute, the court will assess costs. If the case goes to trial, the judge will summarily assess costs at the end of the hearing. In cases which do not go to trial, there should be a shortened form of detailed assessment, of the kind described in the last sentence of Practice Direction 47, paragraph 5.7, with a provisional assessment fee cap of – say – £500.*
>
> [p. 89, paragraph 5.22]

His recommendations have been subject of consultation but not yet brought into law.

Resolving disbursements disputes

Some disbursements are fixed in amount under Section III and Section IIIA and others are not. Where non-fixed disbursements are not agreed, they may need to be assessed. PD44 provides:

> *8.3 Where a party is entitled to costs some of which are fixed costs and some of which are not, the court will assess those costs which are not fixed. For example, the court will assess the disbursements payable in accordance with rules 45.12 or 45.19. The decision whether such assessment should be summary or detailed will be made in accordance with paragraphs 9.1 to 9.10 of this Practice Direction.*

As not all disbursements are fixed, it is obvious there are some circumstances in which an assessment of disbursements will be required. PD44 8.3 codifies what Simon J said in *Nizami v Butt* [2006] 1 WLR 3307 at [25]: '*I have rejected the argument that there is an anomaly in that CPR 45.10 requires a different approach. The reason why the costs under CPR 45.10 call for a different approach is that there are no fixed figures for disbursements.*' PD47 5.7 prepares for such assessments by directing:

> *If the only dispute between the parties concerns disbursements, the bill of costs shall be limited to items (1) and (2) above, a list of the disbursements in issue and brief written submissions in respect of those disbursements.*

Previously it was thought that Part 36 provided for assessment of disbursements in Section IIIA cases. On Part 36 acceptance there would be a deemed order for detailed assessment on the standard basis under CPR 36.13(1) and (3) of the non-fixed disbursements. That would be true for Section II predictable costs cases. CPR 36.20(13) supposedly qualified that for Section IIIA cases by confirming the entitlement was only to disbursements listed in CPR 45.29I, as opposed to any and all disbursements.

However, as *Hislop* has confirmed that CPR 36.20 replaces CPR 36.13 in Section IIIA cases, that approach cannot be right. In *Nema v Kirkland* [2019] EWHC B15 (Costs), Master Leonard struck out a notice of commencement in a Section IIIA fixed costs case, finding that upon the Part 36 acceptance CPR 36.20 did not give the right to detailed assessment. He reached that conclusion with citing *Hislop*, but it could only fortify the decision. (He also concluded that the application which should be made under CPR 36.20(11) would be an interim application. *Parsa v DS Smith plc*, referred to above, was apparently not cited to him.)

HHJ Lethem advised parties to follow this procedure in *Ivanov* at [32]ff:

> *the application should seek two separate forms of relief. Paragraph one of the application should seek an order for costs in favour of the applicant. The second paragraph should ask for the costs to be assessed in accordance with the sum sought by the party. In order to avoid further difficulties, it would be prudent if the application exhibited a Form N260 (statement of costs), or at least the disbursements page where disbursements only are sought. Thus compliance with the indemnity principle would be confirmed by the signature on the form.*
>
> *Once the court has decided to award the costs under paragraph 1 of such an application, paragraph 8.3 of PD44 is engaged and the court will have to decide whether to summarily assess the costs or order a detailed assessment. I would expect that, save in exceptional cases where there is some complexity or point of principle, there will be a summary assessment.*

Under the costs-only procedure, as set out in the previous section, the court could make an order for fixed costs and an order for assessment of non-fixed disbursements. Or all matters could be considered at a hearing under PD46 9.6. Then, if needed, any disbursements could be summarily assessed or made subject to a detailed assessment under paragraph 9.9.

Differing definitions of 'RTA' in the fixed costs regime

The definition of a 'road traffic accident' differs between predictable costs under CPR 45 Section II and portal costs under the RTA Protocol. The differences are in bold:

CPR 45.9(4):

> *'road traffic accident' means an accident resulting in bodily injury to any person* ***or damage to property*** *caused by, or arising out of, the use of a motor vehicle on a road or other public place in England and Wales.*

RTA Protocol, para 1.1(16):

> *'road traffic accident' means an accident resulting in bodily injury to any person caused by, or arising out of, the use of a motor vehicle on a road or other public place in England and Wales* ***unless the injury was caused wholly or in part by a breach by the defendant of one or more of the relevant statutory provisions as defined by section 53 of the Health and Safety at Work etc Act 1974.***

The definition in Part 45 is broader with the result that some claims that may be excluded from the RTA Protocol will fall under predictable costs.

For instance, claims where there is no bodily injury may fall within Part 45. That may include accidents where only property is damaged. However, as the upper limit for predictable costs is £10,000 (CPR 45.9(2)(c)) and the small claims threshold is £10,000, the small claims exclusion in CPR 45.9(2)(d) should separately prevent predictable costs applying to such claims.

The victim

For the purpose of the definitions, it need not be the claimant who suffers personal injury, and it need not be the claimant's property that is damaged. As long as *someone* suffered bodily injury or *someone's* property was damaged, the definition of 'RTA' for predictable costs or the Protocol will be fulfilled, as the case may be.

However, other criteria make it personal to the claimant. Paragraph 4.1(2) of the RTA Protocol requires the claim to include personal injury. If it does not, it may fall under predictable costs as long as the claim includes damages for damage to property, as the alternative to damages for personal injuries under CPR 45.9(2)(b).

Psychological injuries

On the face of it, a psychological injury alone is not enough to fulfil the RTA definitions. These may be claims by secondary victims, for instance. However, CPR 45.9(2)(b) provides that the Section applies if the agreed damages include 'damages for personal injuries', and para 4.1(2) of the RTA Protocol provides that the Protocol applies where 'the claim includes damages in respect of personal injury'. The rules of interpretation in CPR 2.3(1)(c) provide: '"personal injuries" includes any disease and any impairment of a person's physical or mental condition'.

RTA claims against an employer

Where a vehicle is involved in the accident circumstances there is a reasonable chance it is an RTA. Many employees use vehicles at work. *Thomas v Cardiff County Council* (HHJ Vosper QC, Cardiff County Court, 31 January 2008, unreported) is an example of how a claim can be both an RTA and EL claim, but RTA overrides for costs purposes. A piece of hot metal burned through the floor of the works van and injured the claimant's foot. He made a claim against his employer. His solicitors sought standard basis costs with an EL success fee. They came away with RTA predictable costs.

The RTA definition in the Protocol would exclude many such claims. A footnote in the Protocol lists the 'relevant statutory provisions':

- Control of Substances Hazardous to Health Regulations 2002 (S.I. 2002/2677);
- Lifting Operations and Lifting Equipment Regulations 1998 (S.I. 1998/2307);
- Management of Health and Safety at Work Regulations 1999 (S.I. 1999/3242);
- Manual Handling Operations Regulations 1992 (S.I. 1992/2793);

- Personal Protective Equipment at Work Regulations 1992 (S.I. 1992/2966);
- Provision and Use of Work Equipment Regulations 1998 (S.I. 1998/2306);
- Work at Height Regulations 2005 (S.I. 2005/735);
- Workplace (Health, Safety and Welfare) Regulations 1992 (S.I. 1992/3004);
- The Construction (Design and Management) Regulations 2007 (S.I 2007/320).

That list gives the flavour of the exclusions. The mistake can be made at the costs stage to argue that the claim should have been started under the RTA Protocol, forgetting the definition of RTA differs from Part 45 and these exclusions must be borne in mind.

If the claim against the employer settles for less than £10,000 without any Part 7 proceedings, it is more likely that predictable costs will apply.

Use of a vehicle

Another aspect of the definition is that a road traffic accident must be caused by or arise out of the use of a motor vehicle on a road or public place in England & Wales. Knowing if those criteria are met is decisive, for instance, on whether the claim should have started under the RTA Protocol or is within scope of predictable costs. Key questions are:

- what is meant by 'caused by or arising out of';
- what constitutes 'use on a road or public place';
- what additional possibilities arise from the interaction of the parts of the definition?

The paradigm case on 'caused by or arising out of' is *Dunthorne v Bentley* (Court of Appeal, 26 February 1996). The defendant's vehicle ran out of petrol. It was parked on the side of the road and had been for some 10 minutes. The defendant was standing behind her vehicle with hazard lights on. Her friend pulled up across the road. The defendant negligently ran out into the road. She was struck and killed by the claimant's car. The claimant suffered head injuries. The claimant made a claim against the defendant's motor policy. While the facts are grim, the relevant legal point is that the claim succeeded. The accident arose out of the defendant's use of her vehicle. (Of course, it was a road traffic accident anyway because the claimant's car hit the defendant, so it is really a policy coverage case.) The principle is that 'arising out of' embraces more remote possibilities that 'caused by'. There is a full discussion and many examples in *AXN v Worboys* [2012] EWHC 1730 (QB) at [20]-[58], another case with grim facts. It is not a costs case, but nevertheless helpful.

Many criminal law precedents such as *AXN* assist in this area. The courts have construed identically worded provisions, such as those in the Road Traffic Act 1988. The meaning of the words has been considered carefully in criminal cases because there is no offence if there is no RTA. Although the purpose is different, the analyses can be helpful in civil costs cases.

Embarking on and disembarking from vehicles is ordinarily covered by motor insurance and is captured by the scope of 'RTA'. See the examples of *Green v KIS Coaches* (Plymouth County Court, 2008, unreported) and *Schneider v Door2Door* (Master Campbell, SCCO, 18 July 2011, unreported).

'Use' means 'have the use of': *Elliot v Grey* [1960] 1 QB 367. That was a criminal case in which the vehicle had broken down and been left in the road outside the owner's house until it could be repaired, with the engine broken, the battery removed and no petrol in the tank. While it could not be driven, it could be moved, and therefore the owner had the use of the vehicle. Although CPR 45.9(4) defines 'motor vehicle' as 'mechanically propelled vehicle intended for use on roads', it does not exclude broken down vehicles which at the time of the accident may not be capable of mechanical propulsion.

'Use' encompasses any activity that is part of the ordinary use of the vehicle. That does not simply mean then as a mode of transport or driving the vehicle. It includes carriage of goods. Goods transport involves loading and unloading. It is a question of how remote the loading or unloading is from the accident. See *AXN* at [43].

'Road' is self-explanatory, and CPR 45.9(4) advises, with an abundance of caution, that it includes a bridge over which a road passes.

'Public place' requires more thought. It is not to do with ownership of the land. In a criminal context, whether a road was public was considered in *DPP v Vivier* [1991] 4 All ER 18. In coming to the conclusion that a road in a caravan park was public, simplifying somewhat, the approach should be whether people having access were screened for some personal characteristic so that they were a special distinct class of people. Only if they were not would the place be public. If entry screening is merely for payment and agreeing to modest terms while on the land, that did not create a special class. Some instances are obvious. A council car park is a public place (*Clarke v Kato* [1998] 1 WLR 1647, which held a car park was not a road, was concerned with a definition of 'RTA' that did not include 'public place'). A loading bay of a fenced off depot is not a public place. Google's 'Street View' can be invaluable in determining whether there were any special access requirements.

It is not the accident which must be on a road or in a public place, but instead the use of vehicle which causes the accident or out of which the accident arises that must be on a road or in a public place. Combining 'caused by or arising out of' and the 'use' in this way embraces an even wider range of circumstances. Thus if a vehicle flew off a road and hit someone in a field, that would have arisen out of the use of the vehicle on a road. It must be immediately or closely proximate in time to the use of the vehicle on the road or in the public place: see the majority view in *Lister v Romford Ice and Cold Storage* [1956] 2 QB 180. An example is *Randall v Motor Insurers Bureau* [1968] 1 WLR 1900. The vehicle was half on private land and half on the road when the claimant pedestrian was injured. It was held that the vehicle was being used on the road.

In short, if the accident involves a motor vehicle in any way a claimant should give careful thought to whether a claim should start under the RTA Protocol; and at the costs stage, the claimant should give careful thought as to whether to claim only predictable costs; and the defendant at that stage will consider whether the claimant should be limited to RTA Protocol costs because the claim should have started under that Protocol, or whether predictable costs apply.

Allocation

Several issues connected with allocation are covered in Chapter One, such as: the relationships between predictable costs, portal costs and Section IIIA costs and small claims; split liability and the small claims threshold; reallocation; and Section IIIA and the multi-track, including the effect of the important *Qader* judgment.

This section considers other ways in which allocation can have fixed costs consequences.

The effect of allocation can be overstated. Some claims are allocated by the court, some are treated as allocated by effect of the rules (CPR 8.9(c)), and some settle before allocation. Allocation, or non-allocation, or deemed allocation are not determinative of costs issues, because the court has discretion on assessment (or for the small claims track, to make an assessment). Allocation is often a red herring.

For examples, see:

- *Drew v Whitbread* [2010] 1 WLR 1725 – allocation is not decisive;
- *O'Beirne v Hudson* [2010] 1 WLR 1717 – non-allocation is not decisive;
- *Dockerill v Tullett* [2012] 1 WLR 2092 – deemed allocation is not decisive.

For more on non-allocation see Chapter One, 'Applicability of small claims fixed costs.' For reallocation, see Chapter One, 'Reallocation of small claims' and 'Section IIIA and the multi-track'.

Special rules for costs on allocation

The small claims track and the fast track have 'special rules' about costs. The small claims track has rules covering the whole of the costs. The fast track has fixed fast track trial costs (not to be confused with the similar trial advocacy fixed costs in Section IIIA).

CPR 46.11(2) says that the special rules apply to a case once it is allocated to the track, and they also cover the period before allocation as well as after.

There is a specific exception that may be invoked when a claim is allocated to the small claims track because of admissions. See the section below.

The special rules are not always unbreakable or closed rules. If a claim is allocated to the small claims track, small claims fixed commencement costs apply; but the court still has a residual discretion to allow costs for unreasonable behaviour: CPR 27.14(2)(g). In a claim allocated to the multi-track, the court cannot simply apply fixed fast track trial costs; but if the court considers the claim should have been allocated to the fast track, the court can take those trial costs into account when making its assessment: *Drew v Whitbread* [2010] 1 WLR 1725.

In any circumstance where a party contends more than or less than what would be normal on that track should be allowed, the argument is likely open and deserves consideration rather than summary dismissal. Common judicial errors are findings that the claim was allocated to the fast track or there is an order for costs on the standard basis, so therefore the court cannot allow small claims costs or portal costs. Those points are dealt with more fully elsewhere in this book.

<u>Deemed allocation</u>

Part 8 claims are treated as allocated to the multi-track under CPR 8.9(c). It is rule of convenience that allows the whole allocation stage to be avoided in Part 8 claims.

Dockerill v Tullett [2012] 1 WLR 2092 is the leading case. In Part 8 claims brought for the approval of settlements in children's claims, the claimants said that the deemed allocation meant that small claims costs were irrelevant, even though the value of the claims put them within scope of the small claims track. The Court of Appeal held that the deemed allocation was not determinative. When assessing costs, the court is required to look at the underlying claim, and if it decides the normal track for that claim is the small claims track that will be highly material whether it was reasonable to have employed solicitors and thus whether costs should be allowed.

CPR 8.9(c) does not apply to Part 8 costs-only proceedings, per PD46 9.11. Costs-only proceedings are covered in Chapter Seven.

Allocation and partial admissions

There is a specific possible exception to the rule that on allocation to the small claims track, small claims fixed costs will apply to the period before allocation. That is where allocation follows a partial admission.

Allocation is based on the value of the claim at the date of allocation rather than the date of issue (that being the effect of CPR 26.8(2)). Sometimes, a claim may fall below the small claims threshold because of items admitted (and thus no longer being in dispute) after issue but before allocation. PD46 7.1(3) allows the court to assess costs for the admitted items down to the date of allocation, and the costs for the remaining items will be small claims fixed costs. It is an often-overlooked power.

It would surely be wrong to invoke the power to allow costs down to the date of allocation in respect of items which had been admitted prior to proceedings being started and wrongly included in the claim form.

An admission to pay part of a sum claimed, if made properly, stands as an admission rather than merely an offer, and can have the effect of reducing the claim's value so that it is allocated to the small claims track: *Akhtar v Boland* [2015] 1 All ER 644.

Pre-issue, defendants might go so far as to make admissions for partial sums against heads of claim to reduce the disputed value below the small claims threshold, meaning that is more likely that any subsequent proceedings will be allocated to the small claims track and less likely the claimant will get an order for costs down to the date of allocation.

Ramirez v EUI Limited (HHJ Blunsdon, Lambeth County Court, 30 August 2012, unreported) is an example of such an outcome.

CHAPTER THREE
LIMITING TO OR ESCAPING FROM FIXED COSTS

The court has powers to limit a receiving party to fixed costs or fixed recoverable costs, and powers to order a paying party to pay more than fixed recoverable costs. A claim may have left a fixed costs regime and the paying party may argue that the exit was unreasonable in some way, and the costs should be limited. Or, a claim may be within scope of a fixed costs regime but the receiving party will argue that greater costs should be allowed. Arguments in the former category are the most common.

The power to restrict to small claims costs

CPR 46.13(3) provides:

> *Where the court is assessing costs on the standard basis of a claim which concluded without being allocated to a track, it may restrict those costs to costs that would have been allowed on the track to which the claim would have been allocated if allocation had taken place.*

That provision is used to restrict a party to small claims costs: see the section 'Applicability of small claims costs' in Chapter One. The reference to the standard basis impliedly excludes the power where the assessment is on the indemnity basis. PD46 8.2 makes that express.

There does not at present appear to be any other situation in which it might apply. PD46 8.2 does not contemplate any. The only other track specific costs are fast track trial costs. There is no trial without allocation, and the rule could not be used to extend fast track trial costs to a pre-allocation hearing such as a disposal hearing, because PD45 5.3 says fast track trial costs do not apply to disposal hearings. Although Section IIIA costs are understood to be costs for fast track cases, the Section is not triggered by allocation, but rather by starting in a relevant Protocol.

The powers to allow more than small claims costs

The court has discretion to allow more than small claims fixed costs in a claim allocated to the small claims track where the paying party has behaved unreasonably: CPR 27.14(2)(g). Any costs allowed will be summarily assessed.

The power is exercised sparingly. In *Dammerman v Lanyon Bowdler LLP* [2017] 2 Costs LR 393, the Court of Appeal said at [32] that '*it would be unfortunate if litigants were too easily deterred from using the Small Claims Track by the risk of being held to have behaved unreasonably and thus rendering themselves liable for costs.*'

Common complaints by receiving parties are that the paying party delayed matters or should have settled sooner. They are not generally enough.

CPR 27.14(3) provides: '*A party's rejection of an offer in settlement will not of itself constitute unreasonable behaviour under paragraph (2)(g) but the court may take it into consideration when it is applying the unreasonableness test.*'

It is not unreasonable in itself to oppose a claim or to not respond as quickly as an opponent would like. There might be something unreasonable about the way in which it was done, and the receiving party would need to show that.

As to appeals, small claims costs continue to apply and the Court said in *Dammerman* at [32] that '*an appellate court should therefore be wary of ordering costs on appeal to be paid if they were not ordered below, unless circumstances on appeal are truly different.*'

See also the section 'portal costs and small claims' in Chapter One for the circumstances in which portal costs can be allowed in small claims.

The powers to restrict to Protocol costs

CPR 45.24 gives the court the power to limit a claimant to portal costs. That power is available where:

- The claimant did not comply with the RTA or EL/PL Protocol when it applied, or elected to exit the claim from the Protocol; and
- Part 7 proceedings have been started.

The requirement that Part 7 proceedings have been started seems to have been included in the expectation that proceedings would be started promptly when a claim exited the Protocol. However, that often does not happen and it limits the number of cases to which the rule might apply.

CPR 45.24(2) adds the further requirement that a judgment is given in favour of the claimant. The rule does not specify what type of judgment, but a judgment on the claim for damages is the most natural reading. Construed narrowly, CPR 45.24(2) limits the rule to claims concluded at trial. It seems undesirable that a defendant must take damages to trial which may otherwise be capable of agreement simply because he wants to argue the claimant should be restricted to portal costs.

'Judgment' could also be construed more widely to include orders. In *Brown v Ezeugwa* (HHJ Simpkiss, Tunbridge Wells County Court, 23 January 2014, unreported), a claim settled by consent order, the appeal court decided CPR 45.24(2) should be read in its broader sense, to include orders and judgments generally. It was held also that the power in CPR 45.24 is available both when the order for costs in principle is made, and on the assessment of costs. Part 45 is generally about quantification of costs rather than the right to costs, so that makes sense. *Brown* means that CPR 45.24 arguments do not necessarily need to be raised when damages are settled, and can be raised later and more naturally at the assessment stage in claims settled by consent order. Pragmatic though it may be, that judgment may be wrong or at least need to be treated with caution because of the *Williams* case below.

If a claim were started under Part 7 and then settled by Part 36, it is not clear if CPR 45.24(2) would be satisfied. Part 36 acceptance does not make a judgment for damages. There will be a 'deemed order' for costs under CPR 44.9 where CPR 36.20 does not apply. Could that fulfil CPR 45.24(2)? *Williams* (below) was not clear on the point, but was not encouraging. Defendants who intend to raise CPR 45.24 arguments might avoid making or accepting Part 36 offers for damages once the claim has left the relevant Protocol and instead make offers in some other way. Or the defendant could force the claimant to enter judgment for damages (so as to be sure CPR 45.24 applies) by delaying payment of damages: see CPR 36.14(7). This may all be a moot point as the same results may be achievable by applying *Williams*.

The alternative to CPR 45.24

The court can also apply Part 44 to achieve the same result: *Williams v Secretary of State for Business, Energy and Industrial Strategy* [2018] 4 WLR 147. *Williams* concerned a noise induced hearing loss claim which should have been brought under the EL/PL Protocol and which settled pre-issue by Part 36 offer and acceptance. At [40] Coulson LJ held Part 7 proceedings and a judgment were pre-conditions to CPR 45.24 applying. He did not elaborate on what constituted a 'judgment' for the purposes of the rule but went on to find a just alternative to CPR 45.24. At [61] he held: '*In a case not covered by r.45.24, such as this one, a defendant can rely on the Part 44 conduct provisions to argue that only the EL/PL Protocol fixed costs should apply.*' The 'Part 44 conduct provisions' were defined in the judgment as CPR 44.3, 44.4 and 44.11, namely the court's powers to decide the amount of costs and to deal with misconduct.

A question that arises is whether a claimant who unreasonably exits the Protocol into another fixed costs scheme under Part 45, such as Section IIIA costs, can be limited to portal costs by way of the Part 44 conduct provisions per *Williams*. Doubt arises because in the context of fixed success fees, it was said Part 44 cannot be used to adjust the results under Part 45: see *Lamont v Burton* [2007] 1 WLR 2814. The question is how widely *Lamont* is to be understood. It seemingly prevents use of CPR 44.3 and 44.4, but unreasonable or improper conduct was not a factor in *Lamont* and the court did not consider the CPR 44.11 misconduct powers. Arguably that rule might still be applied. There has yet to be a senior courts case to determine the point.

The Civil Procedure Rules Committee has recently rejected proposals to amend CPR 45.24. The minutes of its May 2020 meeting recorded:

> *The* [Lacuna Sub-Committee's] *view is that although there may be an argument to extend CPR 45.24(2) to other non-judgment circumstances where costs liabilities arise, for example, settlements by way of acceptance of a CPR Part 36 offer, the sub-committee can see no need to do so, because the result in* Williams *was no different from that provided for by CPR 45.24(2). If anything,* Williams *adds a useful degree of discretionary flexibility. The discussion highlighted that there is a difference between judgments (where the court has to consider their consequences) and settlements (which are generally more consensual) and thus flexibility may be useful. Accordingly, the matter was noted and it was* ***AGREED*** *that no action is to be taken.*

Were it to prove that *Williams* does not apply to Section IIIA cases because Part 44 can never be used to adjust Part 45 results, a defendant still has some practical options. Say a claimant exits the portal simply to claim Section IIIA costs and does not start Part 7 proceedings. If the defendant wishes to argue that the claimant should be restricted to portal costs, the defendant's first option is to not settle the damages claim without an express agreement that costs will be limited to portal costs. Otherwise as a second option, the defendant could force the claimant to commence Part 7 proceedings by refusing to settle.

A third option, and a very risky one, is trying to secure an order in costs-only proceedings that permits the argument. Although fixed costs apply, some courts still make orders in standard wording which provide for detailed assessment on the standard basis. The costs judge cannot go behind the order made and must give effect to it (*Cope v United Dairies* [1997] 1 Costs LR Core 23), and therefore that may open up the argument. The risk lies in the order still being construed as an order for fixed costs, when considered in context, extending the principles from *Ho v Adelekun* [2019] Costs LR 1963.

<u>Section IIIA, Part 36 and portal costs arguments</u>

Assuming CPR 45.24 can apply to Part 36 settlements (see above), claimants have argued that where a Part 36 offer is accepted within its relevant period in a Section IIIA case, there is no scope to argue that costs should be limited to portal costs by way of the power in CPR 45.24. It is said that CPR 36.20 gives an inalienable right to Section

IIIA fixed costs, e.g. *Cookson v Manchester City Council* (His Honour Judge Main QC, County Court at Manchester, 28 April 2017, unreported). That decision should be treated with considerable caution.

At a high level, the inalienable right is a surprising contention. In *Hislop*, the Court of Appeal implicitly accepted that the power in CPR 45.29J to allow greater costs where there were exceptional circumstances was available in a Part 36 acceptance case. If a claimant can argue for more, why should a defendant not be allowed to argue for less?

Generally, Section IIIA does not oust CPR 45.24. CPR 36.20 appears to preserve that position. CPR 36.20(1) provides:

> *This rule applies where a claim no longer continues under the RTA or EL/PL Protocol pursuant to rule 45.29A(1).*

CPR 45.29A(1) provides:

> *Subject to paragraph (3), this section applies where a claim is started under—*
> *(a) the Pre-Action Protocol for Low Value Personal Injury Claims in Road Traffic Accidents ('the RTA Protocol'); or*
> *(b) the Pre-Action Protocol for Low Value Personal Injury (Employers' Liability and Public Liability) Claims ('the EL/PL Protocol'),*
> *but no longer continues under the relevant Protocol or the Stage 3 Procedure in Practice Direction 8B.*

CPR 45.29A(3) provides:

> *Nothing in this section shall prevent the court making an order under rule 45.24.*

As CPR 45.29A(1) is subject to that qualification, it is logically arguable that so too is CPR 36.20(1).

The argument stems from the wording of CPR 36.20(2): '*Where a Part 36 offer is accepted within the relevant period, the claimant is entitled to the fixed costs in Table 6B, Table 6C or Table 6D in Section IIIA of Part*

45 for the stage applicable at the date on which notice of acceptance was served on the offeror.' [Underlining added.]

Claimants may argue that 'is entitled' is an absolute right which COR 45.24 cannot displace and it replaces the right that would otherwise arise under Section IIIA itself. There are three reasons to doubt that argument.

First, if CPR 36.20(2) replaces Section IIIA, it does so incompletely. It makes no provision for London weighting. It makes no provision even for VAT.

Second, Coulson LJ held in *Hislop* that CPR 36.20(2) was merely duplicative:

> *Finally on interpretation, both Mr Bacon and Mr Benson in their respective cases argued that rule 45.29B and rule 45.29J could not be relevant to the costs consequences of acceptance of a Part 36 offer, because if they were relevant, there would be no need for rule 36.20(2). That is a bad point, for two reasons. First, the draftsman has always striven to make Part 36 self-contained, so it has always contained some provisions which can also be found elsewhere in the CPR. Second and more generally, the fact that there is some duplication within the CPR is, unsatisfactory though it might be, inevitable. Rules should not be construed in reliance on duplication.*

Third, it mistakes the purpose of CPR 36.20(2). It is not to give an absolute right to costs. It is to clarify which stage in the Tables applies. The rule clarifies that the claimant will receive the fixed recoverable costs applicable at the date of acceptance, as opposed to the date of the offer. That may be obvious to some, but the draftsman has merely adapted the provision at CPR 36.13(1) to Section IIIA circumstances. And of course, the entitlement under CPR 36.13(1) is not inalienable. CPR 45.24 can apply to costs entitlements under the rule.

Other rules support the conclusion that CPR 45.24 arguments are available. CPR 36.20(11) envisages that there may be a dispute about the costs liability, because it confirms the court's residual jurisdiction to make an order where there is a dispute. Further CPR 36.14(5)(b) confirms that the stay on acceptance of a Part 36 offer does not affect the power of the court '*to deal with any question of costs (including interest on costs) relating to the proceedings*'.

In *Ansell & Evans v AT&T* (County Court at Oxford, 14 December 2017, unreported), Her Honour Judge Clarke accepted similar arguments on appeal. However the point has not been directly confirmed by the senior courts. District Judge Matthews in *Soud v Lestrade* (County Court at Oxford, 25 October 2018, unreported) thought *Williams* cast doubt on *Ansell*, when *Williams* in fact seems to be an alternative.

Wary defendants wishing to argue CPR 45.24 points might avoid the uncertainty by not making Part 36 offers and making Calderbank offers instead, and only accepting a claimant's Part 36 offer outside its relevant period.

Were it the case that CPR 45.24 is not available at all after Part 36 settlement because there is no judgment (the opposing position to the opening remark of this section), a defendant might alternatively make its argument using CPR 44.11 per *Williams*; that power must be available for the same reasons CPR 45.24 would have been available as described in this section.

One way or another, it seems that the court should be able to reach the just result of limiting a claimant to protocol costs where appropriate.

The discretion in CPR 45.24

CPR 45.24(2) provides that where judgment is given in favour of the claimant but the claim was taken out of the Protocol in one of five ways, 'the court may order the defendant to pay no more than the fixed costs in rule 45.18 together with the disbursements allowed in accordance with rule 45.19'.

'May' shows that it is a discretionary power. His Honour Judge Gregory in *Raja v Day & MIB* (County Court at Liverpool, 2 March 2015, unreported) held that once the defendant establishes that CPR

45.24(2) is engaged, the onus shifts to the claimant to show that costs should not be restricted to Protocol amounts.

Circumstances that engage CPR 45.24

Incomplete CNF

CPR 45.24(2)(a) applies where:

> *The court determines that the defendant did not proceed with the process set out in the relevant Protocol because the claimant provided insufficient information on the Claim Notification Form.*

Paragraph 6.1 of the Protocols requires the claimant to complete and send a CNF. Paragraph 6.3 says:

> *All boxes in the CNF that are marked as mandatory must be completed before it is sent. The claimant must make a reasonable attempt to complete those boxes that are not marked as mandatory.*

Paragraphs 6.8(1) of the RTA Protocol and 6.7 of the EL/PL Protocol provide:

> *where the defendant considers that inadequate mandatory information has been provided in the CNF, that shall be a valid reason for the defendant to decide that the claim should no longer continue under this Protocol.*

The rule does not use the precise words of the Protocol. 'Insufficient information' is broader than 'inadequate mandatory information'; adequate mandatory information may be given but the defendant may still argue that the information overall was insufficient. In reality, a defendant would prefer to keep the claim in the Protocol with its low fixed costs, and is unlikely to exit the claim for anything other than a failure to provide adequate mandatory information. If the defendant shows factually that inadequate mandatory information was provided the onus is then on the claimant to show why he should recover more than Protocol costs.

Where test of reasonableness applies

CPR 45.24(2)(b) applies where 'the court considers the claimant acted unreasonably' in at least one of three ways. The burden is on the defendant to show that the claimant acted unreasonably rather than for the claimant to show that he acted reasonably.

The court must not apply hindsight or speculate about what might have happened: *Ryan v Hackett* [2020] EWHC 288 (QB). The rule against hindsight has been applied by a regional costs judge (*Tennant v Cottrell*, DJ Jenkinson, Liverpool County Court, 11 December 2014, unreported) and a circuit judge (*Dawrant v Part & Parcel Network*, HHJ Parker, Liverpool County Court, 26 April 2016). The general rule against speculation has been affirmed by the Court of Appeal: *Straker v Tudor Rose* [2008] 2 Costs LR 205. (*Ryan* itself is a baffling case on the point, because Stewart J concluded that the particular claim would have inevitably exited the Protocol. It may have been highly likely, but to conclude it was a certainty could only be speculation.)

The first of the three ways is 'by discontinuing the process set out in the relevant Protocol and starting proceedings under Part 7'. It is already a requirement under CPR 45.24(1) that there are Part 7 proceedings.

The second way is 'by valuing the claim at more than £25,000, so that the claimant did not need to comply with the relevant Protocol.' For claims started before 31 July 2013 under the RTA Protocol, the upper limit was £10,000 and there is a transitional provision in rule 10 of The Civil Procedure (Amendment No. 6) Rules 2013 (SI 2013/1695) that continues to apply that cap in the older claims.

Whether it can be shown that the claimant unreasonably overvalued the claim at the outset of or during the claim will depend on the facts of the case. It may for instance be possible if the claim settles for drastically less than the upper limit, or if the claimant was shown to have included a head of claim that should not have been included (for instance, vehicle related damages under the RTA Protocol).

The third way is the claimant acting 'in any other way that caused the process in the relevant Protocol to be discontinued'. If the claimant starts a chain of events which leads to the defendant positively or inadvertently causing the claim to exit, the provision may be engaged. It is often argued in conjunction with the first way as an alternative scenario.

There is a bipartisan group called the Claims Portal Behaviour Committee which considers allegations of portal misuse and abuse. It has issued six guidance notes. They often assist with unreasonable exit arguments. The notes can be found here: https://www.claimsportal.org.uk/about/behaviour-committee/ (accessed 1 July 2020). They are:

- Direct Contact with Represented Claimants – once an insurer knows a solicitor is acting for a claimant because a CNF has been received, there should be no direct contact with the claimant personally.
- Multiple Claim Notification Forms by Multiple Claimant Representatives – it is the responsibility of the claimant's representative to ensure that they have a valid retainer with the claimant. The insurer should pay only once and the claimant's solicitor must resolve the problems created by their actions.
- Credit Hire Claims and inclusion in the Pre-Action Protocol – credit hire claims should not be excluded as a matter of course from the RTA Protocol.
- Concertina Accidents – concertina collisions should not be excluded from the RTA Protocol as a matter of course.
- Pre-Med Offers conditional on the exit of Pre-Action Protocol – offers made before medical reports with conditions about exiting the Protocol so lower costs can be paid should not be made. Paragraph 3.2(4) now makes it an 'aim' of the RTA Protocol that offers are made only after a fixed cost medical report has been obtained and disclosed. When Part 1 of the Civil Liability Act 2018 is brought into force (expected April 2021) then this practice will be unlawful in any event.
- Settlements at Stage 2 and Stage 3 – the committee's view is now enacted in CPR 45.23A.

Case examples of circumstances where the court has found it was unreasonable to discontinue the process or cause the process to end are:

- Where a claimant withdraws an offer so that the claim exits: *Ilahi v Usman* (HHJ Platts, Manchester County Court, 26 November 2012, unreported, and permission for a second appeal to the Court of Appeal was refused on paper by Jackson LJ on 14 January 2013).
- Where the defendant makes a nil offer for a head of claim. Nil is an amount, and defendants are not compelled to offer more: *Glazer v Reid* (DDJ Johnson, Liverpool County Court, 2 March 2012, unreported).
- Where the defendant did not make a further offer in response to the claimant's counter offer: *Uppal v Daudia* (DDJ Matthews, Leicester County Court, 14 May 2012, unreported).
- Where the defendant makes a pre-medical offer which the claimant's solicitors struggled to advise on: *Monteith v Carroll* (Liverpool County Court, 17 October 2012, unreported).
- Changing solicitor after Stage 1: *Mozzano v Riwa* (DDJ Dawson, Birkenhead County Court, 24 April 2012, unreported).
- Where the defendant did not give reasons for the offer: *Modhwadia v Modhwadia* (HHJ Hampton, County Court at Leicester, 20 January 2015, unreported).
- Where the claimant failed to provide proof of identity on request, where there were conflicting details: *Doyle v Manchester Audi* (District Judge Matharu, Manchester County Court, 25 June 2013, unreported).
- Exiting the portal to file witness evidence when witness evidence is allowed in the portal: *Lamb v Gregory* (HHJ Gore QC, Liverpool County Court, 8 July 2011, unreported).
- Exiting for an interim payment which was never sought once proceedings were started: *Woodford v Factair* (County Court at Ipswich, 9 February 2015, unreported).

Disregarding the Protocol

CPR 45.24(2)(c) applies where 'the claimant did not comply with the relevant Protocol at all despite the claim falling within scope of the relevant Protocol'. That may arise where the claimant's solicitor is completely unfamiliar with the protocols, although one would expect the defendant's insurer to invite that the claim is resubmitted via the relevant Protocol upon receiving a letter of claim. More recently, there have been disputes about whether claims belong under the EL/PL Protocol, where in a PL claim it is alleged the defendant is an individual and in an EL disease claim there are said to be multiple defendants (see *Williams* for an example *par excellence*). Those are questions of fact to be decided on evidence. There is no test of reasonableness under this rule, so a claimant could not rely on a reasonable belief.

Rafiania v All Type Scaffolding (DDJ Corscadden, County Court at Manchester, 14 January 2015, unreported) is an example of costs being limited under that rule. Liability had been denied already so the claimant did not use the RTA Protocol when the claim was started, and as a result was limited to RTA Protocol costs.

In *Raja v Day & MIB* (HHJ Gregory, County Court at Liverpool, 2 March 2015, unreported), the claimant failed to send a CNF when presenting the claim to a new insurer after the claim had been presented already to a different insurer with a CNF. The claimant was limited to RTA Protocol costs.

Failure to include CUE reference

CPR 45.24(2A) applies:

> *Where a judgment is given in favour of the claimant but the claimant did not comply with the process in paragraph 6.3A(2) of the RTA Protocol, the court may not order the defendant to pay the claimant's costs and disbursements save in exceptional circumstances.*

Paragraph 6.3A of the RTA Protocol provides:

> *(1) Before the CNF is sent to the defendant pursuant to paragraph 6.1, the claimant's legal representative must undertake a search of askCUEPI (website at: www.askCUE.co.uk) and must enter in the additional information box in the CNF the unique reference number generated by that search.*
> *(2) Where the claimant has sent the CNF without the unique reference number required by subparagraph (1), the defendant may require the claimant to resend the CNF with the reference number inserted. The period in paragraph 6.11 or 6.13 starts from the date the CNF was sent with the unique reference number.*

Although there are no express words limiting its application to the RTA claims, the rule should be purposively read that way. It would make no sense to apply to EL and PL claims and would lead to consistently unjust results in those claims.

As to 'exceptional circumstances', the commentary below on exceptional circumstances to escape fixed recoverable costs may be some assistance.

Failure to improve on interim payment

CPR 45.24(3) addresses claimants who exit the Protocol seeking to obtain payments on account of damages.

A winding path leads to the rule. Under the Protocols, the claimant may send an interim settlement pack and initial medical reports and request an interim payment of £1,000 for general damages. The defendant must make payment within 10 days of receiving the interim settlement pack. The claimant can ask for more than £1,000. Any amount is excess will be for other pecuniary losses. The claimant has to provide details of other pecuniary losses and disbursements with the interim settlement pack, but does not have to ask for more than £1,000. When the claimant asks for more, within 15 days the defendant must pay the amount sought, £1,000 or an amount in between. The defendant has to give reasons why the full amount is not being paid. If the defendant does not pay in time, the claimant may exit the Protocol and start proceedings for an interim payment. If the defendant does not pay as much as the claimant wants, the claimant may similarly exit and start proceedings. The claimant has only 10 days from the date the payment was due to make that choice and give notice that the claim is exiting the Protocol.

The rule applies where proceedings are started.

> *Where the claimant starts proceedings under paragraph 7.28 of the RTA Protocol or paragraph 7.26 of the EL/PL Protocol and the court orders the defendant to make an interim payment of no more than the interim payment made under paragraph 7.14(2) or (3) of the RTA Protocol or paragraph 7.17(2) or (3) of the EL/PL Protocol the court will, on the final determination of the proceedings, order the defendant to pay no more than –*
> *(a) the Stage 1 and 2 fixed costs; and*
> *(b) the disbursements allowed in accordance with rule 45.19.*

Unfortunately, there appears to be several errors in the rule. None of the paragraph references are correct. First, paragraph 7.28 of the RTA Protocol and 7.26 of the EL/PL Protocol are the wrong references. Those are the provisions about the defendant not making the payment in time. The rule should refer to paragraphs 7.29 and 7.27 respectively, which deal with the defendant paying less than the claimant sought in accordance with paragraphs 7.19(2)/7.18(2) (paying £1,000 only) or 7.19(3)/7.18(3) (paying an in between sum). Thus the references to 7.14(2) or (3) of the RTA Protocol and 7.17(2) or (3) of the EL/PL Protocol are also mistaken. It should be 7.19 (RTA) and 7.18 (EL/PL). That is all borne out by the fact that the pre 1 April 2013 version of the rule refers to the paragraph in the old version of the RTA Protocol about the defendant paying less than the claimant sought. The errors are artefacts from revising the RTA Protocol.

It is a convoluted rule and there has been few cases involving it.

It is more common that the claimant exits the Protocol over an interim payment but never then makes an application in proceedings for an interim payment. The interim payment issue then appears to have been a ruse to exit the Protocol. Paragraphs 7.29 and 7.27 say that the claimant shall have no more than Stage 2 costs (presumably this is intended to encompass stage 1 costs as well) if the court makes no award of an interim payment. However, CPR 45.24(3) does not deal with that situation. Instead, CPR 45.24(2)(b) would capture that as unreasonable behaviour.

Premature progress to Court Proceedings Pack or Stage 3

The Stage 2 period is 35 days (with possible extensions). The claimant should let that time elapse before sending a Court Proceedings Pack and starting Stage 3 proceedings: see paragraphs 7.64 of the RTA Protocol 7.48 of the EL/PL Protocol and Claims Portal Behaviour Committee guidance note 6, 'Stage 2 and 3 Settlements'.

CPR 45.23A provides that the claimant gets Stage 3 Type A fixed costs if the claim settles after the court proceedings pack is sent but before Stage 3 proceedings are started. That would appear to be an unfair reward for a claimant who prepared the court proceedings pack prematurely.

Where Stage 3 proceedings are started and then the claim settled, the defendant might seek a remedy under CPR 45.29 (which sets out the procedure for applying to the court to resolve costs disputes after Stage 3 proceedings have been started) and CPR 45.25 (which deals with costs in post-issue settlements). The defendant could seek costs of the application to set off against any unfair reward of Stage 3 costs obtained by the claimant.

A defendant might also consider exiting the claim from the Protocol and forcing the claimant to start Part 7 proceedings in order to raise an argument under CPR 45.24(2)(b)(iii). The defendant will consider proportionality before taking that step and might consider instead or in addition a complaint to the Claims Portal Behaviour Committee.

Late payment after settlement in the Protocol

When a claim settles at the end of Stage 2, paragraphs 7.47 of the RTA Protocol and 7.44 of the EL/PL Protocol which are both headed 'Settlement' require the defendant to pay damages and portal costs within 10 days of the settlement. Unlike paragraphs 6.19 and 6.17 respectively in the Protocols which give the claimant the option of exiting the Protocol when Stage 1 costs are not paid in time, there is no provision allowing the claimant to exit the Protocol if the settlement payments are late.

When the defendant is late, some claimants have given purported notice of exit or have argued that the claim automatically exited the Protocol. They then seek Section IIIA costs.

In *Coggon v Irvine* (County Court at Birkenhead, 17 October 2014, unreported), Regional Costs Judge Jenkinson concluded there was no exit provision because the Protocol has run its course and the claim has by then settled and the appropriate way forward, where reasonable, would be enforcement proceedings.

As payment is typically only a few days late it is doubtful it would be in the interests of the overriding objective to commence enforcement proceedings, although that remains an option. The claimant should reasonably chase the payment first. Tolerating minor delay may seem unfair to claimants, but there should be only minor prejudice.

Section IIIA costs will not apply as the exit will be ineffective. If a claimant starts costs-only proceedings seeking Section IIIA costs, the proceedings must identify the agreement to pay costs and the only agreement on which the claimant can rely is the automatic agreement on settlement in the Protocol to pay portal costs. The claimant is likely to end up paying the costs of the proceedings.

The power to restrict to predictable costs

The court's power – duty even – under CPR 44.3 to allow only reasonable and proportionate costs is the basis of the power to limit to predictable costs. The argument arises when the defendant considers the claimant started Part 7 proceedings unreasonably or prematurely and but for the proceedings predictable costs would have applied.

These arguments apply to few claims now because predictable costs apply to few claims. It may arise in claims that are outside the scope of the RTA Protocol, or claims that are started under that Protocol before

31 July 2013 that exit. The argument is more usually whether the claimant should be restricted to portal costs.

The cases are nevertheless interesting because they grapple with the interaction of the standard basis and fixed costs.

There were two opposing views. Looking at it one way, if the court concludes that proceedings were started unreasonably or prematurely and predictable costs would have applied but for the proceedings, then on a standard basis assessment of what is reasonable and proportionate the court can disallow costs in excess of predictable costs as they were unreasonably incurred. Looking at it in another, if costs are to be assessed on the standard basis the court must consider the bill line-by-line and cannot make the leap to allowing a sum equivalent to fixed costs, and instead if the court finds that proceedings were started unreasonably and prematurely it will disallow the costs of proceedings but still allow costs on the standard basis.

The former view generally prevails now.

The latter viewed is based on an extrapolation from *O'Beirne v Hudson* [2010] 1 WLR 1717 in which the court was considering the fixed costs for small claims. Waller LJ said at [19]:

> *a costs judge has no power to alter the order for costs made by the a judge, and thus make a direction from the outset where costs have been awarded on the standard basis that costs will be assessed on a small track basis. But what lay behind what Judge LJ said reflects what Lord Woolf CJ was saying in the Lownds case [2002] 1 WLR 2450 and provided the costs judge does not purport to vary the original order or tie himself to assessing by reference to the small claims track it is quite legitimate to give effect as far as possible to the philosophy which lies behind the above statements. There is a real distinction between directing at the outset that nothing but small claims costs will be awarded and giving items on a bill very anxious scrutiny to see whether costs were necessarily or reasonably incurred, and thus whether it is reasonable for the paying party to pay more than would have been recoverable in a case that should have been allocated to the small claims track. Was it for example necessary to have had lawyers and is it*

> *reasonable for the paying party to have to pay for lawyers are questions that should arise where a claim should have been allocated to the small claims track.*

Waller LJ did not say there had to be a line by line assessment of the bill. He did say that the court cannot simply apply small claims costs. Based on that, authorities such as *Letts v Royal Sun Alliance Plc* [2012] EWHC 875 (QB) have called it 'heresy' that predictable costs should be applied as a cap. However, on Waller LJ's 'anxious scrutiny' approach the court can end up in the position where no more than small claims costs are allowed. Thus on assessment there is no reason that the court cannot end up allowing a sum equivalent to predictable costs. Confusion arises because unless the court is seen to assess the bill on the standard basis, there is no practical difference between applying predictable costs at the outset of the assessment and applying them at its end; but assessing the bill is hardly a good use of the court's time.

Solomon v Cromwell [2012] 1 WLR 1048 has also been cited to add to the confusion. Moore-Bick LJ was considering the conflict between the general rule in Part 36 for a detailed assessment on the standard basis and the application of predictable costs, and observed at [19]:

> *Although I accept that that regime does involve an assessment of some kind (particularly in relation to disbursements and cases where the court is satisfied that exceptional circumstances exist), I do not think that one can properly regard it as representing an assessment on the standard basis in those cases to which it applies.*

That observation should be understood in context. The court was considering a particular tension in the rules. Predictable costs applied on the face of Part 45, but calculating predictable costs was not the assessment on the standard basis which followed the Part 36 acceptance. The court was not considering arguments about limiting costs to predictable costs when they did not strictly apply. The court did not say than an assessment on the standard basis cannot conclude with predictable costs being found to be reasonable and proportionate, and indeed the conclusion in *Solomon* was that despite the right to costs on the standard basis under Part 36, predictable costs prevailed.

As an aside, *Lahey v Pirelli* [2007] 1 WLR 998 has been cited in support of both views. It does not add anything to the other cases or the rules, but has inadvertently added to the confusion. At [19], Dyson LJ (as he then was) said a costs judge could not allow a percentage of costs because that would amount to varying the order for detailed assessment on the standard basis (impliedly for 100% of the costs). From that, the costs judge cannot vary the order by allowing fixed costs either. As much is said in *O'Beirne*. He also said at [24] that the court can disallow entire sections of the bills when the costs have been unreasonably incurred.

O'Beirne, *Solomon* and *Lahey* are not directly in point. Although their dicta have been sensibly applied by analogy, it was never a perfect fit.

Smith v Wyatt [2011] EWCA Civ 941, a decision on permission to appeal, is directly in point and contains the prevailing statement of the law. On the first appeal the court had limited the claimant to predictable costs and the claimant sought permission for a second appeal, which was refused. Moore-Bick LJ said at [11]-[12]:

> *It is the function of the costs judge to determine whether costs have been reasonably and necessarily incurred and, if he can see that a particular course of conduct has led to a group of costs being incurred unnecessarily, he is entitled to say that and need not to consider each item individually. In my view, the argument to the contrary is not really sustainable.*
>
> *The question whether a defendant can agree to pay reasonable costs to be assessed by way of a detailed assessment and then invite the court to assess costs by reference to a more restrictive regime is not in my view an important point of principle of the kind contemplated by Rule 52.13. If the defendant settles a claim on terms that he will pay the claimant reasonable costs to be assessed, it will be a matter of construction of the agreement whether he is agreeing to submit to a detailed assessment in which the costs judge is to have power to make an assessment by considering all the circumstances or whether he is agreeing that the costs judge is to ignore the possibility that the proceedings might have been conducted in a more economical way. That might vary from case to case although, speaking for myself, I should have thought that a*

> *defendant is unlikely to be taken to have given up a valuable argument unless it is clear that he has done so.*

Letts and *Solomon* were both decided after that judgment was given and the opposing view continued to be expressed by reference to those cases. *Hacket v RSA Insurance* (HHJ Robert Owen QC, Birmingham County Court, 18 May 2012 unreported) is an example. *Javed v British Telecom* (HHJ Mitchell, Central London County Court, 2012, unreported) is an example of the *Smith v Wyatt* approach being preferred, although only the County Court appeal decision is quoted. As *Smith v Wyatt* became better known it was more often followed.

Ultimately, there are policy issues. There is no compelling reason why a party who has behaved unreasonably by starting Part 7 proceedings should profit from it in costs. The *Smith v Wyatt* approach leads to just results.

The uncertainty in this area may have influenced the creation of simple rules confirming the powers to limit to portal costs in CPR 45.24 and small claims costs in CPR 46.13(3).

<u>Were proceedings issued unreasonably and prematurely?</u>

The *Smith v Wyatt* approach applies only when the claimant has unreasonably or prematurely started proceedings. Generally, it needs to be shown that the claimant has done one of the following:

- Failed to follow a pre-action protocol (such as not allowing sufficient time or not providing information or documents that that were reasonably and necessarily requested by the defendant);
- delayed excessively;
- exaggerated the claim, or;
- been involved in some other sort of misconduct or unreasonable behaviour.

The new Pre-Action Protocol for Personal Injury Claims is less prescriptive than its predecessor. The following are examples of expected behaviour under the protocol, and a failure to complete them may mean it was unreasonable to premature to issue:

- Sending a letter of claim (5.1).
- Allowing a three month investigation period (6.3).
- Sending a schedule of special damages (8.1.1(b)).
- Allowing 21 days from disclosing medical report and special damages schedule (8.1.2).
- Considering whether it is appropriate to make a Part 36 offer (8.2).
- Considering ADR (9.1.3).
- Stocktaking to avoid litigation or narrow the issues (11.1).
- Seeking nomination of solicitors to accept service 7 to 14 days before issuing proceedings (11.1).

Short delay by the defendant is unlikely to make issuing reasonable.

Arguments that it is premature issue when the claimant fails to negotiate before issuing have traditionally failed. If the claimant gets more than the defendant offered pre-issue, the courts usually found that it was not unreasonable to issue. *Straker v Tudor Rose* [2008] 2 Costs LR 205 was taken as the authority for that conclusion, although the case had nothing to do with predictable costs. The Court of Appeal said that courts cannot speculate about what might have happened had certain events occurred when they did not in fact occur. Thus the argument that proceedings would have been avoided if the claimant had negotiated before issuing was a non-starter. The court could not conclude that the claim would certainly have settled without proceedings.

Straker led to claimants demanding that defendants provide their best offer immediately and if not acceptable, proceedings rather than negotiations would follow.

That sits uneasily with the overriding objective and the statement in the Pre-Action Protocol for Personal Injury that 'Litigation should be a last resort'. The protocol has been rewritten since the time when these disputes were at their peak and *Straker* was routinely applied. In view of the new requirements under the protocol to consider making offers, to stocktake and narrow issues, if the Court of Appeal were now asked to look at premature issue and predictable costs, it might distinguish *Straker*.

Exceptional circumstances

The court has the discretion to allow more than predictable costs or Section IIIA costs if there are 'exceptional circumstances'. There are several criteria and the tests for each costs regime are broadly identical although the wording differs slightly.

CPR 45.13(1) sets the test for predictable costs claims:

> *The court will entertain a claim for an amount of costs (excluding any success fee or disbursements) greater than the fixed recoverable costs but only if it considers that there are exceptional circumstances making it appropriate to do so.*

CPR 45.29J(1) sets the test for Section IIIA cases, where the potential escape route is available to both parties:

> *If it considers that there are exceptional circumstances making it appropriate to do so, the court will consider a claim for an amount of costs (excluding disbursements) which is greater than the fixed recoverable costs referred to in rules 45.29B to 45.29H.*

Under both rules, the court's discretion is engaged only when there are (a) exceptional circumstances and (b) they make it appropriate to allow greater costs. It follows that not all exceptional circumstances will make it appropriate to allow greater costs.

Both rules are expressed provisionally ('entertain', 'consider') because there are 'snap-back' provisions in the event that a threshold is not reached. That threshold is covered by subsequent rules.

Leveson LJ considered the provisions of CPR 45.13(1) (or 45.12(1) as it was numbered before 1 April 2013) in *Costin v Merron* [2013] 3 Costs LR 391. It was a judgment on permission to appeal so it is not binding, but it is helpful and carries the weight of a decision of an eminent judge. At [11], he said:

> *In my judgment the phrase "exceptional circumstances" in the context of 45.12 speaks for itself. It cannot possibly mean anything other than that, for reasons which make it appropriate to order the case to fall outside the fixed costs regime, exceptionally more money has had to be expended on the case by way of costs than would otherwise have been the case.*

He identified that there must be a causal link between the greater costs and the exceptional circumstances.

At [6], he identified exceptional circumstances which would not make it appropriate to order greater costs:

> *I, for my part, have no difficulty in concluding that the exceptional circumstances to which 45.12 refer must be exceptional in the sense that the case is taken out of the general run of this type of case by reason of some circumstance which means that greater costs are in fact incurred than could reasonably be expected to be incurred. Obviously a claimant's solicitor cannot rely upon their own failure to take some appropriate step…*

Coulson LJ rolled back that position when considering CPR 45.29J *obiter* in *Hislop v Perde* [2019] 1 WLR 201 at [57]:

> *I do not accept Mr Post's gloss on rule 45.29J. His suggestion that a claimant must demonstrate a precise causative link between the exceptional circumstances and any increased costs would, in my view, lead to an unnecessarily restrictive view of the rule. It goes without saying that a test requiring "exceptional circumstances" is already a high one. It is not a proper interpretation of the rules to suggest that there should be further obstacles placed in the way of a party who wishes to rely on that provision.*

That dictum proved important however for establishing that 'exceptional circumstances' was a high threshold, effectively ending arguments that it was lower, such as the 'out of the norm' approach to indemnity costs, and deprecating judgments to the contrary. For instance, Master Haworth's decision in *Udogaranya v Nwagw* [2010] EWHC 90186 (Costs), which pre-dated even *Costin*, caused a spate of copycat applications which were largely unsuccessful. The master made two observations. First, the dictionary definition of 'exceptional' was 'unusual or not typical'. Second, that the claim was not a run-of-the-mill case and that the defendant gave the claimant the run-around. That 'low bar' approach is wrong.

Hislop was followed for the binding decision in *Ferri v Gill* [2019] Costs LR 367. Stewart J held at [44] that 'exceptional circumstances' was not a 'low bar'. He held also at [49] that 'exceptionality' is to be measured against the basket of other claims falling within Section IIIA, and not claims remaining in the RTA or EL/PL Protocols.

Carr J (as she then was) examined *Hislop* in *Parsa v DS Smith plc* [2019] Costs LR 331 and said at [24]:

> *the following four broad propositions can be identified: first, a finding that the party claiming costs has spent an unusual additional amount of time as a result of any given activity on the other side is not a necessary condition for the exercise of discretion to award more than fixed costs under CPR 45.29J, but it may still be a relevant circumstance; secondly, there may be occasions where a paying party's conduct may be out of the norm and amount to an exceptional circumstance, but that will not always be the case; thirdly, the application of CPR 45.29J is always going to be a highly contextual exercise and fact-specific; there is little to be gained from comparisons with the facts of other cases; fourthly, the threshold to be met in order to establish "exceptional circumstances" is a high one.*

Parliament has decided that the costs of many claims will be fixed. A fixed costs regime does broad justice. It is appropriate to have an escape route so the courts can do justice regarding costs when the case demands it. The power is rightly used sparingly.

Procedure

As to procedure, although the rules do not specify it, it would be sensible to make an application on notice for greater costs under this rule, giving reasons. The application may be included in a costs-only proceedings claim form. PD45 2.8 requires for predictable costs cases:

> *Where the claimant is claiming an amount of costs which exceed the amount of the fixed recoverable costs the claim form must give details of the exceptional circumstances to justify the additional costs.*

There is no express mirror provision for Section IIIA costs, but it would be sensible and helpful to follow the same approach. If the application is opposed, the defendant should deal with it briefly in a witness statement when acknowledging service. It is unlikely that the court will decide an opposed exceptional circumstances application on the papers. A hearing is likely to be convened upon consideration of the acknowledgement of service pack.

If the court considers that greater costs should be allowed, it may make a summary assessment or a detailed assessment. That gives the court flexibility.

If the court considers there are no appropriate exceptional circumstances, it will make an order for the appropriate fixed recoverable costs, and in all likelihood will decide the amount of costs there and then.

The court should not be taken to have decided an exceptional circumstances argument on the papers in costs-only proceedings when it makes a standard order for detailed assessment without including clear words indicating that it has done so: Master Campbell at [9] in *Soanes v McDowell* (SCCO, 5 March 2013, unreported).

Snap-back

If the court does assess the costs, it does not end there. There are snap-back provisions, which is why the exceptional circumstances decision is provisional. CPR 45.14 and CPR 45.29K provide that if the assessed amount is less than 20% greater than the fixed recoverable costs, the applicant gets only the fixed recoverable costs, or, if they are really unlucky, the assessed sum if it is less than the fixed recoverable costs. VAT, any success fee and disbursements are excluded for the 20% comparison. If the assessed costs are at least 20% greater, the applicant gets the assessed sum.

Presumably the comparison must be made between the grand total of assessed profit costs and the grand total of the fixed recoverable costs. The test would become muddled if a party sought greater costs for only part of the work; for instance, for one of the stages under the tables in CPR 45 Section IIIA. There is no reported decision on the point to show what a court might do.

Where an exceptional circumstances application fails outright or where the assessed costs are at least 20% greater, the court has further discretion under CPR 45.15 and CPR 45.29L about the further costs generated. The court may decide not to allow the applicant's costs of any costs-only proceedings or detailed assessment proceedings as the case may be, and may order the applicant to pay the other side's costs. The former version of the predictable costs rules made that mandatory, but it was changed to discretionary presumably to enable the court to make a just order depending on what other arguments might have been raised.

CHAPTER FOUR
DISBURSEMENTS

This chapter bridges the parts of the book about fixed costs and assessed costs. It is directed firstly at disbursements in fixed costs claims. Certain restrictions apply in those cases, mostly on the types of disbursements that may be allowed and sometimes on the amounts that may be allowed.

In other claims where the costs are on the standard basis or the indemnity basis, many of those restrictions are lifted. Much of the material in this section is applicable to those claims also, minus the restrictions of the fixed costs schemes. This section does not deal extensively with certain disbursements that may be allowed in non-fixed costs cases, such as reasonable and proportionate counsel's fees.

What is a disbursement?

The Glossary to SRA's Standard and Regulations says 'disbursement' '*means any costs or expenses paid or to be paid to a third party on behalf of the client or trust (including any VAT element) save for office expenses such as postage and courier fees'*. A disbursement is a sum paid by a solicitor in the course of providing services for clients. It includes items such as court fees, counsel's fees, expert's fees and interpreter's fees. Office expenses such as postage, courier fees, telephone bills and routine photocopying are not disbursements and instead are part of the solicitor's overheads. Although, telephone conference fees and unusually heavy photocopying charges could be allowed if the court were persuaded: PD47 5.22(4) and 5.22(5).

As ever, there is more complexity in the authorities, distinguishing "solicitors' disbursements" and "professional disbursements". *Herbert v HH Law Ltd* [2019] 1 WLR 4253 at [57]-[67] goes into the detail, but it does not have much bearing on the everyday practice of costs. The items discussed in this chapter are generally accepted as being disbursements.

List of recoverable disbursements under fixed costs schemes

There are slight differences in the lists of recoverable disbursements between each fixed costs scheme. The court cannot allow a disbursement that is not on the permitted list for the relevant Section: CPR 45.12(1)(b); CPR 45.19(1)(b); CPR 45.29I(1)(b) respectively. The court may allow a disbursement that is on the list, but the permissive language suggests that the court may decide not to allow it, for instance if it is unreasonably or disproportionately incurred.

	Section II Predictable costs CPR 45.12	Section III Portal costs CPR 45.19	Section IIIA costs CPR 45.29I
Medical records	✓	✓*	✓*
Medical report(s)	✓	✓*	✓*
Fixed price medical report		✓	✓
Further fixed price medical report where justified		✓	✓
Non-medical report as provided for by Protocol		✓	✓
Expert's trial attendance fee where the court has given permission			✓
Police report	✓		
Engineer's report	✓	✓	✓
DVLA search fee	✓	✓	✓
Motor Insurance Database search fee		✓	✓
Counsel's fees where they are necessarily incurred by reason of claimant being a child or protected party	✓		
Cost of advice from a specialist solicitor or counsel as provided for by the relevant Protocol			✓
Court fees			✓
Court fees where they are necessarily incurred by reason of claimant being a child or protected party/ Court fees as a result of Part 21 being applicable	✓	✓	
Court fees payable where proceedings are started as a result of a limitation period that is about to expire		✓	
Court fees for the Stage 3 procedure		✓	✓

Witness expenses			✓
Party or witness loss of earnings or loss of leave not exceeding amount in PD45 (at 2A.1, £90 per day for damages up to £10K, £135 over)			✓
Any other disbursements which has arisen due to a particular feature of the dispute	✓	✓	✓

* subject to whether fixed cost medical fees apply instead.

Interesting points of note are that police report fees are not automatically recoverable under portal and Section IIIA costs, and nor are MID search fees under predictable costs. However, if a claimant could demonstrate they were necessarily rather than frivolously incurred, a defendant would likely agree them under the provision for any other disbursement arising due to a particular feature of the dispute – which is addressed further below.

Disbursements in small claims

Only certain disbursements are recoverable:

- **court fees**;
- no more than £750 (as specified currently by PD27 7.3(2)) for each **expert's fees**;
- in an appeal, the cost of any **approved transcript** reasonably incurred.
- expenses which a party or witness has reasonably incurred in **travelling** to and from a hearing or in **staying away from home** for the purposes of attending a hearing;
- no more than £95 per day for each person (as specified currently by PD27 7.3(1)) for any **loss of earnings or loss of leave** by a party or witness due to attending a hearing or to staying away from home for the purposes of attending a hearing;

The first two are the most common in personal injury claims. Few claims go all the way to a small claims hearing because it is uneconomic.

Claimants' solicitors are often reluctant to accept small claims costs because the practical outcome is that they do not get paid for their work. They are even less likely to accept small claims costs if they will be left out of pocket for disbursements. The cap for expert's fees was formerly £200, and that meant defendants would offer less for a GP report than was provided for by the MRO Agreement. The new cap of £750 per expert is helpful for facilitating settlements and defendants are more likely to offer the sum claims for expert reports.

One-line objections for use on portal forms

Under the Protocols, where the defendant does not agree a disbursement he must state his objection and pay what he considers reasonable. These are common objections that might be given to the claimant and used on page 3 of the Court Proceedings Pack Part A.

Medical report fees

Issue	**Reason given by defendant for not paying full disbursement**
Already paid	Fee paid already with stage 1 fixed costs/ direct to medical agency
Fixed price fee	The fixed fee applies for the first report in this soft tissue injury claim
MROA applies	MRO Agreement and its capped fees apply – fee exceeds MROA rate
Fee excessive	Fee is excessive and no breakdown has been provided
Direct report	Fee exceeds rates under MRO Agreement which include agency fees
Shopping around	Undisclosed – claimant relied on other reports – 'report shopping'
Not used	Report not relied upon – unreasonably obtained, other report(s) adequate
Non-attendance	Non-attendance fees are not reasonably recoverable from defendant
Further report	It was not reasonable, proportionate or necessary to obtain a further report

Medical notes fees

Issue	**Reason given by defendant for not paying full disbursement**
VAT added	VAT has been wrongly added to the medical provider's charge
No agency element	Fee exceeds statutory cap of £50 (SI 2001/3223)
MROA applies	MRO Agreement and its capped fees apply – fee exceeds MROA rate

Other fees

Issue	Reason given by defendant for not paying full disbursement
ATE Premium	ATE is not recoverable in claims commenced after 1/4/13
Costs drafting	Fee not allowed under CPR 45.19
Counsel's fees	Fee not allowed under CPR 45.19
Courier	Fee not allowed under CPR 45.19 or PD47 5.22(4)
DVLA Search	DVLA search costs £2.50 directly from DVLA
Engineer's fee	Vehicle was obviously economically repairable – repair estimate sufficient
Engineer's fee	Excessive compared to typical market fees
Enquiry agent	Fee not allowed under CPR 45.19
MID search	MID search costs £4 one off, or is £160 p.a. unlimited use for solicitors
Non-medical report	Not reasonably required to value the claim
Non-medical report	The fee is unreasonable and disproportionate and should be reduced
Postage	Fee not allowed under CPR 45.19 or PD47 5.22(4)
Photocopying	Fee not allowed under CPR 45.19 or PD47 5.22(5)
Referral fee	Agreements to pay referral fees are unenforceable: s57(6) LASPOA 2012
Travelling expenses	Fee not allowed under CPR 45.19 or PD47 5.22(3)

The following pages set out further reasoning on those issues.

Providing disbursement fee notes

When commencing detailed assessment proceedings, the receiving party must serve 'copies of the fee notes of counsel and of any expert in respect of fees claimed in the bill' and 'written evidence as to any other disbursement which is claimed and which exceeds £500': PD47 5.2. They must also be filed at court for when requesting a detailed assessment hearing or provisional assessment: PD47 13.2(h). There is no requirement under PD44 to file or serve fee notes for a summary assessment.

In practice, for the purpose of negotiations, paying parties usually ask to see all fee notes and claimants provide them, often without prompting. The paying party understandably wants the best evidence of the costs claimed. Providing the fee notes facilitates swifter agreement and is welcome co-operation.

In surprising contrast, claimants are often tremendously reluctant to provide information that notable cases say should be provided – such as a breakdown of a medical report fee where the report was obtained via an agency: *Stringer v Copley* (HHJ Cook, Kingston Upon Thames County Court, 17 May 2002, unreported).

Medical agencies (MROs)

Medical fees, or more particularly fees via medical reporting organisations ('MROs') – more simply called medical agencies – have been a blight on the successful operation of the fixed costs schemes because they were not fixed for a long time. That began to change when fixed cost medical reports were introduced in 2014.

Problems began with the predictable costs scheme. Defendants said that the fees of the medical agency were solicitor's work and should be covered by the formula for predictable costs, and not charged separately as disbursements. The case that came to the fore was *Woollard v Fowler* [2005] EWHC 90051 (Costs). It went to the Court of Appeal on the decision that the agency fees were recoverable as disbursements. It was joined with another case called *Crane v Canons Leisure*, also concerned with the nature of disbursements. *Woollard* went for mediation before hearing, which resulted in a settlement and the first MRO Agreement, which set out capped fees for medical reports including agency fees. You may still hear the MRO Agreement called the 'Woollard Agreement'. *Crane* went on to be decided by the Court of Appeal ([2008] 1 WLR 2549) which, inconsistently with the negotiated outcome in *Woollard*, held by a majority that disbursements (here costs draftsman's fees) should be treated as part of the solicitor's charges because of the nature of the work – the solicitor remained responsible for it. *Crane* has been doubted by commentators, and Sir Rupert Jackson proposed to reverse it by statute in his *Final Report* if recoverable additional liabilities were to continue.

The MRO Agreement would have worked well as a solution if everyone had participated in it. While most insurers did, many medical agencies did not. As the years went by, fewer medical agencies participated, seemingly with a view to claiming fees above the cap. Some insurers then withdrew with the aim of paying lower fees, as the capped amounts had become *de facto* fixed fees. Thus, while large sums were involved in aggregate, there ended up being many disputes over low sums in individual claims.

One phenomenon was solicitors owning their own medical agencies, so that they could benefit from the medical agency fees in addition to the fixed costs.

Claimants continue to resist the MRO Agreement's rates being accepted as any benchmark; although it is true that any claimant could obtain a report from a participating agency, so it is difficult to see why the figures are not a proper comparison.

The new system of fixed cost medical reports has sought to tackle some of these problems, and hopefully it will expand in due course.

<u>MRO Agreement</u>

The MRO Agreement was renewed in perpetuity in 2012, although it was amended and restated in 2014. It applies to claims for general damages not exceeding £15,000 where the medical agency and compensatory both participate in the agreement. The participators are listed on AMRO's and DAC Beachcroft's websites. The rates that apply under the agreement are:

	Rate A Paid within 90 days of receipt of the Applicable Invoice and Required Information	**Rate B Paid after 90 days of receipt of the Applicable Invoice and Required Information**
General practitioner Report – No notes	£200	£225
Review notes by General Practitioner	£50	£55
Orthopaedic Report – Including review of notes	£425	£465
Accident and Emergency report – Including review of notes	£375	£410
Addendum	Cost + £25	Cost + £30
Cost of obtaining each set of medical records	Cost charged by data provider + £25	Cost charged by data provider + £30

Some agencies always render a Rate B invoice, and leave it to defendants to apply Rate A instead – defendant claims handlers unfortunately do not always notice.

The 90 days do not start until the invoice and 'required information' is delivered to the insurer. Participating agencies usually provide that information in the invoice, which is:

- Compensators' claim reference number;
- Claimant's name;
- Claimant's date of birth;
- Accident Date;

- specialism of the expert providing the report.

Defendants who may be asked to pay Rate B might check first whether that information has indeed been provided, as if it has not they would be able to pay Rate A beyond the 90 days since receiving the invoice.

There is a row that has never really been resolved over Rate A and Rate B. Is Rate B is the normal rate, and Rate A a discount for early payment; or is Rate A the normal rate and Rate B the penalty for late payment? The distinction is important when the MRO Agreement's rates are adopted as a benchmark for reports not falling within its scope.

Fixed cost medical fees in RTAs

Fixed cost medical fees are payable in 'soft tissue injury claims' started under the RTA Protocol by a CNF dated on or after 1 October 2014.

Although the prices are fixed, it appears from the rules that the court may still choose to disallow the fee, for instance if it was unreasonably or disproportionately incurred. Presumably such arguments will be rare.

Normally there will only be one medical report and it will be provided by a person independent of any treatment provided.

'Soft tissue injury claim' is defined in paragraph 1.1(16A) of the RTA Protocol: 'a claim brought by an occupant of a motor vehicle where the significant physical injury caused is a soft tissue injury and includes claims where there is a minor psychological injury secondary in significance to the physical injury.'

Broadly speaking, this means a 'whiplash' claim. The word 'occupant' is important and has led to some argument. It would exclude a pedestrian's claim, perfectly logically – no one expects a person hit by a car to walk away with only whiplash, for instance. Some claimants have argued that it excludes motorcyclists. As a matter of interpretation of the definition, that seems unlikely. The motorcyclist is the occupant of the motorcycle. Many may see analogies with claims under the Occupier's Liability Act 1957 from hazy memories of Law School if not practice – *Wheeler v Copas* [1981] 3 All ER 405 concerning the occupant of a step ladder, for instance. With motorcyclists, the classification is more likely to turn on the injuries because motorcyclists too are at risk of more serious injuries than whiplash. There are reports that when stakeholders were discussing these provisions, the proposed language was intended to exclude motorcyclists. If so, the language does not clearly achieve that. It is unambiguous and appears to indicate the opposite.

CPR 45.19(2B) and 45.29I(2B) prohibit, save in exceptional circumstances, the recovery of a fee from a person who has provided treatment to the claimant or is associated with someone who does. 'Associated' is defined in the RTA Protocol, and broadly speaking means 'works in the same practice'. The purpose of these provisions is to ensure independent medical evidence. There have not yet been any reported instances of 'exceptional circumstances'; discussions elsewhere in this book show that is a very high threshold.

An occasional misunderstanding around the 'association' prohibition is that it means reports obtained via a medical agency that also arranged treatment are irrecoverable. The rules do not say that. The agency stands in the shoes of the solicitor for making the arrangements. A solicitor can arrange treatment and expert evidence, so the agency can do so as well. The focus must be on the experts themselves. If an agency report did fall foul of the association prohibition, it would follow the agency would not recover anything for its work either because it is covered by the fixed fee.

The recoverable fees are:

First report, whatever discipline	£180
Further reports, where justified:	
Consultant Orthopaedic Surgeon (inclusive of a review of medical records where applicable)	£420
Consultant in Accident and Emergency Medicine	£360

General Practitioner registered with the General Medical Council	£180
Physiotherapist registered with the Health and Care Professions Council	£180
Medical records, per set	no more than £30 plus the direct cost from the holder of the records, and limited to £80 in total for each set of records required
addendum report on medical records (except by Consultant Orthopaedic Surgeon)	£50
answer to questions under Part 35	£80

VAT on medical fees

VAT is recoverable between the parties in addition to the base cost of medical reports and medical records, unless the receiving party is registered for VAT and can recover VAT as input tax.

That is the short answer. The longer answer traces back further.

VAT may be applied at source or by the obtaining solicitor or medical agency. Medical reports usually attract VAT at source because they are not subject to a VAT exemption. They used to be, but a decision of the European Court of Justice changed that in 2006. Treatment is VAT exempt, but a medical report for the court in a damages claim does not fall into that category. So, if a medical expert is VAT registered (which he should be if his incomes exceeds the registration threshold), he would add VAT to his medical report fee and that VAT would appear on his invoice along with his VAT registration number. If the medical expert is not VAT registered he will not add VAT, but the medical agency or solicitor usually will for the reasons given below.

Medical records are subject to various VAT exemptions. There are exemptions when records are obtained under the Data Protection Act 1998 or the Access to Health Records Act 1990 for use in claims. It is difficult to envisage a situation where the records are not obtained for a claim under one of those statutes. The provisions are summarised in paragraph 4.1 of HMRC VAT Notice 701/57. Thus GPs, hospitals and the like do not usually charge VAT when providing copies of medical records.

VAT on medical records fees was a doggedly contentious issue that produced notable judgments for more than a decade. Although very small sums are involved in each case, it arose in so many claims that paying parties took the point.

The law was settled by *Prosser v British Airways Plc* [2019] 1 WLR 4513. Its *ratio* dodges the question of whether VAT is properly added by medical agencies, and concluded it should be allowed because the sums involved were small, and there were seemingly authoritative materials in support, so that the VAT was reasonably and proportionately incurred. That was an inversion of some circuit level decisions, in which doubt as whether the VAT was reasonably incurred was resolved in favour of paying parties. Doubt arose because only the involvement of the medical agency seemed to give rise to VAT: the VAT tribunal decision in *Barratt, Goff and Tomlinson v HMRC* [2011] 3 Costs LR 409 held a solicitor who did not use a medical agency did need to add VAT to a medical fee which does not already have VAT added. That is now doubtful itself following *Prosser*. The Court of Appeal's obiter dicta about the solicitor's obligations is the hard backstop. Where a solicitor uses medical reports and records to provide his service to the client, rather than acting a mere postbox to pass them on, then he must add VAT to the fees if there is not already VAT on them at source.

Other experts

Predictable costs make no provision for the fees of non-medical experts.

Under the RTA and EL/PL Protocols, non-medical reports are permitted where they are reasonably required to value the claim, and hence the fees for such reports are recoverable as disbursements under portal costs: CPR 45.19(2)(a)(ii).

For Section IIIA costs, the cost for any such report provided for in the relevant Protocol for the claim is recoverable: CPR 45.29I(2)(b). Any expert's fee for attending the trial where the court has given permission is also recoverable: CPR 45.29I(2)(e).

Counsel's fees in fixed costs claims

In the general run of claims, counsel's fees are recoverable disbursements and are subject to assessment. In fixed costs claims, counsel's fees are recoverable only where the rules provide.

Until recently, counsel's fees were often allowed as disbursements in fixed costs claims. Treating counsel's fees as disbursements was the old familiar way. Establishing that the intention of the fixed cost regime might be different meant challenging that preconception in every claim. There has been a sea change following the landmark Court of Appeal decision in *Cham v Aldred* [2020] 1 WLR 1276. *Cham* concerned a claim for counsel's advice in a child's claim under Section IIIA. The disallowance of counsel's fee in that particular type of claim because Section IIIA made no provision set the high-water mark. There is now a broader appreciation that fixed costs were always intended to cover the work of all legal representatives, solicitors and counsel (and even costs draftsmen), and counsel's fees will rarely be allowed as disbursements in addition to fixed costs.

There are only a handful of provisions in the fixed costs schemes allowing for recovery of counsel's fees. Often counsel's fees are part of the fixed costs allowance. Counsel may give the advice on quantum in a child's Protocol claim, and his fee is strictly treated as part of the fixed profit costs (Type C fixed costs). Counsel may be the advocate at the trial covered by Section IIIA fixed costs. Any work done by counsel is impliedly treated as legal representative's work and is covered by the fixed profit costs. Thus it is not possible for a solicitor to heavily outsource to counsel and improve his profitability by recovering fixed costs plus counsel's fees as disbursements.

Predictable costs and counsel's fees

Counsel's fees are recoverable in predictable costs cases only where they are necessarily incurred because the claimant is a child or protected party. See 'Predictable costs and children' in Chapter One. See also the further discussion of *Cham v Aldred* below.

Portal costs and additional advice

In portal costs, Type B and Type C fixed costs might cover counsel's advocacy at a Stage 3 hearing and advice in a child's claim respectively. CPR 45.23B allows for recovery of an amount equivalent to Type C fixed costs in Protocol cases with damages over £10,000 where additional advice has been obtained from a specialist solicitor or counsel and it was reasonably required to value the claim. The rule does not specify whether that amount is to be allowed as a disbursement or as part of the fixed costs. In practice, counsel's fees would usually be shown as disbursements.

If the claim exits the Protocol after the additional advice fee has been incurred, it is still recoverable under Section IIIA: CPR 45.29I(2)(c).

Section IIIA and counsel's fees – *Cham v Aldred*

CPR 45.29I(2)(c) is the only provision for counsel's fees as a *disbursement* in Section IIIA. (That rule also allows for a specialist solicitor's disbursement for the same work, an apparent express departure from the statutory definition of a disbursement in s67 Solicitors Act 1974 and the simpler definition in the SRA's glossary.) The rule covers the same additional advice that would be allowed in over £10,000 damages claims under relevant Protocol. Lambert J held in *Dover v Finsbury Food Group plc* [2020] EWHC 2176 (QB) that the fee is not fixed at the same amount as under the Protocol (£150 plus VAT) so will be assessed if not agreed, but it may be disallowed if unreasonable or unjustified. The claimant will need to explain why the advice was needed and justify the fee level.

There is no other provision for counsel's fees as disbursements in Section IIIA. If counsel were the advocate at trial, his fee would be recoverable as the advocacy fee in Part D of the relevant table. Any counsel's fee for advice or drafting would be treated as part of the fixed recoverable costs and not treated as a disbursement.

Counsel's fees will rarely be recoverable under the provision in CPR 45.29I(2)(h) for any other disbursement reasonably incurred due to a particular feature of the dispute. In *Cham v Aldred* [2020] 1 WLR 1276, Coulson LJ said at [48] and [51]:

> *in the vast majority of cases, counsel's fees, although properly described as a disbursement, and although doubtless reasonably incurred, would not be allowed by the court under r.45.29I(1)(a). That is because the work that is the subject of the disbursement has already been allowed for in the fixed recoverable costs (Table 6B)...*
>
> *If an item of work is deemed (or can be said implicitly) to be within the fixed recoverable costs in Table 6B, then it will not be separately recoverable as a disbursement.*

The court did not identify the residual minority of cases in which counsel's fees may not be within the fixed recoverable costs. Coulson LJ did say at [36]:

> *The particular features of the dispute in an RTA claim will commonly be matters such as: how the accident happened, whether the defendant was to blame for the accident, the nature, scope and extent of the injuries and their consequences, and other matters of that kind. For example, the particular circumstances of the accident may be sufficiently unusual to require an accident reconstruction expert, or the injuries may be so complex that they require a number of different experts' reports. Such additional involvement of experts may also require specific advice from counsel. Depending always on the facts, such costs may be said to be a disbursement properly incurred as a result of a particular feature of the dispute.*

At first blush that may suggest counsel's fees for advice on quantum may be recoverable under CPR 45.29I(2)(h) where there are several medical reports. That would not be a remotely safe conclusion. Medical reports are recoverable in their own right, and would not fall under CPR 45.29I(2)(h). Therefore, dealing with many reports will usually be within the fixed recoverable costs.

This in *Coleman v Townsend* (SCCO, 13 July 2020, unreported), Master Haworth disallowed counsel's abated brief fee and skeleton argument fee claimed under CPR 45.29I(2)(h) after the claim settled the day before trial (meaning that the trial advocacy fee was not recoverable).

In *Cusmans v Plumbing Solutions* (County Court at Bristol, 12 October 2017, unreported), a case predating *Cham* by two years, DDJ Humphreys came to similar conclusions and disallowed an abated brief fee, counsel's fee for setting particulars and the fee for attending a CMC. Dealing with a curious point where a trial was started but had to be adjourned when the judge recused himself, the DDJ dis allow a sum equivalent to the trial advocacy fee under CPR 45.29I(2)(h) or alternatively under CPR 45.29J.

The working assumption should generally be counsel's fees aside from the additional advice will not be recoverable in Section IIIA fixed costs cases.

As counsel's work will fall within the fixed recoverable costs, then in an appropriate case counsel's fees might be recoverable as a result of an exceptional circumstances argument under CPR 45.29J. Indeed a case in which counsel's fees might be allowed under CPR 45.29I(2)(h) might involve exceptional circumstances anyway.

The Supreme Court refused permission for a further appeal in *Cham*. The Civil Procedure Rules Committee will consider this issue again in due course. If they decide rule amendment is appropriate then rather than introducing any fees at large, specific rules allowing additional fixed sums in specific circumstances would promote the aim certainty through fixed recoverable costs.

Court fees

Court fees incurred during the period covered by a costs order are recoverable.

Unlike other disbursements, there is no fee note. Instead, evidence that the step has been taken in the proceedings is evidence that the fee has been incurred. The court form with which the fee corresponds should have been served.

The current court fees are set out in the Civil Proceedings Fees Order (SI 2008/1053) as amended. The fees have been varied or increased several times since 2008 with amending statutory instruments. The recoverable fee is the actual fee that was paid in accordance with the Fees Order as it was at the time of payment.

Most court fees are paid by the claimant, but when the defendant takes a step in the proceedings such as making a counterclaim or application the defendant pays the fee.

Some fees are payable on a scale according to the value of the claim, such as issue fees or the fees for requesting a detailed assessment. If the claim was unreasonably overvalued at the time the court fee was incurred which caused a greater fee to be paid, the paying party can argue that the higher fee was unreasonably incurred and a lower fee should be allowed on assessment.

Traditionally issue fees have been set in bands. For claims exceeding £10,000, they are now 5% of the value of the claim. Substantial sums are involved. The claimant is incentivised to make a reasonable valuation of the claim otherwise he will have to pay an unnecessarily high fee. It does not seem so far that the courts are being strict on valuations and seeking top-ups if the payment was short. On the flip side of that, courts are not generally reducing fees on the basis the claim was overvalued. Nevertheless, the defendant can still argue for a lesser fee if the facts support it.

What the defendant cannot do is argue for a court fee based on the final settlement figure. The claimant does not have a crystal ball; the test is whether the claimant made a reasonable valuation at the time the fee was incurred.

DVLA and MID fees

A search of the DVLA records to identify a vehicle's registered keeper – commonly done when the claimant only gets the defendant's vehicle registration at the accident – costs £2.50. There is no fee note from the DVLA, but claimants usually produce the form the DVLA returns with the defendant's address as proof of payment. A one-off search of the Motor Insurance Database costs £4, although solicitors can subscribe for £200 yearly to get unlimited access, in which case there would be no specific fee chargeable to an individual claim.

Costs of 'obtaining'

The word 'obtaining' in the fixed costs rules was one of the justifications for allowing medical agency fees. The various fixed costs rules say that the receiving party is allowed 'costs of obtaining… a medical report', for example. On the face of it, there is no reason why agency fees would not be allowed for obtaining DVLA searches, MID searches, police reports and engineer's reports. Such additional costs are rarely seen. It would be difficult to justify a mark-up on the modest DVLA and MID fees where the solicitor can get what is needed in one or two units of time. Agencies have sometimes gotten involved in providing engineer's reports, but it is not encountered often. The fee would have to be reasonable and proportionate.

Other disbursements arising due to a particular feature of the dispute

There is a 'sweep-up' provision to allow for other disbursements in predictable costs and Section IIIA cases.

As addressed above in the section 'Section IIIA and counsel's fees' this provision will not generally allow for counsel's fees. Although the provision appears to be wide, in *Cham* Coulson LJ said at [58]: '*the rule at rule 45.29I(2)(h), even if it can properly be described as a catch-all, needs to be carefully and narrowly interpreted by reference to Section IIIA as a whole.*'

The rule applies to 'other' disbursements, which suggests it is a provision for disbursements not otherwise listed in the Rules. The disbursement must also arise because of a particular feature of the dispute. Thus pre-emptive disbursements would not pass muster; the particular feature requiring the disbursement must be present.

The meaning of 'dispute' is ambiguous. On a plain reading it would be an aspect of the claim about which the parties were arguing; but other usages in Part 46 suggest it is a term of art meaning the 'claim' more broadly. See CPR 45.9(2)(a) and 45.29(1)(a).

In costs-only proceedings for predictable costs, PD45 2.9 sets out a mandatory requirement:

> *The claimant must also include on the claim form details of any disbursements. The disbursements that may be claimed are set out in rule 45.12(1). If the disbursement falls within 45.12(2)(c) (disbursements that have arisen due to a particular feature of the dispute) the claimant must give details of the particular feature of the dispute that made the disbursement necessary.*

There are no mirror provisions for portal costs or Section IIIA costs, but it would be sensible and helpful if the practice direction were followed.

The types of disbursement that may be allowed under this provision in appropriate cases are fees for photographs (of the accident location, or of scarring) or locus reports.

Translation and interpreting fees were often claimed under this provision. However, the Court of Appeal disapproved that in *Cham*, holding at [35] that linguistic ability was feature of the claimant and not a feature of the dispute, and hence did not fall under the 'sweep-up' provision. Overnight, translation and interpreting fees ceased to be recoverable in fixed costs cases.

Disbursements outside the fixed costs schemes

More disbursements are recoverable beyond the limits set out in the fixed costs schemes.

Travelling expenses

Travelling expenses, where travel is not 'local' as defined in PD47 5.22(3), may be allowed. The mileage rate where allowed should be limited to 45p per mile, being the rate prescribed by HMRC for tax purposes for business mileage. It is important to note that the solicitor may be obliged to add VAT to some travelling expenses, such as train fares. This is because the ticket is not received and used by the claimant personally so the conditions to not add VAT in HMRC Notice 700 paragraph 25.1.1 are not met. If practical, if a client (or ultimately an opponent) does not want the expense increased by 20%, a solution is to ask the client to purchase the train ticket and hand it over to the solicitor.

Counsel's fees

Counsel's fees are recoverable on the standard basis where they are reasonably and proportionately incurred and reasonable and proportionate in amount. There is less transparency about counsel's fees than solicitor's fees from counsel's fee note, but counsel's fees are broadly speaking based on hourly rates and time spent and are amenable to challenge in the same way as solicitor's profit costs (as covered in the next section).

If a senior fee earner had conduct, involving counsel may be unreasonable. That depends on how counsel assists. If counsel drafts statements of case, it may amount to reasonable delegation. It might be unreasonable duplication if counsel gives a senior fee earner a second opinion on liability on quantum. Whether counsel's advice in conference rather than in writing is needed depends on whether there is an evaluative element such as assessing a witness that can be done only at a face to face meeting.

CHAPTER FIVE
RECOVERABLE COSTS

This chapter considers the costs that are recoverable where fixed costs do not apply and instead costs will be assessed.

The indemnity principle

The indemnity principle is a simple rule at common law that a party may not recover from his opponent more costs than he has to pay his own solicitor. It holds true not just for the overall amount but also for individual elements of the costs, such as the hourly rate.

For contentious business agreements only, the indemnity principle is enacted in s60(3) Solicitors Act 1974.

The indemnity principle has been eroded down the years but is still of importance for assessments on the standard basis or the indemnity basis (the indemnity basis should not be confused with the indemnity principle; they are different things with similar names). For fixed costs, Simon J (as he then was) held that amendments to s51(2) Senior Courts Act 1981 meant that fixed costs could be prescribed in the CPR in abrogation of the indemnity principle: *Nizami v Butt* [2006] 1 WLR 3307 at [8]-[10].

Standards basis and indemnity basis costs

Where detailed assessment and summary assessment describe the process the court will follow to decide the amount of costs, the bases of assessment set out how the court will in substance decide what to allow, if anything, for each item of costs.

Costs on the standard basis are reasonable and proportionately incurred and reasonable and proportionate in amount, with any doubt to be resolved in favour of the paying party (CPR 44.3(1) and (2)). Costs on the indemnity basis must be reasonably incurred and reasonable in amount with any doubt resolved in favour of the receiving party (CPR

44.3(1) and (3)). The court should have ensured the case was dealt with at proportionate cost anyway under the overriding objection in CPR 1.1(1).

A pet hate is orders drafted to refer to costs on 'a standard basis'. That shows a lack of appreciation of the fact that the standard basis is a specific thing defined by the CPR and takes the definite article. 'Standard' is not used merely in the general sense of 'the way it is normally done'.

Costs arguments on assessment about reasonableness and proportionality are raised retrospectively, but must not use hindsight. They must be based on what the solicitor knew at the time: *Francis v Francis & Dickerson* [1955] 3 WLR 973 which has also been approved by the Court of Appeal post-CPR.

Most assessments are on the standard basis. Costs judges seem remarkably confident, because often there is no sign they have any 'doubt'; costs which might have been doubtful are allowed when they would have been disallowed if there were any doubt. In practice there seems very little difference to the indemnity basis because of that apparent lack of doubt.

The indemnity basis arises infrequently. If a claimant beats his own offer at trial he gets indemnity costs under CPR 36.17 for the period after the expiry of the winning offer's relevant period. A court may order indemnity costs if a party's conduct was 'out of the norm': *Excelsior Commercial & Industrial Holdings Ltd v Salisbury Hammer Aspden & Johnson (a firm)* [2002] EWCA Civ 879.

Costs on the standard basis or the indemnity basis are not fixed costs; but that does not mean an assessment on the standard basis or the indemnity basis cannot result in fixed costs.

That fact seems to be one of the most confusing to judges and practitioners. An example will demonstrate. A claim concludes with an order for detailed assessment on the standard basis; the claimant presents a bill of costs drawn on an hourly rate; the defendant argues the claimant unreasonably exited the RTA Protocol; the court agrees and the claimant is limited to fixed costs. Nothing in the making of an order for an assessment on the standard basis and conducting that assessment on the standard basis ousts the court's powers on assessment to consider fixed costs arguments.

That breaks any outright correlation between the standard basis, the indemnity basis and hourly rate costs.

The standard basis and the indemnity basis must be understood in a more abstract way, which is as they are expressed in CPR 44.3.

Reasonableness and proportionality

Better minds have tried to define these terms with limited success. There is no firm definition. Some everyday context helps.

Reasonableness is about the going rate. If one shop charges noticeably more for a product than other shops, its price is probably unreasonable. That does not mean the cheapest shop is the reasonable one. Others that are slightly dearer might offer value added services which make it worth paying a little more. So, reasonableness is about making a wider comparison beyond the individual claim.

There is a semantic argument about whether reasonableness is about (a) what is reasonable for the receiving party to have incurred (which may favour the receiving party) or (b) what is reasonable for the paying party to pay (which may favour the paying party). CPR 44.3(1) expressly refers to (a), and whether something is reasonable in amount is probably broad enough to encompass (b). Different cases look at it in different ways; it is an argument to be aware of rather than one to try and resolve.

Proportionality is about gauging the costs relative to the individual's claim's features, such as its value or complexity. If a shop charged £100 for delivery of a small item, that would seem out of kilter. It's much easier to say what is disproportionate than what is proportionate. Proportionality is successful as a long-stop position, to prevent very high amounts being allowed.

There are two proportionality tests. The older one is the test from *Lownds v Home Office* [2002] 1 WLR 2450, usually called the Lownds test. It has two stages. At the start of an assessment, the court will form a broad view as to whether the costs appear proportionate (this is sometimes jokingly called the 'eyebrows' test – if they eyebrows go up, the costs are disproportionate). If the costs are disproportionate, the next step is to only allow the costs that are necessary when allowing the bill. Necessary is a stricter test than reasonable, but may still lead to costs allowances that appear disproportionate.

A new test was inserted into the CPR on the recommendations of Sir Rupert Jackson after his 2009 review of civil costs. Proportionality is now overriding: disproportionate costs will be disallowed even if they were reasonably and necessarily incurred (CPR 44.3(2)(a)). CPR 44.3(5) says:

> *Costs incurred are proportionate if they bear a reasonable relationship to –*
> *a) the sums in issue in the proceedings;*
> *b) the value of any non-monetary relief in issue in the proceedings;*
> *c) the complexity of the litigation;*
> *d) any additional work generated by the conduct of the paying party; and*
> *e) any wider factors involved in the proceedings, such as reputation or public importance.*

Defining proportionality with the word 'reasonable' is a confusing overlap. Under the new test, proportionality can be applied on a broad brush basis at the end of an assessment. Some judges like to look over the provisional assessment arithmetic before making a final decision on proportionality, and ask the parties to write back to the court with figures for that purpose.

The new test was considered by the Court of Appeal in *West v Stockport NHS Foundation Trust* [2019] 1 WLR 6157. The Court held at [81]-[82]:

> *when the judge comes to consider proportionality, there are some elements of costs which should be left out of account. The exceptions are*

> *those items of cost which are fixed and unavoidable, or which have an irreducible minimum, without which the litigation could not have been progressed. Court fees are perhaps the best example.*

That approach to the proportionality test may mean that the final total may still appear disproportionate if large items are 'unavoidable'. It seems to reintroduce something similar to the Lownds proportionality test's 'necessary' criterion. Unavoidable items are necessarily incurred. Parties may dispute which items are 'unavoidable', but it should be a narrow category. Aside from court fees, other examples covered in the judgment are VAT and the costs of preparing the bill, which are said to distort the perception of whether the costs are proportionate, plus any still recoverable ATE premium.

The Court's guidance on applying proportionality in detailed assessments is set out in Chapter 8.

CPR 44.3(7) deals with which test applies. It does not refer to the Lownds test by name, but refers to the old wording of the relevant rule under which it was applied. If proceedings were started before 1 April 2013, the Lownds test applies to the whole bill. If proceedings were started after 1 April 2013, the Lownds test applies only to work before that date. Part 47 and its practice direction requires that bills are split between the two proportionality tests so that they can be more easily applied: PD47 5.8(7).

Exaggeration

What happens where a party pleads a claim for damages for a very much greater sum than is eventually agreed or allowed? In many cases, the consequences are dealt with when the order for costs is made. There may be no order for costs, or an order to pay the opponent's costs, or an order for only a percentage of costs, or an order for costs of certain issues only. There is a huge array of possibilities.

This section is concerned mainly with the assessment of costs where the damages claim was exaggerated.

Check whether the costs order has already dealt with exaggeration. Double jeopardy does not apply. Although there is no reason in principle why the court could not assess costs down where the claim had been exaggerated, if the costs order has already dealt with exaggeration then the court is not likely to think such an assessment was fair. Thus if a party is only to get a percentage of costs or costs of certain issues that is the end of the exaggeration issue. In particular, if the court decides the exaggeration was an intentional deception, it is very likely the costs order will deal with it.

If the exaggeration was instead that the claimant put its case at its very best and recovered very much less, the court may not have dealt with the issue in the costs order, or the claim may have concluded on a Part 36 acceptance so there was no chance to deal with the issue. The exaggeration issue is then dealt with on assessment. The defendant will argue that some costs will have been unreasonably and disproportionately incurred. In *Lahey v Pirelli Tyres* [2007] 1 WLR 998, Dyson LJ (as he then was) said at [24]:

> *the costs judge can disallow entire sections of a bill of costs. If the costs judge considers that the claimant acted unreasonably in refusing an offer to settle made before proceedings were issued, he is entitled to disallow all the costs post-issue on the footing that they were costs 'unreasonably incurred': rule 44.4(1). Similarly, where he decides that a party was unreasonable to raise and pursue an issue, the costs judge is entitled to disallow the costs relating to that issue on the grounds that they were unreasonably incurred.*

Thus, although reasonableness and proportionality are simple and abstract, they are powerful and facilitate justice on assessment for all manner of situations.

The court has a power in CPR 44.11 to deal with misconduct in proceedings, including the assessment proceedings, by disallowing all or part of the costs. In most cases it adds little to what can be done already with reasonableness and proportionality.

If the costs claim itself is exaggerated, the principles are similar; and the paying party can protect itself by making a reasonable offer.

Hourly rates

Uncertainty

Hourly rates introduce uncertainty into assessments. Receiving parties would like as high hourly rates as possible. Paying parties want them to be low. In personal injury claims, claimant lawyers' rates creep up year on year; defendants would prefer to have them fixed at set rates.

A survey of decisions on assessments would not produce a predictable pattern of hourly rates allowed. Hourly rates are treated as being within the discretion of the court – which they are; but more consistent application of principles in all cases would save costs in the assessment process, as parties would not gamble so often on getting a particular result.

Composition

Hourly rates reflect:

1. The direct cost of doing the work, including:
   a. Fee earner's wages
   b. Overheads: rent, rates, bills, support staff, office sundries.
2. A profit element, covering care and conduct and the complexity of the case.

You may occasionally hear reference to 'Factor A' and 'Factor B'. That was the old system of setting hourly rates, in which the 'direct cost' and the 'mark up' were separated. It no longer has any relevance. That process of setting hourly rates was abandoned at the turn of the century. In *Various Claimants v TUI* (SCCO, 11 August 2005, unreported), the Senior Costs Judge Master Hurst said:

> *The Claimants argue that the guideline rates are composed of a base rate plus a notional 50% uplift for care and conduct. This is not in fact the case. When the first guideline rates were produced in July 1999 they were replacing the previous A+B method of arriving at hourly rates, which the Lord Chancellor had indicated that he wished to cease. In arriving at the first figures for guideline rates a 50% uplift was*

taken as the starting point. Since that time however, the guideline rates have been revised four times, each time after a consultation conducted by the Designated Civil Judge for each area of the Country. This court has no way of knowing the basis upon which the rates recommended by the Designated Civil Judge have been arrived at. It must however, be borne in mind that there has, inevitably, been inflation since the original guideline rates were given and, in addition, the Master of the Rolls asked that the rates be banded into areas, rather than having different rates for individual locations. The most recent revision was based only on the Retail Price Index for the period. Thus, all that can be acknowledged is that the guideline rates contain an element for care and conduct. The precise percentage of that element is not ascertainable.

Guideline rates

The guideline rates were devised for summary assessments, to provide a ready chart of rates to assist judges who were making assessments on the fly under time pressure.

The association with summary assessment has fostered the misconception that guideline rates are for fast track claims only. A claim is suitable for the fast track if the trial will last less than a day (CPR 26.6(5)(a)); and at the conclusion any hearing that lasts less than a day including a fast track trial, the court should make a summary assessment of the costs (PD44 9.2). In fact, as PD44 9.2 shows, guideline rates could be applied in a multi-track claim on interim hearings at least.

Guideline rates are built on two concepts: the 'grade' of fee earner, i.e. the person doing the work; and geographical 'band', i.e. the place where the work was done.

Grades

Grades reflect the **person** that handled the case. There are four grades.

Grade A

Solicitors and Fellows of CILEx with 8 years' or more post qualification experience.

Formerly there were only three grades, 1, 2 and 3, corresponding to B, C and D. Grade A was added as a 'super-grade'. The mantra across judgments is 'Grade A rates for Grade A work.' There are very few personal injury claims that warrant the super-grade. An example might be a catastrophic claim where there has been minimal reliance on counsel. Grade A should be claimed or allowed sparingly. It is often claimed liberally, and not restricted only to the tasks that warranted Grade A. Grade A fee earners should delegate work.

Grade B

Solicitors and Fellows of CILEx with four years' or more post qualification experience.

Claims that may warrant Grade B are multi-track cases and higher value fast track claims with some complex issues, where counsel and the experts are not taking that burden.

Where counsel is instructed to advise on liability or quantum, then it is less likely that a Grade B rate can be justified, because the Grade B fee earner's experience has not brought anything to the case if counsel has been relied upon for the complicated questions. That principle is not as relevant if counsel's involvement has only been to draft documents such as the particulars of claim, because that could be seen as delegation of work.

Grade C

Solicitors and Fellows of CILEx with less than four years' post qualification experience and fee earners of equivalent experience, including Costs Lawyers in appropriate cases.

> In the vast run of personal injury claims, the concept has emerged that this is the 'normal' rate. It is right that for most claims a Grade C fee earner is reasonable, but Grade C will not be allowed if the fee earner does not have the qualifications and experience needed. Thus Grade C is the downwards tipping point at which the person becomes more important than the facts of the case. It is straightforward to determine whether or not a person is a solicitor or fellow of CILEx; there are online directories. Whether a person has equivalent experience can be opaque. Generally, taking the lead from the notes accompanying the guideline rates as published by the SCCO, if a person has 6 years' experience of litigation work, that gets Grade C.
>
> Grade D
>
> Trainee solicitors, members/associates/graduate of CILEx, paralegals, and any other fee earner.
>
> Many junior fee earners are in fact Grade D but the work is more profitable if they can get Grade C rates. And thus: the game is on! There must be adequate proof that the fee earner is in fact Grade C, which claimants will be reticent to provide, and defendants will hunt down.

Uncertainty stems from grades because they are part of a system of guidelines, and thus they are not treated as closed categories in accordance with their definitions. There would be greater certainty if unqualified persons could not claim above Grade C, for instance. However, some courts allow it.

A statement of a fee earner's grade is treated as an opinion, and is open to challenge.

Bands

Bands address the **place** where the work was (or should have been) done.

There are five bands: three for London, and two national bands for the rest of the country. There used to be six bands. There was a third national band. Everything in that band was uprated to national band 2 in 2009. National band 3 is relevant only in cases where work was done when it was in force and in a place where that rate applied.

The bands group places together because the costs of living and working in those areas are broadly similar.

The London bands are:

Band	**Area**	**Postcodes**
London band 1	City of London	EC1–EC4
London band 2	Central London	W1, WC1, WC2, SW1
London band 3	Outer London	other London postcodes

This non-exhaustive table sets out bands for many towns, cities and regions, and includes historic information about places that were in band 3. For work since 2009, they can be treated as Band 2.

Accrington	3	Cambridge County	2
Aldershot	1	Canterbury	1
Altrincham	2	Cardiff (Inner)	1
Basingstoke	1	Cardiff (Outer)	2
Bath	2	Chelmsford North	2
Bedford	2	Chelmsford South	1
Birkenhead	1	Cheltenham	2
Birmingham Inner	1	Chester	2
Birmingham Outer	3	Chorley	3
Blackburn	3	Cornwall	3
Blackpool	3	Coventry	2
Bolton	2	Cumbria	3
Bournemouth	1	Derbyshire	2
Bradford	3	Devon	3
Bristol	1	Dewsbury	3
Burnley	3	Doncaster	2
Bury	2	Dorset	1
Bury St Edmunds	2	Dudley	2
Cambridge City	1	Epsom	1

Essex	1
Evesham	3
Exeter	2
Fareham	1
Farnham	1
Gloucester	2
Grimsby	3
Guildford	1
Halifax	3
Hampshire	1
Harlow	1
Harrogate	2
Hereford	3
Hertford	2
Hitchin	2
Huddersfield	3
Hull (City)	2
Hull Outer	3
Isle of Wight	1
Keighley	3
Kidderminster	3
Kingston	1
Lancaster	3
Leeds Inner (within 2km of City Art Gallery)	1
Leeds Outer	2
Leicester	3
Leigh	2
Lewes	1
Lincoln	2
Liverpool	1
Lowestoft	2
Ludlow	3
Luton	2
Maidstone	1
Manchester Central	1
Manchester Outer	2
Medway	1
Nelson	3
Newcastle – City Centre (within 2m of St Nicholas Cathedral)	1
Newcastle (other than City Centre)	2
Newport	2
Norfolk	2
Northampton	3
Norwich City	1
Nottingham	2
Nottingham City	1
Nuneaton	2
Oldham	2
Oswestry	3
Oxford	1
Peterborough	2
Plymouth	2
Pontefract	2
Poole	1
Portsmouth	1
Preston	3
Rawtenstall	3
Redditch	3
Reigate	1
Ripon	3
Rugby	2
St Albans	2
St Helens	2
Salford	2
Scarborough	3
Sheffield	2
Shrewsbury	3
Skegness	3
Skipton	3
South Yorkshire	2
Southampton	1
Southport	2
Stafford	3
Stockport	2

Stoke	3
Stourbridge	2
Stratford	2
Suffolk, East	1
Swansea	2
Swindon	1
Tameside	2
Tamworth	3
Taunton	2
Teesside	3
Telford	3
Thames Valley	1
Tunbridge Wells	1
Wakefield	2
Wales, North	2
Wales, South	3
Wales, West	3
Walsall	2
Warwick	2
Watford	1
Wigan	2
Wiltshire	1
Winchester	1
Wolverhampton	2
Worcester	3
Yeovil	2
York	2

Some places have 'inner' and 'outer' rates, e.g. Birmingham, Cardiff, Leeds and Newcastle. Inner is generally a one mile radius of the city centre, unless otherwise stated in the table. It reflects the fact that prices such as rent are significantly higher in the city centre than in the suburbs.

Again, as the bands are guidelines, solicitors jostle to get paid a higher band.

The rates

Grade	Fee earners	London band 1	London band 2	London band 3	National band 1	National band 2	National band 3
A	Solicitors and legal executives with over 8 years' experience	£409	£317	£229–£267	£217	£201	£201
B	Solicitors and legal executives with over 4 years' experience	£296	£242	£172–£229	£192	£177	£177
C	Other solicitors or legal executives and fee earners of equivalent experience	£226	£196	£165	£161	£146	£146
D	Trainee solicitors, paralegals and other fee earners	£138	£126	£121	£118	£111	£111

The London band 3 rates with brackets are intended to cater for the diversity of firms in those areas. Generally, the larger the firm and the closer to central London, the higher up the bracket will be allowed.

The guideline rates are broad approximations. Claimants often treat them as baselines, but that is incorrect. In some cases, a lower rate could be appropriate. In practice though, lower rates are unheard of. That is a reason to be cautious about allowing higher rates, because applying the same rates is more likely to be fair across the board.

The rates have not increased since 2010.

<u>Relevance of guideline rates for detailed assessment</u>

Guideline rates are useful and gradually became relevant in detailed assessments also. Writing on 28 July 2014 to give his conclusions on a review of guideline hourly rates, Lord Dyson MR accepted the recommendation that:

> *separate rates should not be introduced for detailed assessments of costs, but that there should be greater flexibility in detailed assessments than*

> *would ordinarily be shown in summary assessments... GHRs are needed to guide summary and detailed assessments of costs.*

Writing on 7 April 2015 to confirm that current guideline rates would remain in force for the foreseeable future, he said that guideline rates:

> *also form a part, even if only a starting reference point, in the preparation of detailed assessments.*

Receiving parties may argue that guideline rates are irrelevant to detailed assessment. If that were once the intention, it is no longer true. It is also difficult to logically justify why different rates should apply depending on whether the costs are assessed summarily or in detail. Detailed assessment may result in a more accurate conclusion, but there is no reason to have a different starting point.

Information for summary assessment and detailed assessment

A statement of costs for summary assessment must state the hourly rate and grade of fee earner: PD44 9.5(2). Form N260, which is the standard statement of costs, interprets that as '(name) (grade) (hourly rate claimed)'. The name of the fee earner is a common sense addition.

A bill of costs for detailed assessment must include: 'a statement of the status of the legal representatives' employee in respect of whom costs are claimed and (if those costs are calculated on the basis of hourly rates) the hourly rates claimed for each such person' (PD45 5.11(2)). The model bill of costs in Precedent A does that by stating 'Except where the contrary is stated the proceedings were conducted on behalf of the claimant by an assistant solicitor, admitted November 2008.' Again, there is no requirement to give the fee earners' names, but doing so is likely to smooth things along. The paying party will want to verify the fee earner details and withholding the names will cause delay in negotiations.

Stating a grade only for a fee earner in a bill of costs is not adequate. A statement of the grade is an opinion, and does not convey the fee earner's status. However, the status is likely to be converted to a grade in the background to cross-refer to the guideline rates.

Verifying fee earners

Paying parties (and costs draftsmen drawing bills) can verify fee earner details online. The Law Society's 'Find a Solicitor' webpage allows solicitors to be searched by name and firm, and will also give dates of admission, which is essential for determining the grade. Similarly, the CILEx website includes the Practitioners Directory.

http://solicitors.lawsociety.org.uk/?Pro=True

https://cilexportal.cilexgroup.org.uk/CILEx-Directory
(accessed 6 July 2020)

Assessing the grade

On assessment, the task is not simply to decide the grade to which the fee earner belongs. That is one step. Applying the principles of reasonableness and proportionality and so on, the court must also decide what grade fits the claim.

There are some basic principles for assessing the grade. The grade should be the grade applicable to the case, not the person doing the work. As the years pass, qualified fee earners advance to the next grade. The work they are doing may not have changed. Attention should be on the facts and circumstances of the claim and the disputes that arose.

Work ought to be delegated to the most junior grade capable of doing it competently. That may vary from task to task, but there should be no assumption that because some of the work requires a higher grade, that grade is reasonable for all of the work.

It may be useful to cross-check the grade of fee earner assigned by the paying party.

If the receiving party insisted on the involvement of a particular fee earner, that is not determinative of the reasonable grade. If a solicitor is a sole practitioner and does not have anyone to whom to delegate the work, that is not determinative either. It is always a question of what is reasonable and proportionate for the case.

Receiving parties may argue that the higher grade of fee earner brought the case to a conclusion more quickly, or they needed to spend less time on it. That is a difficult argument. Saving a unit here and there is likely outweighed by the difference between the rates for each grade. A favourable comparison with a bill from a similar claim run by a more junior fee earner where the time spent was significantly higher would give weight to the argument.

Where counsel was instructed to advise, thus taking the burden away from the fee earner, a lower grade may be reasonable for the remaining work done by the fee earner.

Assessing the rate

The starting point is the rates agreed between solicitor and client in the retainer. Because of the indemnity principle, that is the ceiling for what can be allowed between the parties. The certificate to a bill of costs is taken to confirm that the rates do not exceed those in the retainer: *Bailey v IBC Vehicles Ltd* [1998] 3 All ER 570. If the paying party is ever able to demonstrate that the rates do exceed the retainer rates, it should be treated as a serious disciplinary matter because of the breach of the trust placed in the signature on the certificate.

The same principle of giving weight to the certification is applied on summary assessments, partly by necessity. The court has less time to assess the costs, and less time to investigate retainers.

The retainer may say that the hourly rates will increase in line with the rise in the retail prices index ('RPI'). That was a common provision in CFAs. In the years when guideline hourly rates increased each year or every other year, that was a yoke. The rise in the RPI was less than the rise in guideline rates. In order to calculate an RPI increase, take the hourly rate, divide by the RPI headline rate at the time of inception, and multiply by the headline rate at the review date. The Office for National Statistics maintains a useful index of the RPI:

https://www.ons.gov.uk/economy/inflationandpriceindices
(accessed 6 July 2020).

As the guideline rates have been frozen since 2010, retainers permitting an increase in accordance with RPI may be more useful, but increases in the rates each year may not be allowed on the basis they are unreasonable in the recent economic climate.

CPR 44.4(3) contains the 'eight pillars': a list of eight factors for the court to consider when making any assessment. They are:

> *(a) the conduct of all the parties, including in particular –*
> *(i) conduct before, as well as during, the proceedings; and*
> *(ii) the efforts made, if any, before and during the proceedings in order to try to resolve the dispute;*
> *(b) the amount or value of any money or property involved;*
> *(c) the importance of the matter to all the parties;*
> *(d) the particular complexity of the matter or the difficulty or novelty of the questions raised;*
> *(e) the skill, effort, specialised knowledge and responsibility involved;*
> *(f) the time spent on the case;*
> *(g) the place where and the circumstances in which work or any part of it was done; and*
> *(h) the receiving party's last approved or agreed budget.*

Factors (b), (d), (e) and (g) are the most relevant to the hourly rate.

On detailed assessments in particular, those guiding criteria seem to be taken as broad licence to allow hourly rates by unscientifically weighing up the factors. That leads to the unpredictability.

Higher hourly rates are less likely to be allowed for low value claims because they will lead to disproportionate costs.

<u>Enhancements for complexity</u>

Bald assertions that the claim is complicated are unlikely to justify enhanced rates. There is an example in *Various Ledward Claimants v Kent & Medway Health Authority* [2004] 1 Costs LR 101.

Contentions that a claim is complex are more likely to carry weight when used sparingly, but receiving party's solicitors characterise many claims as complex. Where the costs judge is persuaded there is complexity, then a percentage uplift may be allowed against the guideline rates. It is a lottery.

Enhanced rates should be claimed or allowed only for senior fee earners. It is not impossible that more junior fee earners may justify enhanced rates, but less likely as most have relatively few years' experience.

Enhancements for specialism

Receiving parties often seek enhancements against the guideline hourly rates on the basis that the solicitor specialises in the work.

The burden is on the receiving party to produce evidence to justify higher rates. *Jones v Secretary of State for Wales* [1997] 1 WLR 1008 describes the required evidence:

(a) the claimant's solicitor is in fact a 'specialist';
(b) the facts and circumstances warranted the instruction of a specialist; and
(c) the overheads of the claimant's solicitors exceed the local average.

Specialism alone should not result in a greater allowance between the parties; the solicitor must actually have higher overheads. Perhaps that would be the specialist's salary.

Such evidence is rarely produced. An enhancement for specialism should not therefore be allowed, but, regrettably in that it adds to uncertainty on assessment, the court might sometimes do so – even when the *Jones* criteria have been drawn to the court's attention.

A local firm could always instruct specialist counsel; the client does not necessarily need to instruct a specialist solicitor: *Gazley v Wade* [2004] EWHC 2675 (QB).

Location

Location is an issue on which the paying party gets to have his cake and eat it. The rate that will be allowed will usually be the lower of the rates where the receiving party lives or where the solicitor practises.

In a retainer with his client and consequently in a statement or bill of costs, a solicitor will set out the hourly rates for his area.

Wraith v Sheffield Forgemasters [1998] 1 WLR 132 provides the general principle that if a receiving party chooses to instruct a distant solicitor when the hourly rates in his own locality are lower than the rates in the solicitor's locality, then the solicitor will be restricted to recovering the rates of the client's locality. *Wraith* is a pre-CPR case, but it remains good law. There needs to be a reasonable distance involved before a *Wraith* argument should be applied: client and solicitor 25 miles apart is probably a safe minimum distance.

There is no complementary rule that a solicitor can charge more because his client lives in a more expensive area.

It is sometime argued that *Wraith* has no application where panel solicitors (i.e. solicitors on an insurer's or trade union's pre-selected panel of approved firms who get all their work) are instructed. That is a dead giveaway of not looking at the judgment: it was a case about panel solicitors.

Other cases develop the *Wraith* principle, but seem to make it less certain and harder to apply. In *Sullivan v Co-Operative Insurance Society Ltd* [1999] 2 Costs LR 158 the Court of Appeal added that the test was whether it was objectively reasonable for the receiving party to have instructed the solicitors in all the circumstances. The receiving party's subjective wishes are not relevant. The choice of solicitor may be reasonable in some ways, but unreasonable in others, particularly the increase in costs. The court will have to balance the factors. The objective test is qualified by the client's particular circumstances: *Griffiths v Solutia* [2001] 2 Costs LR 247.

Kelly v Hays plc [2015] 5 Costs LO 595 is a recent restatement of *Wraith*. Jeremy Baker J said that the correct way to approach a *Wraith* issue was to ask 'what type of firm should have been retained?' There must be good reasons to conclude that a solicitor in a more expensive area than the claimant's locality should have been retained. Simple statements of the legal principles are helpful and welcome. That said, the question was put equally simply and slightly differently in *Sullivan* and as a Court of Appeal decision, its formulation takes precedence.

Potential exceptions to *Wraith* are:

- the complexity of the claim calling for specialism not available locally;
- the convenience of the solicitor's office, which might be near the client's place of work;
- instructing solicitors closer to the court where the claim would be heard;
- initially instructing local solicitors but becoming dissatisfied with their service and then instructing a more distant firm that was recommended (the point in *Truscott v Truscott*, a claim heard with *Wraith*);
- where local solicitors said the claim had no real prospect of success (*Royal Devon and Exeter NHS Foundation Trust v Acres* [2013] EWHC 652 (QB)).

London

There is generally no place for London band one rates, or 'City rates', in personal injury litigation. Master Hurst coined the phrase 'City rates for City work' in *King v Telegraph Group Ltd* [2005] EWHC 90015 (Costs) at [92], although it is an abbreviation of what he said:

> *City rates for City solicitors are recoverable where the City solicitor is undertaking City work, which is normally heavy commercial or corporate work.*

Paying parties will be on the look-out for London 'post-boxing': where solicitors have a London address for the purpose of claiming London rates, but the work is actually done outside London.

Date when work was done

The hourly rates allowed should correspond to the rates in force at the time the work was done. Today's prices for yesterday's work would be an unjustified windfall. As the guideline rates have not increased since 2010 this is not currently a significant issue in practice.

Delegation and supervision

Some elements of work might be allowed at a higher hourly rate where a more senior fee earner is justified. Other elements of work should be allowed at lower hourly rates where the work was straightforward enough to be delegated. Allowing the same hourly rate throughout a claim is attractive as it makes it easier to calculate the result, but taking the time to make different allowances will give a more just result. An alternative is to allow a 'blended' rate, being a composite rate derived from the various reasonable rates for fee earners who should have done the work. If work should have spread evenly across Grade B, C and D fee earners, a rate close to Grade C might be allowed overall.

Delegation arises when a more senior fee earner enlists the help of a junior fee earner for a specific task. Supervision is when a senior fee earner oversees the work of a more junior fee earner. Supervision should be present in all cases, not just those in which there is delegation.

Delegation and supervision both involve interaction or communication between fee earners. There is cost to that interaction and the issue becomes whether that is recoverable time.

There is a distinction to be drawn between what is an overhead of the practice and what is a cost of a specific claim.

Generally work should be delegated to the most junior grade competent to do it; otherwise how will juniors learn?

Time spent supervising is not recoverable, and forms part of the overhead of the firm covered by the hourly rates: *R v Sandhu* [1997] 1 Costs LR Core 451, and *In re Radcliffe* [2004] EWHC 90039 (Costs) shows the same principle applies since the implementation of the CPR.

Checking that everything is running efficiently and instructing or training junior fee earners will be an overhead of the firm, even if the instruction or training is given in the context of a particular claim.

When allowing the work of the junior fee earner, no more overall should be allowed than would have been the cost if the senior fee earner had done the work. There will inevitably be some small allowance for reading in; but the court will not allow time for wholesale duplication. Any claim exceeding half an hour is not likely to be allowed for that.

If there is a claim for supervision that amounts merely to time for checking the work, then that will be an overhead. However, if the senior fee earner has materially contributed by spending time making amendments, such that the overall cost is still less than if he had done it himself, then it may be allowable. Also, if the senior fee earner gave advice on how to deal with difficult and unexpected issues, or briefly stepped in to deal with those issues directly, that is likely to be recoverable also.

Internal memos are never likely to be recoverable. *Radcliffe* deals with that; they are an overhead of the firm. Instead, reasonable time should be allowed for reading relevant attendance notes.

The same principle will apply to discussions between fee earners.

Litigants in person

'Litigant in person' is the CPR's name for a party without a solicitor who represents himself.

A litigant in person can include a 'legal person' such as a company and will also include a lawyer representing himself. A partner represented by his own firm is excluded though, as he will no doubt deploy his firm's arsenal in the claim and should not be treated as unrepresented.

The special rules for litigant in person costs are in CPR 46.5 and PD46 3.1 to 3.4. First, there is a cap on the amount a litigant in person can recover in costs. It cannot exceed two thirds of the amount of costs that would have been allowed if the litigant had retained a legal representative. Presumably the logic is to remove a notional element for the profit that a solicitor is allowed to make. That cap does not apply to disbursements.

Second, a litigant in person is allowed costs for the same disbursements and work that a legal representative is allowed. Costs of occasional legal assistance (a list of permissible lawyers is in PD46 3.1) and expert assistance may also be allowed.

Third, and this is the crux, the hourly rate of the litigant in person will depend on whether he can show 'financial loss'. The starting point is he gets the hourly rate of £19 per hour. If he can show financial loss, i.e. that he would have spent that time doing something else for better remuneration, he can recover a higher hourly rate up to the two-thirds cap. PD46 3.2 requires the litigant in person to file and serve written evidence of the financial loss at least 24 hours before the hearing at which the issue will be decided or with a notice of commencement of detailed assessment. Without evidence, it is likely £19 per hour is all that will be allowed.

Chargeable units

The unit system

The unit of measurement of legal costs is called a 'unit'. One unit is six minutes, so there are ten units in an hour, and one unit is charged at one tenth of the hourly rate. It's a decimal system.

Letters, emails and calls

PD47 5.22 sets out these provisions for work done by legal representatives:

(1) Routine letters out, routine e-mails out and routine telephone calls will in general be allowed on a unit basis of 6 minutes each, the charge being calculated by reference to the appropriate hourly rate. The unit charge for letters out and e-mails out will include perusing and considering the routine letters in or e-mails in.

(2) The court may, in its discretion, allow an actual time charge for preparation of electronic communications sent by legal representatives, which properly amount to attendances provided that the time taken has been recorded.

'Routine' is not defined, but means in practice a simple or straightforward letter. Such a letter may be generated from the case management system or may be a short one-off letter, to enclose documents perhaps. A routine telephone call might be a short impromptu call for a quick update or to provide some information.

If an item is not routine, it is timed (although items charged as routine items might have been timed as well). Timed work is still charged in complete units. Thus work timed at ten minutes is charged as two units; it is rounded up as if it were twelve minutes. The unit system is used in practice to mean that everything should be rounded up to the nearest six-minute block. There are no fractions of units.

Any letters, emails and calls that have taken more than six minutes are charged often as timed items, on the argument such an item cannot be routine. That is doubtful. Also, letters may be several pages long but they are still routine – especially in this era of letters generated by case management systems. Rounding up would be wrong, because anything that falls into the category of 'routine' should be charged as a single unit, including very quick communications that take only one or two minutes to generate, as well as those that may take seven, eight, nine or ten minutes. Overall, the allowance would be fair.

Attendance and Document time

Attendances in person and work on documents must be timed. Timed items are presented in hours and minutes, even though it will nearly always be in multiple of six minutes based on the unit system.

Rounding up on timed items can add up to considerable overcharging, but that is an inevitable feature of the system. That layer can be negotiated or assessed out of the final figures.

The unit system can also be abused; one method is known as 'padding' where extra units might be added to individual attendances so that they still appear reasonable, but where the cumulative effect is very valuable; another is 'thin-slicing', where a task that only took a few minutes is sliced up into several separate constituent elements charged at one or more units each.

Time on some activities is not recoverable:

Solicitor and own client work

A solicitor cannot recover costs that are overheads of having clients. This is a narrow category, and covers standard steps such as conflict checks, identity checks, anti-money laundering checks, and pure client care work.

This rule is sometimes misunderstood as being very wide; at its worst, some wrongly say that it means a solicitor cannot recover any communications and attendances on his own client. That is absurd; the client must give instructions and the solicitor can charge the client for communications and attendances and thus recover the costs of the work under the indemnity principle.

Funding arrangements

The costs of making funding arrangements (i.e. a solicitor working out how the client will pay his fees) and keeping funders apprised of developments are not recoverable: *Motto v Trafigura* [2012] 1 WLR 657 at [104]-[114]. Lord Neuberger's reasoning was that the solicitor was not acting for the client in making those arrangements but was acting for himself. This could be seen as an extension of the solicitor own client rule. *Motto* was a decision about arranging conditional fee agreements and after the event insurance, but the principle would extend to other types of funding arrangements.

Unrecorded time

If there is no record of time spent, any claim for it must be an estimate, and it will be difficult to show that the claim is reasonable. It will generally be disallowed entirely (see, *Brush v Bower Cotton & Bower* [1993] 1 WLR 1328 at 1349G) and the more substantial the claim the less likely it is to be allowed in the court's discretion because more doubt must arise as to why substantial time was not recorded.

Routine attendance notes

Routine notes of routine telephone calls and other short attendances should be treated as included in the unit allowance for the attendance and not charged separately and additionally. Longer attendances, where the claim is reasonable and the time is recorded, may be charged: *Brush v Bower Cotton & Bower* [1993] 1 WLR 1328 at 1349B.

Travelling time

Time spent travelling is recoverable in principle. Under the CPR, there is no principle that such time should be allowed at a lower rate, for instance to strip out any profit element. However, travelling time must be reasonable. A party cannot recover costs of travelling to attend his lawyers or experts (*McIlwraith v McIlwraith* [2005] EWHC 90010 (Costs) at [34]), and thus if the solicitor chooses to travel to attend on the client that is not generally recoverable either. There may be an exception where there is a good reason why written communication or telephone (or these days, video calling) is not adequate, and the time is reasonable and proportionate. Travel disbursements are covered in the chapter on disbursements.

Setting up a trust

The costs of setting up a trust in which the receiving party may choose to place the damages are not costs of and incidental to the claim. What the receiving party chooses to do with the damages is a matter for the receiving party, and nothing to do with the paying party.

Inquest attendance

Costs of attending an inquest have been allowed but procedural changes means attendance is less likely now. Inquest attendance costs are recoverable in principle as costs of the subsequent damages claim: *Roach v Home Office* [2010] QB 256.

The Coroners (Inquests) Rules 2013 came into force on 25 July 2013. Disclosure should take place under those rules prior to the inquest. Where necessary evidence could have been obtained via the pre-inquest disclosure it is not reasonable, proportionate or necessary to attend at all. See *Lynch v Chief Constable of Warwickshire Police* (Master Rowley, SCCO, 14 November 2014, unreported).

Costs of other proceedings generally

Costs of proceedings other than the proceedings in which the assessment is being made cannot generally be recovered. The exception is set out in *Roach v Home Office* [2010] QB 256. The purpose for which the costs were incurred is not relevant; instead they can be allowed if they were relevant to the current proceedings (and, presumably, have not already been recovered from another paying party).

Pre-issue costs

An order for costs in proceedings includes the costs incurred before proceedings are started: *Re Gibson's Settlement Trusts* [1981] Ch 179. CPR 36.13(1) now spells out that a deemed order for costs on acceptance of a Part 36 offer within its relevant period includes recoverable pre-issue costs.

Generally pre-issue costs will be the costs of complying with a pre-action protocol. If there are no proceedings, such costs are recoverable only if the parties agree that they are recoverable (and note that the RTA and EL/PL Protocols incorporate automatic agreements). See the sections 'No proceedings and no agreement to pay costs' for more detail.

Restoring the defendant company before starting proceedings

Before proceedings can be started, including costs-only proceedings, it is sometimes necessary to apply to restore a defendant company to the register at Companies House because the company has been dissolved. A claimant cannot sue a company that does not exist. An occasional workaround, by agreement with the defendant's insurer in claims other than RTA claims, is to commence proceedings against the insurer. Where the restoration application does need to be made, costs should be modest. It is not complex work. The Government Legal Department has a guide, including the necessary precedents at https://www.gov.uk/guidance/company-restoration-guide (accessed 6 July 2020). The costs of the application are recoverable as costs of the proceedings.

Changing solicitors – are costs still recoverable?

It is not uncommon for a party to change solicitors during a claim. There are all sorts of reasons: the solicitor's firm may close down, the client may be unhappy with the solicitor, the solicitor's firm may merge with another to become a new legal entity, the fee earner may change firm and the client moves with him.

If that party goes on to obtain an order for costs of the claim, often his costs claim will include the costs of his former solicitors. However, those costs may not be recoverable.

The general rule at common law is that a solicitor's retainer is an 'entire contract'. That means the solicitor must finish what he was instructed to do in order to have the right to be paid. Doing part of the job is not enough. A solicitor could not get halfway with a personal injury claim and charge half his fee. It is all or nothing. This general rule is found in *Underwood, Son & Piper v Lewis* [1894] 2 QB 306. A conditional fee agreement should logically be construed as an entire contract, or more precisely an agreement of 'entire obligations', because the solicitor can only get paid when the claim is won. However, it is beyond the scope of this book to consider that further.

The general rule can be displaced. It depends on two things: the reason why the client and former solicitor parted ways, and the terms of the retainer between them.

A broad distinction might be drawn between situations where the client ends the retainer and situations where the solicitor ends the retainer. It is more likely that the costs are still payable by the client and therefore recoverable from an opponent where the client ends the retainer. The retainer will usually make provision for the client having to pay if the client ends the retainer.

The retainer is much less likely to provide for the solicitor to be paid if he ends the retainer for his own reasons that have nothing to do with the client, for instance because the firm is closing. It is not impossible, just less likely. If on the other hand the solicitor ends the retainer because the client is in breach in some way, such as failing to pay the fees or failing to give instructions, the solicitor may still be paid. See *Richard Buxton (a firm) v Mills-Owen* [2010] EWCA Civ 122 and *Minkin v Cawdery Kaye Fireman & Taylor* [2012] EWCA Civ 546.

To avoid application of the general rule, the receiving party should be forthcoming in providing reasons why it should not be applied supported by evidence where needed and a copy of the retainer to show the clauses relied on. Merely asserting that all is in order is a difficult position to take when the burden of proof on a standard basis assessment falls on the receiving party.

Lien

When a retainer ends during a claim, a solicitor may hold a lien over the client's file until his fees are paid – if he is justified in doing so. That can raise practical problems for the client, who might need to continue his claim to successful conclusion in order to get the money to pay those fees. In those circumstances, the file may be handed over to the new firm on the condition that the new firm preserves the lien of the former solicitor by holding the file to the former solicitor's order.

Assignment

The solicitor may be able to assign his right to be paid to a new firm who assumes conduct, and they may then collect the fees owed to the former firm. The deed of assignment should be produced for assessment to displace the general rule. The law of assignment would mean that only the benefit of being paid could usually be assigned, not the burden of continuing the work. The new solicitor would need a new or novated retainer.

Separate claims

In *Harris v Moat Housing* [2008] 1 WLR 1578, the second solicitors claimed their costs which were assessed by the court. The first solicitor then tried to claim his costs. The court refused to allow any of the first solicitor's costs because the assessment had been made already and that was the end of the matter. It shows that current and former solicitors should collaborate on costs recovery. PD47 5.8(1)(a) requires that a single bill must contain costs of all the receiving party's solicitors during the claim.

Bill certificates

Note that the requirements for certifying bills of costs would still require the former solicitor to sign a certificate. The model certificates in Precedent F provide:

> *Where the bill claims costs in respect of work done by more than one firm of solicitors, certificate (1), appropriate completed, should be signed on behalf of each firm.*
>
> *(1) CERTIFICATE AS TO ACCURACY*
>
> *(other cases where costs are claimed for work done by a legal representative) [in respect of Parts(s).... of the bill] the costs claimed herein do not exceed the costs which the receiving party is required to pay me/my firm.*

It is difficult to see how the successor firm could sign that certificate on behalf of the former firm, even when there has been an assignment.

Representation

The currently retained solicitor will have to present the claim for all costs, including those of the client's former solicitors. The former solicitors are no longer instructed and have no *locus standi*, and do not have authority to negotiate or agree costs on behalf of the former client cannot give a valid receipt for any costs paid. That is often to the chagrin of the current solicitor, who ends up with more work for no pay unless some arrangement is reached with the former solicitor.

VAT

Value added tax applies to legal costs. The only outright exception is small claims fixed costs and other fixed costs in CPR 45 Section I, which makes no provisions for VAT being payable in addition. An order for costs is usually treated as covering applicable VAT; the court would not usually order 'costs and applicable VAT'. The definition of 'costs' in CPR 44.1(1) is wide enough to capture VAT.

VAT registered clients and between the parties costs

Some parties in litigation are VAT registered. They will typically be businesses or business people. A solicitor should not charge VAT between the parties when the client is able to recover it as 'input tax'.

A very crude summary of VAT will assist here. Once a business' turnover reaches a certain threshold, that business must register for VAT. That business will then charge VAT on its sales of goods and services, and pay VAT when it purchases goods and services. The VAT it charges is output tax, and the VAT it pays is input tax. At the end of the VAT accounting period, the input tax is set off against the output tax, and the net amount is paid to HMRC. End consumers (customers or clients) are not VAT registered and shoulder their VAT bills.

Strictly speaking, including such VAT in a statement or bill of costs would not be technically wrong in the sense that the statement of bill is certified to say the amount claimed does not exceed the amount the client is liable to pay, and the client must pay the VAT even though it is not recoverable between the parties. But that approach is actually wrong because of the provisions of PD44 2.3:

> *VAT should not be included in a claim for costs if the receiving party is able to recover the VAT as input tax. Where the receiving party is able to obtain credit from HMRC for a proportion of the VAT as input tax,*

only that proportion which is not eligible for credit should be included in the claim for costs.

PD44 2.4 continues: *'The receiving party has responsibility for ensuring that VAT is claimed only when the receiving party is unable to recover the VAT or a proportion thereof as input tax.'*

Disputes can arise sometimes because the claimant is an individual who is VAT registered in connection with his business and the defendant says VAT is not payable between the parties on his costs. The answer turns on whether the claim is for the benefit of the individual or for the benefit of the business. If no money is being recovered for the business, then the VAT on the solicitors' fees would not go through the company books. If some of the work was done to claim money for the business, such as loss of income, a proportion of VAT on the costs, or VAT on the costs of that work, should not be claimed between the parties.

Where there is any continuing dispute, PD44 2.5 says a certificate in the form of Precedent F must be produced.

Change of VAT rate, tax points, apportionment and dividing bills

The VAT rate has changed several times in recent years. The work on a claim can span the changes in VAT rates. VAT may be 'apportioned' so that it is charged at the rate in force at the time the work was done.

This topic requires some understanding of 'tax points', even if just to understand how they are not decisive. The tax point is the time the taxable supply is made, and it is needed so that VAT can be accounted for in the correct tax period. A basic tax point arises when the work is done. In personal injury claims that will be when the claim has been won and damages paid, but before the costs claim is made. The costs have to include the VAT, so it must have already arisen. A basic tax point can be overridden by an actual tax point. An actual tax point will be created if an invoice is raised or costs are paid **before** the basic tax point, or if an invoice is rendered within 14 days **after** the basic tax point. There can be more than one tax point in a claim, depending on whether the costs are invoiced or paid in parts.

Confusion often arises between tax points and apportionment. The mistaken logic runs: the tax point arises at the end of the claim. The VAT rate at that date is, say, 20%. The VAT rate on the bill must therefore be 20% throughout. That is mistaken because the rules on tax points are separate from the rules on apportionment. A tax point means that tax must be charged but does not oust the apportionment rules.

Where work spans VAT rate changes, a solicitor may elect to apportion work between the different rates.

PD44 says:

> *Form of bill of costs where VAT rate changes*
>
> *2.7*
>
> *Where there is a change in the rate of VAT, suppliers of goods and services are entitled by sections 88(1) and 88(2) of the Value Added Tax Act 1994 in most circumstances to elect whether the new or the old rate of VAT should apply to a supply where the basic and actual tax points span a period during which the rate changed.*

That practice direction's wording is the source of some of the confusion about tax points and apportionments. The sections of the Act cited do not refer to tax points. HMRC stated the position more clearly in a note called 'VAT – Change of the Standard Rate to 20 Per Cent: a Detailed Guide for VAT-Registered Businesses' (22 June 2010). Section 9.5 covered solicitors:

> *If you are a solicitor most of your supplies are covered by the normal tax point rules including a tax point on completion of the work. Where you issue a VAT invoice or receive a payment on or after 4 January 2011 for work that was completed before 4 January 2011 you may use the special rules and account for VAT at 17.5 per cent (see section 3.3). Where work commenced before 4 January 2011 but will not be completed until on or after 4 January 2011 you can apportion the supply between that liable to 17.5 per cent and that liable to 20 per cent (see section 3.4).*

There is a presumption in favour of electing to apportion VAT in PD44 2.8:

> *It will be assumed, unless a contrary indication is given in writing, that an election to take advantage of the provisions mentioned in paragraph 2.7 and to charge VAT at the lower rate has been made. In any case in which an election to charge at the lower rate is not made, such a decision must be justified to the court assessing the costs.*

It would be a strange assumption to make if the bill had been drawn without apportioning VAT, but nevertheless that is the position. PD44 2.9 says:

> *Subject to 2.7 and 2.8, all bills of costs, fees and disbursements on which VAT is included must be divided into separate parts so as to show work done before, on and after the date or dates from which any change in the rate of VAT takes effect.*

The final sentence of PD44 2.8 about justifying a decision is important. One can understand why a solicitor might elect not to apportion VAT; it might be a huge hassle. But that in itself would not be justification. It is difficult to see any justification. Even if there were some justification it may not be enough. On assessment, the receiving party may not recover costs which have been unreasonably incurred. VAT at the higher rate which could have been apportioned to a lower rate would be unreasonable, and likely to be disallowed. For example, see *Hutton v Lloyd Fraser* (HHJ Kay QC, Luton County Court, 13 September 2011, unreported).

The same principles apply to disbursements. The disbursement provider, including experts and counsel, can exercise the same options about apportioning VAT and charging the rate applicable at the time the work was done.

Outside EU – place of belonging

Solicitors in England & Wales may sometime represent clients who are outside the jurisdiction. There are some general rules which assist in deciding whether or not VAT should be charged. These rules will be subject to change following the Brexit transition period. The UK is scheduled to leave the EU VAT regime on 31 December 2020. This section addresses the current law.

The first step is to decide where the services are supplied. The options are (a) the UK, where the solicitor is based and where the work is physically done, or (b) the country where the client 'belongs', where he receives the benefit of the work.

Note for this purpose and many other EU purposes, the law is applicable to the UK rather than England & Wales. The EU views England, Scotland, Wales and Northern Ireland as a single sovereign state, rather than separate jurisdictions.

B2B

The general rule for B2B (business to business) supplies of services is that the supply is made where the client belongs. If a solicitor supplies services to a business outside the UK, no UK VAT should be charged, but local taxes – especially VAT in other EU member states – may apply.

B2C

The general rule for B2C (business to consumer) supplies of services is that the supply is made where the supplier belongs. Most clients in personal injury claims are consumers, and therefore this general rule is generally the one to apply.

There is an exception to the B2C general rule where the client lives outside the EU. The Value Added Tax Act 1994, Schedule 4A, Part 3, para 16(1) says that a supply of services covered by that paragraph which is made to a person who is not a 'relevant business person' and 'belongs in a country which is not a member State (other than the Isle of Man)' is to be treated as made in the country where that person belongs (like the B2B rule). Paragraph 16(2)(d) covers the services of lawyers and similar services. Therefore the solicitor's fees would be outside the scope of UK and EU VAT. No VAT should be charged on the solicitor's costs.

Sometimes the client may be in the UK at the start of the claim and instructs solicitors here, and then at some point during the claim the claimant leaves the country and at the end of the claim is outside the EU. (Holidays do not count; a more permanent living arrangement is required.) The basic tax point arises when the work is completed. The basic tax point can be overridden by an actual tax point if a bill is rendered sooner or an invoice is sent within 14 days of completion. At the date of the tax point, basic or actual as the case may be, if the client 'belongs' outside the EU no VAT should be claimed.

More information

See HMRC VAT Notice 741A: place of supply of services for more information.

Part 20 and multi-defendant claims

Part 20 claims include counterclaims and claims by a defendant against an existing party or against a new party. Various special costs rules can apply.

Counterclaims - the rule in *Medway Oil*

Where there is a claim and counterclaim and the PI Protocol has run its course, there is then a rush to issue because the costs are at stake.

The position is straightforward if the claimant or counterclaimant wins outright. The successful 'claimant' gets all the costs of bringing his own claim and defending his opponent's claim.

When the claim and counterclaim both succeed to an extent, there is a special rule for the costs of a counterclaim. It is the rule in *Medway Oil v Continental Contractors* [1929] AC 88. It is an old case but has been approved post-CPR. The rule in Medway Oil is that the costs of a counterclaim are the costs by which the costs of the proceedings have been increased by the counterclaim.

That brain-teaser means in practice the costs of the claim will include the costs of liability, but the costs of the counterclaim will not. The costs of the counterclaim will be the costs of quantum of the counterclaim and the costs of the statements of case solely for the counterclaim.

It is arguably an unfair rule that creates an unnecessary rush to issue. The parties can agree to or the court can disapply it and divide costs on a percentage basis perhaps, and that may be the preferred approach under the CPR. But where there is nothing expressly to the contrary, by default Medway Oil applies on assessment.

Note that Medway Oil is a rule of assessment, not a rule concerned with the making of an order for costs in principle. His Honour Judge Gregory held in *Farnworth v Davis* (County Court at Liverpool, 2 June 2016, unreported) that a Part 36 offer and acceptance regarding the counterclaim did not oust Medway Oil; the deemed order for cost of 'proceedings' was for the costs of the counterclaim only. *Medway Oil* would still apply on an assessment.

Co-defendants and co-insurers

Assessments of costs where there are multiple paying parties are complicated for the paying parties. In the interests of co-operation, it helps if the claimant appreciates those difficulties because they may mean more time and patience is needed in costs negotiations.

Co-insurers arise typically in EL disease claims. The claimant was exposed over a period of time, during which his employer changed insurer. Thus those insurers share the 'time on risk'. The convention is the last insurer on risk will deal with the claim. That can be advantageous because earlier insurers may no longer be trading or traceable. On costs, it is sometimes necessary for the lead insurer or his representatives to obtain authority from the other contributing insurers, and if anyone lags behind that stalls the whole negotiations.

Sometimes there are co-defendants who are paying the claimant's costs between them. They are often jointly and severally liable for the costs. They will typically have separate representatives who need to liaise. The defendant with the lion's share often takes the lead, but sometimes the defendants negotiate separately.

Matters can be further complicated where there are co-defendants and one or more of those defendants have co-insurers.

Where a claimant brings a claim against multiple defendants, but succeeds against only one or some, then it depends on what terms the parties agree whether the defendant(s) who pay damages also have to pay costs of the claimant pursuing the other defendants. If one defendant makes a Part 36 offer to settle his liability, the costs he must pay are the costs of the claim against him only: *Haynes v Department of Business Innovation & Skills* [2014] EWHC 643 (QB) at [21].

If the defendant does in principle have to pay costs of the claimant pursuing other defendants, it is a matter for assessment whether those costs are reasonable and proportionate. If the claimant was on wild goose chase, the costs may be reduced.

Defendants who do not settle the claim may seek their costs against the claimant, and if they obtain such orders the claimant may be unable recover his costs of pursuing those defendants; but he may be able to recover the costs he has to pay those defendants – which leads into the next topic.

Sanderson and *Bullock* orders

Bullock order: C sues D1 and D2. C wins against D1 only. C loses against D2. C has to pay D2's costs, but can recover those costs from D1 as part of his costs against D1.

Sanderson order: C sues D1 and D2. C wins against D1 only. C loses against D2. D1 has to pay C's costs and D2's costs.

Whether either such order is made is within the discretion of the court. Depending on the facts or the parties' respect bargaining position, D2 may not recover its costs. That may be the inevitable effect of QOCS.

Common costs: non-specific and specific

On assessment of costs incurred for multiple purposes, such as claims against multiple defendants, theoretical and practical difficulties arise.

Costs may need to be split up; for instance the claimant can recover costs against one defendant but not the other.

Some costs may clearly relate to one or other part of the claim. Other costs may relate to the claim as a whole: those are 'common' costs.

Haynes v Department of Business Innovation & Skills [2014] EWHC 643 (QB) at [26]ff has a useful analysis of the law. Jay J, sitting with Senior Costs Judge Hurst as an assessor, said:

> *common or generic costs effectively fall into two categories. First, there are the non-specific costs such as court fees, medical reports and travel expenses which would have been incurred in any event, regardless of the number of other defendants. Secondly, there are the specific costs which are, in principle, capable of identification and division. For example, if there is a conference with Counsel concerning the liability of all ten defendants, the total fee may be envisaged as ripe for division.*

Common non-specific costs will be allowed in full against the paying party, as they would have been incurred anyway even without such other part of the claim for which costs are not recoverable.

Common specific costs must be divided, and only the part relating to the claim against the paying party should be allowed. Patten J (as he then was) in *Dyson Technologies Ltd v Strutt* [2007] 4 Costs LR 597 said that this must be based on analysis of the work done. The practical difficulty that arises is that parties do not record time so that it is divided between different parts of the claim. That led to earlier decisions such as *Fourie v Le Roux* [2006] EWHC 1840 (Ch), in which Warren J took a more 'rough and ready' approach to 'apportioning' costs. It appears that is permissible although a more imperfect solution. Such approach has an older mandate under *Lavery v Ewing* [2015] 3 Costs LR 443, which despite the year of reporting is actually a 1995 case. 'Apportioning' is distinct from 'dividing' in the eyes of the law (see *Hay v Szterbin* [2010] EWHC 1967 (Ch) at [12]), although that may be a semantic difference for the purposes of this short summary.

Whether dividing or apportioning that does not mean splitting into equal 'moieties'. Bills used often to be drawn on the basis of a moiety of one half for certain items where they related to more than one part of the claim. That is OK when the paying party will be paying 100% of the costs anyway; for instance when a moiety has been made of common costs of two successful claimants. But it would now seem impermissible for claims where only a part of the costs can be recovered.

A problem arises on the standard basis. If an item of cost resists division even on a rough and ready basis, and the approach is simply to say 'it relates to two things so let's apportion it 50/50', i.e. the *Lavery v Ewing* approach, doubt must arise as to whether the paying party will end up paying too much. Doubt must be resolved in favour of the paying party, and that may result in the whole item being disallowed. The court must be satisfied that some allowance should be made. The receiving party should present a rational basis for the division of such items especially if more than half is sought, or likely get only half or risk not recovering them at all.

Foreign costs – costs where there is a multi-jurisdictional element

Claims involving choice of laws

There are claims in which the courts of England & Wales may accept jurisdiction, but apply the laws of another jurisdiction to the dispute. On costs, the question is whether costs should be allowed in accordance with the CPR or in accordance with the rules of that other jurisdiction. The answer is straightforward. Costs are a matter of procedural law, and they are decided in accordance with the laws of the forum. Therefore the CPR would apply to costs.

Work of lawyers outside the jurisdiction

There are two possible scenarios.

First, a party instructs a lawyer in this jurisdiction, but there is some element of the claim that requires the assistance of a lawyer outside of England & Wales. Therefore the English lawyer instructs the foreign lawyer as an agent. In those circumstances, the fees of the foreign lawyer may be recovered in this jurisdiction as disbursements. The fees should be assessed according to the rules of the jurisdiction in which they were incurred: *McCullie v Butler (No 2)* [1962] 2 QB 309.

Second, a party instructs a lawyer outside this jurisdiction who, with the help of an English agent, brings a claim in this jurisdiction. The costs of the foreign lawyer would not be recoverable, and nor would the costs of the agent be recoverable as a disbursement. That is the result of a prohibition under the Solicitors Act 1974. Section 20(1) provides that 'no unqualified person is to act as a solicitor'. Under s1, a qualified person has been admitted as solicitor, appears on the roll and has a practising certificate. A lawyer in a different jurisdiction is very unlikely to count as a qualified person in this jurisdiction. Section 25(1) of the Act states:

> *No costs in respect of anything done by any unqualified person acting as a solicitor shall be recoverable by him, or by any other person, in any action, suit or matter.*

Westland Helicopters Ltd v Sheikh Salah Al-Hejailan [2006] 4 Costs LR 549 is an example of the court disallowing costs for those reasons.

Damages Based Agreements

The extension of damages based agreements ('DBAs') was part of the Jackson reforms. DBAs have had little take up, in part because of concerns about the DBA Regulations. Thus, this is a short section.

A DBA is a form of retainer in which the solicitor gets paid a percentage of the damages. The client does not necessarily lose the damages; he can recover costs still if he gets a costs order in addition to his damages. CPR 44.18(1) says that costs orders should be made as normal, and under CPR 44.18(2) although costs will also be assessed as normal, the amount that the party has to pay his solicitor in costs under the DBA acts as a cap on how much that party can recover from an opponent. That is a reason why DBAs may be unpopular in low value litigation. The cap on the deduction from damages in personal injury claims is 25% under the DBA Regulations. 25% of the damages is likely to be less than the predictable costs, portal costs or post portal costs.

There is no obligation to give notice that the claim is funded by a DBA. In those circumstances, the application of CPR 44.18(2)(b) might be innocently or deliberately overlooked.

CHAPTER SIX
COSTS BUDGETING

Costs budgeting could by now fill a book of its own. It will not fill too much of this book, because costs budgeting has more to do with claims handling procedure than it does with costs procedure. This chapter relates costs budgeting to the eventual allowance of costs.

Terminology

The template for a costs budget is Precedent H.

Two keys terms for following along with this commentary are 'incurred costs' and 'budgeted costs'. Incurred costs are all costs incurred up to and including the date of the first costs management order, unless otherwise stated. Budgeted costs are all costs to be incurred after the date of the first costs management order.

Thus incurred costs is not to be taken literally; at the time of drafting the costs budget, the costs management hearing at which the costs management order stands to be made will be in the future, and therefore some of the incurred costs will be future costs, and therefore estimated for inclusion in the costs budget.

Costs Management Orders

A costs management order is made under CPR 3.15(2) and records the extent to which budgeted costs are agreed between the parties, the court's approval after revising budgeted costs which have not been agreed, and the extent to which incurred costs are agreed.

On any subsequent assessment of costs, the approach differs depending on whether a costs management order has been made.

Where no costs management order has been made

It is entirely conceivable there may be no costs management order. Budgets may be filed and exchanged, but the claim settles before the CCMC. Or, the budgets are agreed and the court does not consider that a costs management order is necessary, or perhaps runs out of time to make the order. To be clear, agreed budgets do usually still find their way into a costs management order.

PD44 paragraph 4 applies where no costs management order has been made. It sets out how the costs budget will be relevant to the detailed assessment.

The costs budget will not have the same near immoveable weight if there is no costs management order, but it is still important. If the bill of costs totals 20% or more than the costs budget, there must be a statement of explanation in the bill of costs: PD44 3.2. If the court is not convinced by the explanation, the court may draw an inference that costs claimed are unreasonable or disproportionate: PD44 3.7.

If the paying party claims to have relied on the budget and wants to refer to it in disputing the bill, he must serve a statement setting out his case in his points of dispute: PD44 3.3. Reliance is difficult to prove, but the cases where it can be proved are the ones most likely to generate results. Mere assertion that the paying party relied on the budget is often unconvincing. Linking a decision to go ahead with a particular aspect of the case because of the budgeted costs may be more compelling for succeeding in the argument. If costs claimed are 20% or more than the budget (PD44 3.5) and the court considers there was reasonable reliance it may restrict the costs to such sum as is reasonable for the paying party to pay: PD44 3.6. If that 20% difference is absent, the paying party's statement may simply help him succeed on any reasonableness and proportionality arguments: PD44 3.4.

The court has to have regard to the receiving part's last approved or agreed budget on assessment, and may have regard to any other budget: PD44 3.4.

These provisions are similar to the old provisions on having regard to costs estimates, and rather like those provisions they do not have great effect on detailed assessment.

Where a costs management order has been made – 'good reason' test

CPR 3.18(2) provides that on a standard basis assessment, the court will not depart from budgeted costs covered by a costs management order unless there is good reason to do so. A 'departure' might be upwards or downwards from the budgeted costs; there needs to be a good reason for movement in either direction.

> *Where there is a proposed departure from budget – be it upwards or downwards – the court on a detailed assessment is empowered to sanction such a departure if it is satisfied that there is good reason for doing so. That of course is a significant fetter on the court having an unrestricted discretion: it is deliberately designed to be so. Costs judges should therefore be expected not to adopt a lax or over-indulgent approach to the need to find "good reason": if only because to do so would tend to subvert one of the principal purposes of costs budgeting and thence the overriding objective.*

Davis LJ, *Harrison v University Hospitals Coventry and Warwickshire Hospital NHS Trust* [2017] 1 WLR 4456 at [44].

Whether there is a good reason is a matter of discretion and will be fact sensitive. Davis LJ suggested analysing the good reason in line with the well-known three-stage Denton principles.

Although Davis LJ was unconvinced by leading counsel's '*doom-laden predictions of detailed assessments becoming mere rubber stamps of CMOs and of injustice for paying parties*', they seem well-founded. The effect of CPR 3.18(b) is that in most claims, if the actual costs in the bill of costs match or do not exceed the budgeted costs, they will be allowed as claimed. That is because of the difficulty in finding a good reason to depart downwards that the court will accept, or the unattractive proposition of risking costs in attending a detailed assessment hearing with uncertain prospects of convincing the court there is a good reason to depart downwards.

The most obvious circumstance in which departing downwards from the budgeted costs may arise is where the actual costs are less. The receiving party will draw a bill of costs corresponding to the budget phases and can only show the actual costs. In *Harrison*, the court held that the application of the indemnity principle may indeed be a good reason to depart downwards at [41]. That was applied on the circuit appeal in *Barts Health NHS Trust v Salmon* (His Honour Judge Dight, County Court at Central London, 17 January 2019). The judge also held that once a good reason had been established, neither party had to establish a further good reason as a necessary precursor to persuading the court to make any further adjustment.

Other possible good reasons for departures downward may include:

- Mistaken assumptions. The budget will state assumptions and if they do not transpire there may be a good reason to adjust the costs downwards.
- Experts differ. Where a CMO states figures on the basis there would be certain experts but those experts were not in fact instructed, costs might be reconsidered.
- Irrecoverable in law. Chapter 5 covers Recoverable Costs. If the bill contains irrecoverable items it would be perverse to allow them and there should be an adjustment downward. Such items may only involve trivial sums however, e.g. costs in respect of funding arrangements.

Departures upwards can be similarly problematic for receiving parties. They will face the challenge of why a prompt application was not made to vary the budget once the overspend became apparent.

The court will assess incurred costs on the usual principles, without needing to find a good reason for any departure from the incurred costs in the budget (*Harrison* at [47]), save that it will have regard to any comment made on the incurred costs in costs management order (or elsewhere). The court is not bound by such comment, and might have enough further information in the detailed assessment to feel confident in putting it aside. A receiving party who did attract comment on his incurred costs in the costs management order should actively try and produce counteractive material for the detailed assessment so as to have a chance of recovering more in respect of incurred costs.

Hourly rates

A criticism of costs budgeting and its interaction with detailed assessment is that the court abdicates any detailed assessment of hourly rates, which are a key element of any costs claim and may often be seen as the principle driver of disproportionate costs. Solicitors have an obvious incentive to seek recovery of ever higher rates.

PD3E 7.10 provides:

> *The making of a costs management order under rule 3.15 concerns the totals allowed for each phase of the budget. It is not the role of the court in the cost management hearing to fix or approve the hourly rates claimed in the budget. The underlying detail in the budget for each phase used by the party to calculate the totals claimed is provided for reference purposes only to assist the court in fixing a budget.*

Thus the court will not make a decision on hourly rates at the CCMC. In *Yirenki v Ministry of Defence* [2018] 5 Costs LR 1177, Jacobs J held it was inappropriate to above specific hours and disbursements at the CCMC and to hold over the assessment of hourly rates for detailed assessment.

As a result, the court will not get into the nuts and bolts of hourly rates on the CCMC.

Come detailed assessment, CPR 3.18(b) requires the court not to depart from the budget in respect of budgeted costs unless there is a good reason, and unless there is such good reason the court will not direct its analysis to the hourly rates. Thus hourly rates are not generally subject to detailed scrutiny on detailed assessment either. That is unsatisfactory.

There is some comfort. The court held that finding a substantial overstatement of the hourly rate in the budget may be a good reason to depart downwards in respect of budgeted costs: *MXX v United Lincolnshire NHS Trust* [2019] Costs LR 1151. But few cases may feature a 'substantial' overstatement, and in that case it emerged because the rates in the bill differed from those in the budget.

The SCCO's approach has varied. Master Campbell found a reduction to the hourly rate of incurred costs should extend to budgeted costs: *RNB v Newham LBC* [2017] EWHC B15 (Costs). But Master Nagalingam declined to do the same in *Nash v Ministry of Defence* [2018] EWHC B4 (Costs). Actual costs were already less than budgeted costs and he found adjusting hourly rates downwards would be double jeopardy in respect of the budgeted costs. Although expressed differently, Master Nagalingam's approach appears to accord more closely with the *Harrison* approach.

Failure to file a budget

A total failure to file a costs budget in time results in the sanction that the party will be treated as filing a budget comprising only of court fees: CPR 3.14.

If however that party makes a claimant's Part 36 offer which he betters at trial, he can recover half of his assessed costs: CPR 36.23(2).

Practical points for detailed assessment

The requirements for detailed assessment proceedings are described in Chapter 8. Care should be taken so as to avoid orders to redraw the bill or causing delay in detailed assessment for the correct documents to be produced.

Where a costs management order has been made, a bill of costs must be divided into separate parts '*so as to distinguish between the costs claimed for each phase of the last approved or agreed budget, and within each such part the bill must distinguish between the costs shown as incurred in the last agreed or approved budget and the costs shown as estimated*': PD47 5.8(8).

Along with the various other reasons for different parts in a bill, the bill may contain an unwieldy number of parts. The electronic bill (see Chapter 8) does what it can to make this easier.

Among the other requirement is a need for Precedent Q or equivalent, which allows the court to compare the costs in the bill to the budgeted costs. Precedent Q has sometimes been prepared wrongly. Instead of comparing budgeted costs in the bill to budgeted costs under the CMO, examples have been seen that compare the total of incurred and budgeted costs to the bill. Per *Harrison*, the incurred costs will be assessed in the usual way. Only the budgeted costs need be compared in Precedent Q as only those costs are subject to the 'good reason' test in CPR 3.18(b).

Where there is no costs management order, do not forget the statements in the bill or points of dispute described above in the section 'Where there is no costs management order'.

Costs of budgeting

The costs of the budgeting process are capped. They were in PD3E 7.2, but from 2 October 2020 they will be in CPR 3.15(4). A rule is binding on the court in a way that a practice direction is not. The caps are:

> *Save in exceptional circumstances—*
> *(a) the recoverable costs of initially completing Precedent H (the form to be used for a costs budget) shall not exceed the higher of—*
> *(i) £1,000; or*
> *(ii) 1% of the total of the incurred costs (as agreed or allowed on assessment) and the budgeted costs (agreed or approved); and*
> *(b) all other recoverable costs of the budgeting and costs management process shall not exceed 2% of the total of the incurred costs (as agreed or allowed on assessment) and the budgeted (agreed or approved) costs.*

The exceptional circumstances are not addressed further here.

Master Gordon-Saker, Senior Costs Judge, confirmed in *Marbrow v Sharpes Garden Services Ltd* [2020] EWHC B26 (Costs), those caps, like the budget itself, do not include VAT. That is entirely logical and must be right.

Breakdowns of those costs will not appear in the budget, just the percentages in the box on the first page of Precedent H. The breakdown will be stated in the bill of costs, and for demonstrating that the costs are within the cap it would be helpful to place them in a separate section of the bill.

CHAPTER SEVEN
COSTS PROCEDURE

Presenting the claim for costs – what format?

To start the ball rolling for costs negotiations or assessment, the receiving party must present the claim for costs.

For detailed assessment, the receiving party must present the claim for costs in a bill of costs along the lines of Precedent S (see the end of PD47 on the Ministry of Justice's Civil Procedure Rules website)., the electronic bill of costs based on phases and tasks adopted from the costs budgeting process. It has superseded Precedent A.

For a summary assessment, the costs must be presented in a statement of costs in Form N260. At the time of writing, a pilot scheme running until 31 March 2021 under PD51O, which is testing N260A for interim applications and N260B for trials.

A bill of costs is expensive to prepare and the detailed assessment procedure can be time consuming. Parties often try to negotiate first and for that purpose the claim for costs is often presented in a less formal, less expensive way.

Some practitioners produce a 'schedule of costs', by which they might mean an N260 or a bespoke hybrid between a statement of costs and a bill of costs, prepared for negotiations. These are often in-house idiosyncratic documents but all tend to convey the same basic information: the fee earner(s) and hourly rates(s), the number of letters, emails and calls with each correspondee, the amount of time on attendances and documents, disbursements, and a grand total.

There is no standard format for presenting a claim for fixed costs. There is a box for fixed costs on Form N260, but often receiving parties will send a single sheet setting out the calculation and listing the disbursements. That enables the paying party to more quickly agree the workings or identify any disagreements.

Costs-only proceedings

Where negotiations fail, the next step is to bring the claim before the court. If proceedings have not already been started, the CPR provide the remedy.

The costs-only procedure is in CPR 46.14. It's designed for claims where damages were settled without proceedings but the parties cannot agree the amount of costs. It sets out a simplified process to start proceedings so the court can make an order for assessment.

Conditions precedent

CPR 46.14(1) sets out that the rule applies where three conditions are met:

> *(a) the parties to a dispute have reached an agreement on all issues (including which party is to pay the costs) which is made or confirmed in writing; but*
> *(b) they have failed to agree the amount of those costs; and*
> *(c) no proceedings have been started.*

Agreement confirmed in writing

Under condition (a), if the parties have not agreed that one will pay costs to the other, the procedure does not apply. The costs-only procedure cannot be used to force a party to pay costs when that party will not agree to do so. It is for quantum disputes only. The agreement might be by written exchange of correspondence. A Part 36 offer and acceptance will suffice as confirmation. An agreement confirmed in writing is also acceptable, allowing for settlements made over the telephone. *Thomas v Home Office* [2007] 1 WLR 230 considered what constituted a 'written agreement of the parties'. At [26] and [29], Neuberger LJ (as he then was) said:

> *where, following the oral agreement, the two solicitors exchange letters confirming what they have agreed, the exchange of letters amounts to an agreement in writing...*

> *an oral agreement between two solicitors, subsequently recorded in a letter sent by one solicitor to the other but not replied to by the other, cannot possibly be said to constitute a written agreement of the parties.*

A written agreement might be a higher threshold than an agreement confirmed in writing, or it might be a semantic difference. If there is correspondence from both parties there is plainly an agreement confirmed in writing which will suffice for CPR 46.14(1)(a). In practice, courts are not strict. Under CPR 46.14(4) and PD46 9.5 the claimant must attach the documents to the claim form. A letter from one party confirming a telephone agreement accompanied by a cheque stub for the agreed damages is often accepted. The court will know also that the defendant is likely to oppose the proceedings if the defendant does not think that there is an agreement to pay costs.

Failed to agree

Condition (b) has long been construed to mean that the parties must have made 'a proper attempt to agree' costs before proceedings are started. That phrase is derived from Senior Costs Judge Hurst in *Bensusan v Freedman* [2001] EWHC 9001 (Costs) at [59]. It appears in the current SCCO Guide, showing the masters of the SCCO still ascribe to it. The parties cannot have failed to agree the amount of costs unless they have tried. The requirement is not the simpler 'the costs have not been agreed'. The provision is in keeping with the overriding objective and the approach that proceedings should be a last resort.

What constitutes a proper attempt to agree varies from case to case. Typically, an exchange of offers, and narrowing issues by dealing with any queries raised by the paying party would be a minimum. Also, if the receiving party has allowed enough time for the paying party to make any offers and there has been no reply, it would then be reasonable to start proceedings.

There have been several circuit level appeals about premature issue of costs-only proceedings, and many first instance decisions. See in particular *Knowles v Goldborn* (HHJ Gregory, County Court at Walsall, 6 January 2014, unreported) and *Eager v TC Cleaning* (HHJ Simpkiss, County Court at Brighton, 23 September 2014, unreported). As a rule of thumb, issuing only 7 or 14 days after sending the claim for costs is likely to be premature; 21 days is likely to be the bare minimum to allow, and even then it would be prudent to telephone the paying party to make sure the costs claim was received if there has been no acknowledgement.

No proceedings started

Condition (c) is the simplest requirement. If the claimant has already started proceedings under Part 7, he cannot commence Part 8 costs-only proceedings. The provision has also been construed to mean that costs-only proceedings can be brought only once: see for instance *Eager* at [25]. If an initial set of costs-only proceedings is dismissed, say, because there has not been a proper attempt to agree, the claimant has squandered his one chance to use the procedure. However, some claimants and commentators have argued that the rule should be read purposively. It is to stop costs-only proceedings being brought when there are other extant proceedings in which an order for assessment could be made. Proceedings which have been dismissed or which have lapsed do not count. They point to PD46 9.12 which makes the costs-only procedure mandatory where the only dispute is the amount of costs. Defendants may say in response that the practice direction did not contemplate misuse of process.

<u>Limitation</u>

There is no general limitation period for costs-only proceedings. They can be brought at any time. Occasionally a solicitor finds a long dormant file at the back of the filing cabinet.

Limitation may arise in rare cases where there is a breach of contract. Costs-only proceedings require an agreement to pay costs. If the paying party refuses to pay costs under that agreement (as opposed to simply arguing, for instance, that the indemnity principle means costs under the agreement are nil), then the six year limitation period for breach of contract would start running from the date of breach (rather than the date of the costs agreement).

In practice, limitation does not arise. Instead, any interest on costs that would otherwise have accrued had proceeding been issued sooner will be lost. Interest would only accrue from the date of the order for costs.

Sanction for not following the costs-only procedure

Despite PD46 9.12, there is nothing to physically stop a party commencing a Part 7 or 'full' Part 8 claim for costs. CPR 46.14(6) deals with that:

> *(6) Where this rule applies but the procedure set out in this rule has not been followed by a party –*
> *(a) that party will not be allowed costs greater than those that would have been allowed to that party had the procedure been followed; and*
> *(b) the court may award the other party the costs of the proceedings up to the point where an order for the payment of costs is made.*

CPR 46.14(6) could refer both to the costs being claimed and the costs of the proceedings. It is framed in broad terms but these provisions seem to tackle an observation in *Solomon v Cromwell* [2012] 1 WLR 1048. Predictable costs apply in costs-only proceedings but would not apply in other proceedings, so if the claimant commenced other proceedings for costs he might get more than predictable costs. Moore-Bick LJ said at [21], talking about the old rule numberings:

> *It is true that the procedure in rule 44.12A is not exclusive and that a claimant may start proceedings under Part 7 or Part 8 to recover costs under the terms of a settlement agreement: para 17.11 of the Costs Practice Direction makes that clear. However, it is very doubtful whether he could recover more than the fixed costs for which Section II of Part 45 provides.*

Under CPR 46.14(6), a party who might have lost his one chance at costs-only proceedings and was forced down the route of starting a Part 7 claim would not only recover no more for his costs than he would under the costs-only procedure, he would also recover only a £55 issue fee (the fee for commencing costs-only proceedings) when he might have paid more, and he might have to pay the defendant's costs of the proceedings down to the making of an order for costs. It adds up to a strong incentive to use the costs-only procedure correctly, and is in keeping with the requirement of the overriding objective at CPR 1.1(2)(f) to enforce compliance with rules.

Procedure under CPR 46.14

The costs-only procedure modifies the Part 8 Alternative Procedure for Claims under the auspices of CPR 8.1(6). Think of Part 8 as a framework. The costs-only procedure takes that framework and for ease strips out certain steps. For instance, costs-only proceedings are not treated as allocated to the multi-track under CPR 8.9(c) because PD46 9.11 says they are not. There is no need for costs-only proceedings to be treated as being on any track, as they are merely a bridge to assessment proceedings.

The claim form

The claimant prepares the Part 8 claim form. There are four requirements for the Part 8 claim form under PD46 9.3. It must:

(a) identify the claim or dispute to which the agreement relates;
(b) state the date and terms of the agreement on which the claimant relies;
(c) set out or attach a draft of the order which the claimant seeks;
(d) state the amount of the costs claimed.

It is also helpful to spell out that it is a claim brought under CPR 46.14 for costs only. The particulars of claim are usually short and do not spill onto a continuation sheet.

The draft order will specify the type of order the claimant seeks. Most simply it would be:

The defendant do pay the claimant's costs to be assessed if not agreed.

If it were a fixed costs claim, it might be:

The defendant do pay the claimant's costs in accordance with CPR 45 [Section II/ Section III/ Section IIIA], with disbursements to be assessed if not agreed.

In addition in most cases there will be an order for:

Costs in the assessment.

That means the costs of the costs-only proceedings will go to the winner in the assessment. Some claimants seek their costs of the costs-only proceedings in any event, but the defendant will usually object and the court will not usually make such an order. The court deals with costs-only proceedings on paper and does not have a full view of the case. It would not be in a position to conclude such an order was appropriate.

Some claimants seek a suite of directions for service of the bill, points of dispute, replies and listing for assessment. That is otiose; it is covered by Part 47.

Some claimants also seek an order for a payment on account of costs under CPR 44.2(8). That is procedurally acceptable; the rule applies concurrently to the making of an order for an assessment. However, courts rarely order payments on account in costs-only proceedings in practice perhaps because the judge knows no more about the case than is stated in the claim form and any witness statement with the acknowledgement of service. He would not know what amount was appropriate. Paying parties often volunteer payment on account though to mitigate interest.

It is sometimes impossible to state the amount of costs being claimed. The parties may have negotiated before proceedings were started on the basis of a schedule of costs. Only a bill of costs can state the amount of costs claimed, and there is no requirement to accompany costs-only proceedings with the bill of costs. It might be prepared later. Therefore the amount of costs might be stated provisionally, with a caveat that the bill will subsequently clarify the precise amount.

Additional information for the claim form in fixed costs cases

There are additional requirements for predictable costs cases set out in PD45:

- PD45 2.8 says '*Where the claimant is claiming an amount of costs which exceed the amount of the fixed recoverable costs the claim form must give details of the* ***exceptional circumstances*** *to justify the additional costs.*'
- PD45 2.9 says '*The claimant must also include on the claim form* ***details of any disbursements****. The disbursements that may be claimed are set out in rule 45.12(1). If the disbursement falls within 45.12(2)(c) (disbursements that have arisen due to a particular feature of the dispute) the claimant must give* ***details of the particular feature of the dispute*** *that made the disbursement necessary.*'

There is no mirror requirement for portal costs or Section IIIA costs, but it would be best practice to follow suit.

Attachments to the claim form

The documents confirming the agreement to pay costs must be attached to the claim form per CPR 46.14(4). A draft order must be attached if it is not set out in the claim form already.

Filing at court

The claim can be issued in a County Court hearing centre of the claimant's choosing. Costs-only proceedings are not started in the County Court Money Claims Centre at Salford. The claim should be started in the High Court **only** if the claim to which the costs relate would itself have been issued in the High Court. If such a claim is to be issued in London, it would be issued in the Senior Courts Costs Office as a division of the High Court (PD46 9.2). Outside London, the claim may be issued in a District Registry.

There is a reduced court fee payable, presently £55 (Civil Proceedings Fees Order fee 1.8(b)).

Send three copies of the claim form for the court to seal: one each for the court, claimant and defendant. Send extra copies if there are additional parties.

The covering letter should state whether court service is sought or whether solicitor service will be effected. If it is court service, the court will send a sealed copy of the claim form to the defendant by way of service. If it is solicitor service, the defendant's copy of the claim form will be sent back to the claimant's solicitor, and the claimant's solicitor must then serve it. Some solicitors choose solicitor service for certainty about service, but court service is the most common method for costs-only proceedings.

There is no requirement to send an unsealed copy of the claim form to the defendant before issue, but if the defendant does not even know proceedings are being started there is no additional pressure on the defendant to settle. The claimant may not want to apply that pressure until after proceedings have been issued, but claimants should be wary of the risk that proceedings started unreasonably may be dismissed.

Acknowledgement of service

Once served, the defendant has 14 days under CPR 8.3(1)(a) to file and serve an acknowledgement of service. That must be in Form N210A. If the defendant has solicitors, they should file a notice of acting at the same time.

The defendant has five options in Form N210A:

- Not contest the claim – an order will be made for the costs as claimed.
- Dispute the amount of costs – the most common response, which will usually result in an order for assessment.
- Dispute the making of an order for costs – typically because the defendant disputes that the costs-only procedure applies, or because costs have been agreed or paid and an order is not required.
- Seek a different remedy – very rarely used.

- Dispute the court's jurisdiction under Part 11 – where the defendant contends that the claimant should not be bringing proceedings in England & Wales, usually because there is an argument that any costs are governed by the rules of a different jurisdiction.

The first two options require a tick on the form, and no more.

The last three options all amount to opposing the claim. (The second does not amount to opposing the claim per PD46 9.10). PD46 9.10 requires the acknowledgement of service to be accompanied by a witness statement setting out the opposition with reasons. Any documents to which the defendant refers should be exhibited.

The defendant should attach to the acknowledgement any alternative order that it proposes. That is not restricted to occasions when the claim is opposed. Sometimes the specific wording of the claimant's proposed order may be disagreeable.

Defendant's default

If the defendant does not file and serve an acknowledgement of service within 14 days, there is a sanction in CPR 8.4(2). The defendant may only attend the hearing but may not take part. As costs-only proceedings are usually decided on the papers, that is a toothless sanction in most cases. It would be a problem for the defendant if the court decided to deal with the costs-only proceedings at a hearing. The defendant would need to apply for relief from sanction in accordance with CPR 3.9. There is no reported instance of that sanction being interpreted so widely that it extends to a detailed assessment hearing in the detailed assessment proceedings commenced on the back of the order made in the costs-only proceedings; and indeed that would seem a stretch.

Also, if the defendant is in default, that should not result in order for costs as claimed. Instead, it should result in an unopposed order for the costs to be assessed, in accordance with CPR 46.14(5).

The court's decision

Costs-only proceedings are usually dealt with as part of a judge's 'box work'. The court staff will pass the court file to a judge once an acknowledgement of service has been filed or once the 14 days to do so has expired (the claimant can assist by writing to point out the default to the court, per PD46 9.7).

Some courts make an order immediately upon issuing the claim form. The laudable aim seems to be to progress the claim swiftly, but the practice would appear to be irregular. The defendant will need to make a decision whether to apply to set aside or vary the order upon service, or to live with it.

More normally the court will consider the papers filed by both parties. In most cases, the court will make an order on the papers. Notwithstanding any draft orders filed by the parties, many judges have their own form of standard order for costs-only proceedings. The court has a broad discretion as to the form of order. CPR 46.14(5) provides:

> *In proceedings to which this rule applies the court may make an order for the payment of costs the amount of which is to be determined by assessment and/or, where appropriate, for the payment of fixed costs.*

PD46 9.6 elaborates:

> *A costs judge or a district judge has jurisdiction to hear and decide any issue which may arise in a claim issued under this rule irrespective of the amount of the costs claimed or of the value of the claim to which the agreement to pay costs relates. The court may make an order by consent under paragraph 9.8, or an order dismissing a claim under paragraph 9.10 below.*

PD46 9.4 advises to assist with the subsequent assessment that:

> *Unless the court orders otherwise or Section II of Part 45 applies the costs will be treated as being claimed on the standard basis.*

In cases where CPR 45 Sections III and IIIA apply, arguably the court should go so far as to say one of those sections applies; or perhaps it is unnecessary because of the principle in *Solomon v Cromwell* [2012] 1 WLR 1048 that special rules about costs prevail over general rules. Certainly, follow the *dicta* in *Ho v Adelekun* [2019] Costs LR 1963 about clarity in parties' agreements in fixed costs cases, it would be helpful if courts adopted similar clarity.

Both parties should check the order upon receipt. If there is a problem (for instance, it orders assessment of costs on the standard basis where fixed costs apply procedurally and the claimant then seeks to disavow the fixed costs), there are only seven days from deemed service to apply to set aside or vary under CPR 3.3(5) and (6).

Sometimes the court decides that a dispute between the parties requires a hearing. PD46 9.6 does say that court may 'hear and decide any issue'. Under PD46 9.10, if the defendant opposes the claim '*The court will then give directions including, if appropriate, a direction that the claim shall continue as if it were a Part 7 claim.*' Such directions may include a hearing. At a hearing, the court may make an order for costs, dismiss the claim, or direct that the claim continues under Part 7 (and it would also assist if the court gave directions for amended particulars of claim and a defence to put the process on the right track). Equally the court could make any of those orders on the papers.

If the court makes an order for assessment after such a hearing, PD46 9.9 reminds that summary assessment of the costs is then a possibility:

> *Where costs are ordered to be assessed, the general rule is that this should be by detailed assessment. However when an order is made under this rule following a hearing and the court is in a position to summarily assess costs it should generally do so.*

That works especially well for costs-only proceedings for fixed costs. It does not work so well for standard basis costs claimed on an hourly rate. The receiving party may have prepared a bill of costs rather than an N260 for summary assessment. Detailed assessment would be a better fit.

When Stage 3 proceedings have already been started

There is an alternative costs-only procedure in CPR 45.29 for claims that settle after Part 8 Stage 3 proceedings have been started but before the court decides the claim. Instead of a claim form, either party can make an application using Form N244 for the portal costs to be decided. That is a rare occurrence. There is no further guidance, but it would sensible to follow the same or equivalent steps that one would follow in 46.14 proceedings.

Costs of costs-only proceedings

If the claim is dismissed on the papers upon opposition by the defendant there is usually no order for costs. If there is a hearing the court is likely to deal with the costs there and then.

If an order for costs is made on the papers, one or other party will get the costs of the costs-only proceedings. Although the costs claimed in the proceedings may be fixed costs, the costs of the costs-only proceedings themselves are not fixed. It appears to be a glaring omission. In *Tasleem v Beverley* [2014] 1 WLR 3567, Sharp LJ observed at [22]: '*the costs of bringing such Part 8 proceedings may be, or should be, relatively minimal.*' The steps are formulaic and many practitioners use templates. The claimant must prepare the claim form and draft order, consider the acknowledgement of service and the order. The defendant must consider the claim form, prepare an acknowledgement of service and consider the order. There are a few letters in addition. 'Minimal' should mean no more than a few hundred pounds for either party.

The costs of these proceedings may be fixed in any future expansion of fixed costs.

No proceedings and no agreement to pay costs

In the law of England & Wales, there is no free-standing cause of action to bring a claim for the costs of a dispute that settled without proceedings and without an agreement to pay those costs. Although s51 Senior Courts of Act 1981 gives the court a broad discretion over costs where the court is already seised, it does not create a cause of action.

In order to recover costs, there must be an agreement that a party will pay another party's costs, or the court must have made an order for costs in pre-existing proceedings. Without an agreement, costs-only proceedings cannot be brought (CPR 46.14(1)(a)).

A Part 7 claim to force a party to pay costs is likely to fail. Lord Diplock said in *Hobbs v Marlowe* [1977] AC 16 at 40:

> *to commence proceedings or to inflate a claim for the sole purpose of obtaining costs or of increasing the costs that defendant may have to pay is an abuse of the process of the court.*

There is a string of cases in which claimants (or their solicitors) have recklessly started proceedings for costs on the misunderstanding that they have a right to costs. Most ways of pleading such a claim have been tried down the years. Some have unsuccessfully sought judgment on pre-action admissions. Some have tried to litigate the damages claim even though it was agreed: see *Smith v Springer* [1987] 1 WLR 1720. They run the risk of not beating pre-issue offers and losing costs for unreasonable conduct. That tactic is particularly difficult when the claim is for a specified sum. The defendant will plead a defence of tender before claim and pay the monies into court. There is a grey area whether the defence of tender has extended to a claim for a specified sum under the CPR, or whether it still only applies to a claim for liquidated damages (which, in substance, is barely distinguishable). The senior courts may come to reconsider that area of law.

Tugendhat J summed up the law in a judgment approved subsequently on appeal by the Court of Appeal. In *Citation plc v Ellis Witham Ltd* [2012] 5 Costs LR 826, he said at [16]:

> *In summary I take the law to be: (1) if no claim form is issued, then there is no litigation and so there are no costs of litigation, whatever costs may have been incurred in complying with a Pre-Action Protocol; but (2) if a claim form is issued, the costs incurred in complying with a Pre-Action Protocol may be recoverable as costs "incidental to" any subsequent proceedings.*

Citation was a defamation claim. The judge held the claimant had an arguable case, but struck out the claim on the basis that the claimant had achieved all which would be of any value to it in vindicating its reputation by the time the claim was issued. The claimant nevertheless sought costs. The claimant's submission was noted at [9]:

> *"it would not be an abuse of the process of the court for a claimant to decline to settle the dispute in question, notwithstanding that he had been offered all that he was entitled to by way of substantive relief, unless the offer included an acceptable offer in relation to costs. In such a situation, it would be perfectly proper for the claimant to decline the offer, commence proceedings and leave the defendant to decide whether to concede the claim for substantive relief in the context of the litigation. As has frequently been observed judicially, costs are, regrettably but in current conditions inevitably, often the most significant elements of a party's claim."*

The judge went on to conclude in the defendant's favour at [27]-[28]:

> *I accept [the defendant's] submission that in the absence of a finding or admission of liability in this case, or an undertaking in the terms sought by the claimant, I cannot make an order for costs against the defendant. I also accept her submission that the claimant should be ordered to pay the costs from the service of the claim form on the defendant on 28 October 2011.*
>
> *As to the costs up to the service of the claim form, I make no order. If the claimant had not commenced the proceedings (and I have held that it ought not to have commenced the proceedings) then the defendant could not have sought an order for its costs for that period to be paid by the claimant. The fact that the claimant did commence proceedings in this case ought not to lead to the result that it becomes liable to pay to the defendant costs which it would not have been liable to pay if it had not commenced proceedings.*

This problem does not arise very often in injury claims. Claims settling in the RTA or EL/PL Protocol have an automatic term for payment of costs. The court has jurisdiction in litigated claims over the costs. It could apply only to unlitigated claims outside the portal. In most injury claims, defendants will agree to pay costs. The dispute arises where defendants or their insurers consider that it was not reasonable for the claimant to involve solicitors. For instance, 'bent metal' claims following RTAs from which there is no injury claim. Many of those will be within the remit of the small claims track anyway. For the few that exceed the small claims limit, that are essentially debt recovery claim for specified sums, the insurer may object to the extra layer of costs of having a solicitor involved.

The cautionary message is that a claimant should take care to secure an agreement to pay costs when finalising the damages claim, and defendants should not carelessly agree to pay costs in all cases and thus occasionally throw away a valuable argument.

Children's (and protected parties') costs claims

Settlements in children's and protected parties' (such as patients') claims must be approved by the court before becoming final. Regarding the costs there are three options: agree them before the hearing, summarily assess them at the hearing, or deal with them on a later date (either by an adjourned summary assessment before the same judge or by detailed assessment).

Such claims are not excluded from fixed costs. The specifics of fixed costs in this context are covered in the fixed costs section.

Procedure ahead of an approval hearing

It is often a conundrum for defendants whether to attend the approval hearing. Damages are likely to be approved without incident, or if they are not, they are unlikely to be increased arbitrarily at the hearing. The court will give directions. Instead, defendants are more likely to attend over costs issues if costs have not been agreed in advance.

It is in the claimant's interest to agree costs in advance of the hearing. There will be greater confidence that approval will be given by the court and the hearing will run more smoothly. Claimants generally provide details of their costs for agreement well in advance of the approval hearing.

Under CPR 46.4(2), the general rule is that if the child or protected party is paying another party's costs there must be a detailed assessment. That is not a common situation. Usually another party will be paying the child or protected party's costs. In those circumstances, CPR 46.4(3) says that the court does not have to order a detailed assessment if the one of the circumstances in PD46 2.1 applies. The most commonly satisfied circumstances are:

> *(b) where another party has agreed to pay a specified sum in respect of the costs of the child or protected party and the legal representative acting for the child or protected party has waived the right to claim further costs;*
>
> *(c) where the court has decided the costs payable to the child or protected party by way of summary assessment and the legal representative acting for the child or protected party has waived the right to claim further costs.*

They allow the parties to agree costs before the approval hearing or for the court to make a summary assessment at the approval hearing. Waiving the right to claim further costs means the claimant's solicitors must agree to accept the sum agreed or summarily assessed and not seek the balance from the child or protected party's damages. Form N292, the standard order for an approval hearing, makes appropriate provision.

Deducting success fees from damages

A problem arose in claims funded by CFAs under the new regime after 1 April 2013 in which success fees are not recoverable. (As this book does not otherwise address the now historic additional liabilities regime, briefly a 'success fee' is the percentage of profit costs a solicitor may charge in addition if he wins the claim for his client.) The rules did not provide for a deduction from the child's damages to cover the solicitor's success fee. That was resolved by rule change. The provisions are at CPR 21.12(1A)(b).

Some judges have expressed concern at the amounts sought to be deducted from the damages by solicitors for their success fees. An example judgment is *A & Anor v Royal Mail Group* [2015] EW Misc B24 (CC) (14 August 2015). There is concern that solicitors are placing very high success fees on claims so as to take the maximum cut (25%) from the damages, even though the claim is low risk and does not justify so high a success fee or so large a deduction from damages. In *Herbert v HH Law Ltd* [2019] 1 WLR 4253, the Court of Appeal held that a success fee that was set without regard to the risks of the individual claim was payable only if the informed consent of the client had been obtained, and in that case it had not been obtained. It is difficult to imagine a client who gives informed consent to a greater reduction from his damages that would apply if a case specific risk assessment is made. That may be the client who is unable to obtain representation otherwise, but 'shopping around' may turn up a solicitor willing to run the claim on better terms. In remaining competitive on children's claim particularly, perhaps the former fixed success fee under Part 45 (12.5% for RTA, 25% for EL – some children do work) would be accepted as reasonable.

In terms of procedure, CPR 46.4(5) says the solicitor and own client assessment procedure under CPR 46.10 may be dis-applied in favour of summary assessment. That is sensible for equality of arms, otherwise the litigation friend may need a new solicitor for the dispute with the old solicitor. If CPR 46.10 does apply the solicitor and litigation friend should note the short timescales.

Summary assessment

Summary assessment is the rough and ready way to decide the amount of costs quickly at the end of a hearing. A summary assessment should be made only by a judge who has decided the case or the relevant issue. That judge will have the background knowledge of the case to make the quick decisions about what is reasonable and proportionate.

Applicability

PD44 paragraph 9 sets out the guidance on and requirements for summary assessment.

The court is encouraged to make a summary assessment when it makes an order for costs other than fixed costs. Plus, as a general rule, the court will summarily assess costs at the end of a fast track trial or any other hearing which has lasted less than a day. If it was an application hearing, the court will summarily assess only the costs of that application. The court can order detailed assessment instead if there's a good reason, such as the paying party raising a substantial issue that is better dealt with by detailed assessment.

N260

Both parties should prepare for a qualifying hearing as if there will be a summary assessment. That means that a statement of costs in Form N260 must be prepared. Form N260 is largely self-explanatory, and if all the relevant boxes are completed the party will have complied with the requirements in PD44 9.5(2) and (3).

Optionally, a party may use Form N260A for an interim application or Form N260B for a trial, while the PD51O pilot is ongoing (until 31 March 2021).

Some parts are difficult to complete ahead of the hearing and may be left blank. For instance, it may not be possible to insert the name of the judge because the court list especially in the County Court is not published far enough in advance. If counsel is instructed to attend the hearing, it may not be possible to insert counsel's brief fee because it has not yet been agreed with counsel's clerk (busy counsel often prepares the day before for short hearings). PD44 9.5(2) lists the things that must appear in the N260, and they include at (d) 'the amount and nature of any disbursement to be claimed, other than counsel's fee for appearing at the hearing', which seems to acknowledge the solicitor's problem; but then (f) says 'counsel's fees' must be shown, leaving doubt as to whether that is other or all counsel's fees. The confusing wording probably intends that counsel's fees are shown separately from other disbursements, and indeed N260 is laid out that way. Generally, if counsel's brief fee is marked 'tbc', counsel will report his own fee to the court and the court will often accept that. That said, there have been instance of the court disallowing counsel's fee because it was not in the statement of costs. Best endeavours should be made with counsel's clerk to include something, even if it is only an estimate.

Timing

N260 must be filed and served not less than 24 hours before the time fixed for the hearing, or for a fast track trial not less than two days before. Under the rules on time in CPR 2.8(4), if the 24 hours or two days spans a Saturday or Sunday, a bank holiday, Christmas Day or Good Friday, those days don't count. So for a hearing at 10am on a Monday, the statement of costs must be filed and served by 10am the preceding Friday (or Thursday for a fast track trial).

PD44 9.6 says a failure to comply with the provisions on content and timing will be taken into account by the court when deciding what order to make about costs. A failure to file and serve a statement of costs does not necessarily mean all costs should be disallowed: *MacDonald v Taree Holdings* [2001] 1 Costs LR 147. Neuberger J (as he then was) held that the court's reaction would be proportionate. That may result in the disallowance of some, but not all, costs. In particular if the statement of costs was only marginally late and there was no prejudice to the paying party, the court would summarily assess as normal. If there were 'aggravating factors', such as a deliberate failure to provide the statement of costs, that may result in disallowance of all or most of the costs.

The court's approach

At a summary assessment, the paying party raises brief objections to the statement of costs and the receiving party replies. The court then makes its decisions, applying the principles described in Chapter Five, often on a broad-brush basis resulting in allowance of a round figure.

Restrictions on ordering summary assessment

PD44 9.7 says that a court awarding costs cannot make an order for summary assessment by a costs officer (defined by CPR 44.1(1) as a costs judge, district judge or authorised court officer, not to be confused with the 'costs officers' in the SCCO). Either the judge makes the summary assessment himself (by adjourning to a later date if necessary) or he orders a detailed assessment. That was the conclusion of the Court of Appeal in *Mahmood v Penrose* [2002] EWCA Civ 457. It is pinned on the principle that a summary assessment can be made fairly only by a judge who already knows the case.

However, Coulson J (as he then was) said in *Transformers And Rectifiers Ltd v Needs Ltd* [2015] EWHC 1687 (TCC) that another judge may make the summary assessment. It is difficult to square that decision with PD44 9.7. Because the practice direction says 'the court may give directions as to a further hearing before the same judge', he construed 'may' as permissive and not exclusive of a hearing before a different judge. He distinguished *Mahmood* because in 2002, the practice direction had said 'must' rather than 'may'. He gave examples of where the judge died (costs hearings can be very long…) or became indisposed before making the summary assessment. No doubt it would be convenient but the solution might instead to be to set aside the adjournment of the summary assessment and make an order for detailed assessment instead.

The practice of holding open a disposal hearing when damages had been agreed for the purpose of summary assessment was observed to be irregular by Wilson LJ (as he then was) in *Thenga v Quinn* [2009] EWCA Civ 151, although having not heard full argument on the point he did not go so far as to condemn the practice. If there were full argument, one would expect the Court of Appeal to rule that the practice must stop.

Costs orders in consent orders

If the parties agree an application by consent before a hearing, PD44 9.4 exhorts the parties to agree a specific figure for costs or agree that there is no order for costs and insert that in the order. They cannot agree a summary assessment. Although it is not stated, there is no reason in principle why the costs might not be 'in the assessment' or 'reserved', or the parties could agree an order for detailed assessment. The rules on timing of detailed assessment in CPR 47.1 mean that the detailed assessment will generally be held off until the claim as a whole has concluded.

CHAPTER EIGHT
DETAILED ASSESSMENT

Detailed assessment timetable

Part 47 is set out in a broadly sequential structure. These are the key events, gathering information from some practice directions also:

Starting point	'Event' giving the right to detailed assessment: a court order, a consent order, a Tomlin order, a Part 36 offer accepted within its relevant period, or a notice of discontinuance.
Within three months of start	Service of notice of commencement
Within 21 days of service of notice of commencement	Service of points of dispute
Within 21 days of service of points of dispute	Service of optional replies to points of dispute
Before detailed assessment hearing/ provisional assessment	Filing and service of any supplementary points of dispute and/ or replies
Within six months of start	Request for detailed assessment hearing/ provisional assessment
Between 14 and 7 days before detailed assessment hearing or as directed by court	Receiving party files supporting papers
No later than 24 hours before detailed assessment hearing	Parties file and serve statements of costs of detailed assessment
Date fixed by court	Detailed assessment hearing/ provisional assessment
No later than 14 days after receipt of provisional assessment	Parties agree arithmetic
Within 21 days of receipt of provisional assessment	Filing and service of any request for an oral hearing
Date fixed by court	Oral hearing following provisional assessment, where requested
Within 21 days after conclusion of detailed assessment hearing or oral hearing	Filing and service of any appellant's notice

Right to detailed assessment

A party cannot commence detailed assessment proceedings simply because his opponent has agreed to pay costs. The agreement must be embodied in some form of order. Alternatively, the court may make an order for costs at the end of a hearing.

The following give the right to detailed assessment:

- An **order** for costs or for detailed assessment;
  - If it's a Tomlin order, the order must be in the body of the order not the schedule, which is not part of the order (see PD40B 3.5).
  - Obviously this does not include an order specifying summary assessment.
  - Nor does it include an order for fixed costs: see the section 'Can there be an assessment of fixed costs?'

- **Acceptance of a Part 36 offer** within its relevant period;
  - See CPR 36.13(1) and (2) and CPR 44.9(1)(b) – it is the deemed order under CPR 44.9(1)(b) that creates the right.
  - Acceptance outside the relevant period will require the parties to agree a consent order or apply for an order under CPR 36.13(4)(b) and (5).
  - Where Section IIIA costs apply, see the section 'Section IIIA and Part 36' for more information.
  - Where the Part 36 offer is accepted pre-issue, there is no deemed order and no right to detailed assessment: CPR 44.9(2). '*An order for costs cannot exist in a vacuum divorced from any substantive proceedings*': *Solomon v Cromwell* [2012] 1 WLR 1048 at [16]. The party will need to commence costs-only proceedings relying on the Part 36 acceptance to obtain an order giving the right to detailed assessment.

- A **notice of discontinuance** (as long as the claim is not allocated to the small claims track);
  - This creates a deemed order for the defendant's costs under CPR 38.6(1) and CPR 44.9(1)(c), unless the court orders otherwise.

There are also some rarely occurring rights under CPR 3.7 and 3.7B for not paying court fees or dishonouring a cheque.

Deemed orders

CPR 44.9 creates deemed orders. A deemed order is an order where the court is deemed to have made an order for detailed assessment on the standard basis where the court has not in fact made in order and there will be no piece of paper setting out that order. It is an order made by automatic effect of the rules rather than an order made by a judge.

Deemed orders were created to avoid the inconsistency that some parties could be left without a right to interest because there was no order for costs: *Legal Aid Board v Russell* [1991] 2 AC 317.

The existence of deemed orders is proved by production of the documents that trigger its creation, such as the Part 36 offer and acceptance.

The court has no power to vary an order deemed to be made by effect of the rules: *Walker Residential Ltd v Davis* [2005] EWHC 3483 (Ch) at [49] approved by *Lahey v Pirelli Tyres* [2007] 1 WLR 998 at [19]. Parties who do not want to be trapped by a deemed order should avoid taking the steps that cause them to arise, such as making Part 36 offers or accepting Part 36 offers within their relevant periods. Parties may not want the costs consequences to apply because they want non-standard costs consequences or want something alongside the order for costs, such as a payment on account of costs.

Preparing a bill of costs

Detailed assessment is modernising. Electronic bills must be prepared for all work done after 6 April 2018 per PD57 5.1(b). An example electronic bill can be found at Precedent S at PD47. It is a spreadsheet intended to be filled out on screen. That format is not mandatory, as PD47 5.A2 permits an alternative spreadsheet that reports and aggregates costs based on the phases, tasks, activities and expenses, reports summary totals, allows the user to identify, in chronological order, the detail of all the work undertaken in each phase, automatically recalculates totals if the data is changed, and is transparent in its workings so other parties and the court can work it. There are several freely available electronic bill templates. The ACL offers one with useful additional functionality at: https://www.associationofcostslawyers.co.uk/ACL-Bill (accessed 16 July 2020). It is currently on its 21st revision. Some costs software can now produce bills in the electronic format.

When some of the costs must be shown in an electronic bill, it may be easier to include any costs preceding 6 April 2018 in the same format. However, as costs draftsman often find the electronic bill more time consuming to prepare, earlier costs may still appear in a 'paper bill', based on one of Precedents A to D (all costs precedents can be found on the CPR website at the end of PD47). Presenting costs disparately can often also result in a higher overall allowance at the end of assessment.

The actual drafting of bills of costs is still usually done by costs draftsmen. We are gradually moving towards the position where case management systems can output ledger information in the correct format, but the ledger entries still need review to determine what is recoverable and what is not. PD47 paragraph 5 details the format of a bill, and coupling that guidance with Precedent S and the information in the Chapter on 'Recoverable Costs', the adventurous may be able to draft their own bill.

Commencing detailed assessment proceedings

If the receiving party has the right to detailed assessment, he may start detailed assessment proceedings by serving on the paying party (or parties) a notice of commencement of detailed assessment in Form N252, his bill of costs, counsel's and expert's fee notes, any other disbursement fee note exceeding £500 and, where a costs management order has been made and the information is not already in an electronic bill of costs, a breakdown of the bill by budget phase in Precedent Q or similar document.

The N252 must be fully completed, signed and dated; otherwise the paying party may legitimately argue it is defective and ineffective. (If that happens, it is normal to fix the problem and re-serve the N252 with an updated due date for points of dispute rather than argue over the validity of the incomplete notice.) The bill must also be signed; but if it is served with its certificates unsigned it is not a nullity. The paying party may attack the bill while it is unprotected by the presumption of trust of the bill's accuracy which comes from that signed certificate per *Bailey v IBC Vehicles* [1998] 3 All ER 570, but ultimately that could be fixed by the solicitor signing the bill late.

Three figures are needed for insertion on N252:

- the grand total of the bill;
- the grand total of the bill plus the court fee for requesting an assessment of a bill of that value (see the Civil Proceedings Fees Order fee 5.2);
- the grand total plus the fixed costs for obtaining a default costs certificate (£80 fixed costs and £66 court fee – see PD47 10.7 and the Civil Proceedings Fees Order fee 5.3).

The second figure is a strange requirement as it will never arise. If the receiving party gets as far as incurring that fee, he will have assessment costs to add on as well, as the wording of N252 says. Correspondingly, PD47 5.3 requires only the first and third figures to be completed on the N252.

The due date for points of dispute must be inserted. It is at least 21 days after service of the N252, bill and accompanying documents. In order to fill in the date you need to know when and how you intend to serve. If it will be electronic service (where permitted) and it's before 4.30pm, it is 21 days from that date. If it's by post, deemed service under Part 6 will be two days later (or if that is not a working day, the next working day). Count 21 days from then.

Even though that date must be completed it is not technically possible to extend or shorten the time for points of dispute simply by entering the date. The sanction in CPR 47.9(3) kicks in if points of dispute are served later than 21 days after service of the N252. The rules never refer to the date in the N252. If the date is wrong but stuck to, the paying party could end up falling foul of the sanction (although the misleading date on the N252 would be a factor lying in favour of relief). Still, it is best to complete the date with care.

Accompanying Documents

CPR 47.6(1)(c) says that if PD47 requires it, the N252 and bill must be accompanied by a breakdown of the costs claimed for each phase of the proceedings. PD47 5.2(f) requires that breakdown where the information is not already included in an electronic bill. Precedent Q, found at the end of PD47 online, shows that what is needed is a breakdown of the bill's total between budget phases, pre and post budget. Anecdotally, there seem to have been cases where parties have agreed costs budgets and the court has omitted to make a costs management order under CPR 3.15(2)(a), so in some cases there may not be a strict requirement – but it would nevertheless be useful.

CPR 47.6 contains a signpost that PD47 deals with 'other documents which the party must file *when requesting detailed assessment*'; and that's true, it does. It would have been more relevant if there were a signpost saying that PD47 deals with documents that must be served with the notice of commencement. PD47 5.2 requires the receiving party to serve:

- copies of the fee notes of counsel and of any expert in respect of fees claimed in the bill;
- written evidence as to any other disbursement which is claimed and which exceeds £500; and
- a statement giving the name and address for service of any person upon whom the receiving party intends to serve the notice of commencement;

It does not specifically say when those documents should be served, but the courts have generally accepted those documents should be served at the same time as the N252, bill and Precedent Q (which are also listed in the same practice direction): see for example Barling J in *Long v Value Properties* [2014] EWHC 2981 (Ch) at [21] to [41]. It also appears to be generally accepted that omission of those documents does not mean detailed assessment proceedings have not been commenced. A paying party should reasonably contact the receiving party to request them, and if they are still not provided the paying party can raise appropriate points of dispute.

'Written evidence' about a disbursement is not taken to mean a witness statement. The fee note or disbursement voucher will do. Although the strict requirement is to supply evidence only for fees over £500 for detailed assessment (other than counsel and expert fees), in practice all fee notes are provided, which is welcomed in the interests of transparency and openness. It would not be unreasonable for a paying party to ask to see them in any event for the purposes of negotiations. Compare for instance that under the RTA and EL/PL Protocols the claimant must attach evidence of all disbursements to an interim settlement pack or stage two settlement pack.

Points of dispute and replies

'Points of dispute' is the name of the document in which a paying party lists his challenges (with reasons) to the bill of costs.

Preparation

Preparing points of dispute can be time consuming and the ordinary time limit to prepare them is not long: they must be served within 21 days of service of the notice of commencement. Before a paying party embarks on preparing points of dispute, there are some basics to check:

- Does the receiving party have the right to detailed assessment?
    - If not, and the receiving party won't concede that, the paying party can make an application to set aside the notice of commencement under PD47 1.3.

- Has the N252, bill and any Precedent Q been validly served?

    - Was service effective under Part 6?
    - Is Precedent Q missing when it should have been served?
    - Are any pages missing?

- Does the amount in dispute make it proportionate to draft points of dispute and risk incurring the additional costs of detailed assessment?
    - Always value the receiving party's bill before starting to draft points of dispute – it's frustrating to find it is not worth proceeding part way through drafting.
    - Has there been an attempt to negotiate settlement before preparing points of dispute?
    - Has an offer been made in advance of the points of dispute? It's not always practical, but an early offer may protect the paying party against the costs of assessment.

Format and content

Points of dispute should be in the format of Precedent G (found online at the end of PD47). Some electronic bills allow for points of dispute to be incorporated into the electronic bill, but that can often be too constrictive. Each point takes the format of three rows: the challenge, a space for a reply, and a space for the court's decision. To the left of those three rows is a label column for numbering and identifying each point.

PD47 8.2 prescribes:

> *Points of dispute must be short and to the point. They must follow Precedent G in the Schedule of Costs Precedents annexed to this Practice Direction, so far as practicable. They must:*
> *(a) identify any general points or matters of principle which require decision before the individual items in the bill are addressed; and*
> *(b) identify specific points, stating concisely the nature and grounds of dispute.*

> *Once a point has been made it should not be repeated but the item numbers where the point arises should be inserted in the left hand box as shown in Precedent G.*

Each point is numbered consecutively, then identified as a 'general point' or 'point of principle' or as a specific point by giving the item number or name from the body of the bill. Use item numbers where every item in the bill is numbered. Resort to names when the bill gives one number to all profit costs. The important thing is always to be clear so the judge can follow the challenges and relate them to the bill. State the part number and page number if necessary as well as the item name.

Generally there is one point for every challenge or legal issue. There may be more than one point about an item in the bill. If the same challenge or legal issue applies to multiple items, list all those items in the left column, don't repeat the challenge. It is wrong to repeat the same challenge.

General points should be ordered by importance: start with those that have the biggest value, and work downwards. Usually all general points are made before starting on specific points.

Specific points are ordered by item number in the bill, so the judge can work through the bill and points of dispute side by side. If a specific point covers multiple items, it is ordered by the lowest numbered item it covers.

If the assessment turns on an item in the bill which carries great value, then it may be sensible to bump the challenge to the general points section – especially if the challenge is based on a point of law. That way, the court won't be running out of time and interest by the time it comes to decide that point.

While each point must be short and to the point, it must also be long enough to be cogent. The judge must be able to follow the argument.

Points of dispute are based on extrapolation from the paying party's file of papers and knowledge of the case. The paying party does not get to see the receiving party's file (although the court may do so at a detailed assessment hearing).

A simple format for a point of dispute is:

- One sentence to succinctly state the issue;
- One sentence to cite the relevant rule or authority; it is OK to quote cases by name, but avoid quoting from them;
- Apply the law to the facts – this is where points are won or lose;
- Conclude by proposing what the court should do, which will usually be to disallow or reduce the item – there is no requirement to make an offer per item, but it often helps to suggest an allowance.
- Plead in the alternative – if you have argued that the item should be disallowed but there is a chance it will not be, propose an alternative allowance. Use with care as this may undermine your point by suggesting you have no faith in it.

It's a drafting convention, as with any pleading, to draft points of dispute in the name of the paying party, so that they say for example 'the paying party offers', rather than the capricious 'we offer'.

In the interests of keeping points short and to the point, state facts as such rather than with introductory padding phrases such as 'the paying party contends that…'

It is common to use precedents for each point of dispute, because the same sorts of issues arise time and time again. However, a point of dispute that engages with specific facts of the case is more likely to be successful on the assessment. Precedents are only a starting point for good drafting.

Common general points or points of principle address:

- Validity of receiving party's solicitors' retainer;
- Overall proportionality of the bill;
- Costs in excess of budget;
- Contentions that fixed costs should be allowed;

- Hourly rates;
- VAT issues; and
- Recurring issues in the bill like funding costs or supervision.

There is no requirement to sign points of dispute, but they often are signed. Precedent G ends with a statement of the date of service and who effected service, but not a space for a handwritten or electronic signature.

Service

Allow enough time for service. If service will be by post, deemed service is two days later. Posting points of dispute 21 days after service of the N252 is too late.

There are no restrictions in the rules on who can effect service, so an external costs draftsman can serve the points of dispute on behalf of a solicitor.

Be clear on whom to serve the points of dispute. The address for service should be given in the N252. That can be trusted to an extent, but be circumspect. It is not uncommon that the receiving party will instruct a costs draftsman, who may have completed the N252. He may have given his address, but technically the address for service remains that of his instructing solicitor unless he has filed notice of change under Part 42 (Costs Lawyers can go on court record). If points of dispute are served on the address in the N252 and that later becomes a problem, a paying party should get relief from sanction arising from failure to serve. It may be better to be more cautious and serve points of dispute on both the solicitor and costs draftsman.

Replies

Replies to points of dispute are optional: CPR 47.13(1). The logic of that is the claim has already been presented in the bill of costs. The time for serving replies is within 21 days of service of points of dispute. The same issues about service apply.

PD47 12.1 prescribes:

> *A reply served by the receiving party under Rule 47.13 must be limited to points of principle and concessions only. It must not contain general denials, specific denials or standard form responses.*

The intention of the practice direction is to get rid of useless replies that maintain everything.

Both the timescale for service and the prohibitions on content have not been strictly enforced in practice. That is an anomaly in the post-*Mitchell* and *Denton* litigation landscape. Replies are often served late with impunity (although in the provisional assessment process the court will not have information on dates of service immediately to hand) and they often introduce long-winded factual information in breach of the practice direction. (In return, many also level similar criticism at points of dispute.) There is no express requirement that replies must be short and to the point like points of dispute, but it is implied that they should be.

If there is no reply to a point of dispute, the default position is that the item remains in dispute. A common judicial mistake is to treat the absence of a reply as a concession; but as a concession may be made expressly one would expect it to be stated.

A reply on a point of principle will take a similar format to a point of dispute. A concession may be more shortly stated.

PD47 12.2 says 'Whenever practicable, the reply must be set out in the form of Precedent G.' Whether that is practicable depends on whether the receiving party has the Precedent G started by the paying party in an editable format. Points of dispute are unlikely to be served in an editable format because service is usually by post or fax because the practice direction on email service is onerous. Gone is the requirement from before 1 April 2013 that an electronic copy must be provided on request; although it will usually be provided on request. Alternatively, optical character recognition is now cheaply available, and it may be a quick and easy task to convert a scan into an editable document.

For provisional assessments especially, it helps the court if receiving parties consider the space the court is likely to need to write out its decision on each point and edit the box size accordingly. The court is unlikely to work with an electronic copy. More difficult points need bigger boxes for the handwritten decision.

There is no requirement to sign replies, but they often are signed.

As replies tend to reveal important new information, sometimes in non-compliance with the practice direction, paying parties should carefully review their arguments and valuations when they are served. The paying party may choose to settle. Disputes about whether information should have been provided sooner would affect the incidence and amount of assessment costs.

Amendments and supplementary points and replies

The paying party has the option under PD47 13.10(1) of amending the points of dispute, or serving a supplementary point of dispute. That may be appropriate where new information has only just been revealed. It can make the assessment process cumbersome and repetitive and may be disproportionate. A receiving party can similarly amend his bill or replies under that provision. Per PD47 13.10(2), the court's permission is not needed – at this stage the court is not usually involved in the assessment process – but the court may strike out the amendment later on if there is a reason to do so.

Default costs certificates

A default costs certificate is an order is a specific format (N255) for the paying party to pay the bill of costs in full plus the fixed costs and court fee for obtaining the certificate. Those same fixed costs also cover the costs of commencing detailed assessment: CPR 47.11(3). On the one hand, that may leave the receiving party slightly out of pocket; on the other, that is compensated for by getting costs in full.

A receiving party may obtain a default costs certificate if it has been more than 21 days since the notice of commencement was served and the receiving party has not been served with any points of dispute (CPR 47.9(4)).

If there are multiple paying parties, service of points of dispute by one, even if not on behalf of all paying parties, appears to prevent a default costs certificate.

The receiving party requests a default costs certificate by completing and filing an N254 with the enclosures and court fee (currently £66).

Even then, a race is on. If points of dispute are served before the court issues the default costs certificate, the court may not issue the default costs certificate: CPR 47.9(5). The courts have construed that as a mandatory prohibition: see Jackson LJ in *Hallam Estates v Baker* [2014] EWCA Civ 661 at [36], and for a fuller practical example see *Cadwallader v Akzo Nobel* (His Honour Judge Wood QC, County Court at Liverpool, 16 June 2014, unreported). In order to take advantage of the prohibition the party serving the points of dispute should make sure the court knows it is being done; usual practice is to file as well as serve late points of dispute for that reason. If the court nevertheless issues the default costs certificate, prior service of points of dispute will be a ground to set it aside.

Avoiding the default costs certificate is not the end of the paying party's problems: the sanction in CPR 47.9(3) still applies. See below.

Tactically better to get sanction?

Receiving parties might be cautious in obtaining a default costs certificate. They are often set aside, and the receiving party risks losing time and costs in the process. It is a gamble. Sometimes default costs certificates are upheld, e.g. *Edray Ltd v Canning* [2015] 5 Costs LR 877.

The receiving party may have other costs associated with the detailed assessment that he will not recover if he obtains a default costs certificate. If proceedings were started under Part 7 he can get no extra costs; if he commenced Part 8 costs-only proceedings he can recover a reasonable sum only for commencing the proceedings in addition to the fixed costs for the default costs certificate: *Tasleem v Beverley* [2014] 1 WLR 3567.

The alternative for the receiving party is to chase the paying party for points of dispute once the 21 day period has expired. The advantage to the receiving party is that the paying party will be on the back foot. If the paying party serves points of dispute, he will trigger the sanction in CPR 47.9(3). He may not be heard further in the assessment proceedings unless the court gives permission (it is debatable whether that is a problem for a provisional assessment, which is made on the papers without hearing orally from either party – but it would be a problem if either party sought an oral hearing). That may encourage the paying party to pay a bit extra to get the claim settled. Absent a settlement, he will have to apply for relief from sanctions and will probably end up paying the receiving party's costs of that application.

Setting aside

The paying party may apply to set aside a default costs certificate. There are two grounds in CPR 47.12. First, the court will set aside the default costs certificate if the receiving party was not entitled to it. Second, the court will set aside or vary the default costs certificate if there is a good reason why the detailed assessment should continue.

An application to set aside a default costs certificate is not strictly an application for relief from sanctions. CPR 47.12 sets out its own test distinct from CPR 3.9. However, *Gentry v Miller* [2016] 1 WLR 2696 held that an application to set aside a default judgment under Part 13 was an application for relief. Therefore, as well as addressing the specific criteria under CPR 47.12, the application must also address the well-known *Denton* criteria for relief. An analysis of those criteria goes beyond the scope of this book. The *Denton* criteria must be addressed not only to the failure to serve points of dispute but another step that is required alongside the application for relief, which is addressed below.

CPR 47.12(1) is expressed in mandatory terms. As long as it can be shown the receiving party was not entitled to the certificate, it will be set aside. The court may conclude that the receiving party was not entitled to the default costs certificate if he did not have the right to detailed assessment, if the costs had been agreed before it was issued, if the certificate had been issued before 21 days since service of the notice of commencement had passed, or if points of dispute had been served before the certificate was issued (per CPR 47.9(5)). There may be other reasons.

PD47 11.1 provides that the court may set aside the default costs certificate at the request of the receiving party. If the receiving party realises he was not entitled to the certificate, he should make that request without further ado.

CPR 47.12(2) is discretionary. The rule is not concerned with whether there is a good reason why points of dispute were not served. It is concerned with whether there is a good reason for the assessment to continue. That usually means showing that there are features of the bill which mean it is likely to be reduced by more than a *de minimis* amount if it were assessed. The *Denton* criteria will also play a significant role here as the paying party must obtain relief for not serving points of dispute in time. The practice direction sets out additional requirements for an application under this rule. It must be supported by evidence; the court will have regard to the promptness of the application (i.e. the less promptly made, the less likely the certificate will be set aside); the applicant has to show there is a good reason to set aside (presumably this is the same good reason to show the assessment should continue as per the rule, rather than a good reason to show why points of dispute were not served in time – although that will be needed in any event under the *Denton* criteria); copies of the bill, default costs certificate and proposed points of dispute must be filed with the application.

An application under CPR 47.12(2) and, depending on the facts, perhaps also an application under CPR 47.12(1) needs to be accompanied by an application for relief from a specific sanction under CPR 47.9(3). That sanction is the late serving party will not be heard further in the assessment and it is triggered by late service of points of dispute. Note that the late serving party may not be heard *further* in the detailed assessment proceedings. That seems to mean the points of dispute will be considered once served, but any further material or oral submissions will not be allowed. The court must still make an assessment using the material it has. As a helpful comparison, that was the approach taken by Langley J in *Days Healthcare UK Ltd v Pihsiang Machinery Manufacturing Co Ltd* [2006] 5 Costs LR 788 at [30] when the paying party failed to comply with an order for making a payment on account of costs. Relief from sanction may be sought by the paying party addressing CPR 3.9 and the *Denton* criteria. The application would usually be granted if the default costs certificate is set aside, otherwise that would be rendered nugatory. An alternative is to apply for an out-of-time extension of time to serve points of dispute; but as that is treated as a quasi-relief from sanctions application and the *Denton* criteria will still apply, there is no real benefit to doing it that way.

Unless the receiving party requests that the certificate is set aside (which might be in the form of a letter or consent order), the paying party must make an application in Form N244. An application under CPR 47.12(1) is likely to be simpler than an application under CPR 47.12(2), but it is often prudent (unless the CPR 47.12(1) application is very strong) to apply in the alternative under CPR 47.12(2) when applying under CPR 47.12(1).

The guidance in *Denton* would suggest that a receiving party who unreasonably or opportunely resists setting aside a default costs certificate may end up paying the costs of the application hearing.

Enforcing payment of agreed costs

Many costs claim settle before going all the way to a provisional assessment or a detailed assessment hearing.

If the costs are finalised by acceptance of a Part 36 costs offer, then CPR 47.20(4)(d) allows the receiving party to apply for a final costs certificate for any outstanding sum if payment is not made within 14 days of acceptance.

There is no strict timescale in the CPR for making a payment following any other agreement. Parties might agree a time, or more commonly the receiving party will try to unilaterally impose a deadline (typically 14 days). Most payments are made reasonably promptly. Insurers and compensators are geared up to make payments promptly as they know it is something likely to cause extra expense if not done.

Where payment is unreasonably delayed, a final costs certificate is the way forward. Under CPR 47.10(1), either party may apply for a final costs certificate on notice, or they can join in a consent order. The parties may also apply for an interim costs certificate, but that will be a rarer circumstance. It is not clear whether the application for a final costs certificate must be accompanied by a 'completed bill'. That is the name for a copy of the bill amended to show the final figures. A completed bill is required to get a final costs certificate after a detailed assessment hearing: CPR 47.17(2). Often the receiving party does not bother after a hearing because payment is received anyway. It would be harder to produce a completed bill where the bill has not been assessed because parties tend to agree round number settlements, which could only be subjectively divided up between all the items.

A final costs certificate includes an order to pay the costs to which it relates. The time to pay costs under an order is 14 days: CPR 44.7. If payment is not made in that further time, then enforcement procedures may be started, such as a writ or warrant of control under Parts 83 and 84 for instance.

Unfortunately in practice, there seems to be all sorts of weird and wonderful and wrong ways of enforcing payment. Common mistakes are that applications are made seeking an order for payment rather than a final costs certificate, or fresh proceedings are commenced to enforce. Such steps often have the desired effect, but proceeding with a just aim in the wrong way may affect the costs recovered for taking those steps.

Delays and extensions of time in detailed assessment proceedings

Parties may agree extensions of time for the key dates in detailed assessment proceedings. Those dates are for: commencement of detailed assessment; service of points of dispute; service of optional replies; requesting an assessment from the court.

There are two provisions in the CPR allowing parties to agree to extend time. CPR 3.8(4) applies where there is a sanction associated with missing the deadline. Parties may agree to extend time for no longer than 28 days and only if it does not put at risk a hearing date. If longer is required, an application must be made to the court seeking an extension under CPR 3.1(2)(a). Where no automatic sanction is associated, CPR 2.11 allows parties to agree a general extension, but it would be plainly unwise to jeopardise a hearing date with such an agreement.

The time for commencing detailed assessment proceedings is ordinarily three months from the date of the order, Part 36 acceptance (within an offer's relevant period), or notice of discontinuance as the case may be: CPR 47.7. There is a sanction for delay in CPR 47.8(3), but it is discretionary. The court may disallow interest for the period of delay. The existence of that sanction may be enough to engage CPR 3.8(4), meaning the period could be extended by no more than 28 days. However, the sanction is relatively minor. Busy legal representatives often breach it without seeking an extension. The receiving party commonly seeks a payment on account, and where a payment on account is made interest is substantially reduced anyway.

An inordinate and inexcusable delay in commencing detailed assessment proceedings which causes prejudice to the paying party may attract further sanction for misconduct under CPR 44.11: *Haji-Ioannou v Frangos* [2008] 1 WLR 144.

In contrast to the time to commence detailed assessment proceedings, the time to serve points of dispute is strikingly short. The period is 21 days from service of the notice of commencement: CPR 47.9(2).

There is a sanction associated with failing to serve points of dispute in time. CPR 47.9(3) provides that the late serving party may not be heard further in the detailed assessment proceedings. In advance of the deadline, an extension may be agreed under CPR 3.8(4).

Jackson LJ has said that a paying party's reasonable request for an extension of time to serve points of dispute should ordinarily be agreed by the receiving party: *Hallam Estates Ltd v Baker* [2014] EWCA Civ 661. Some receiving parties may seek a payment on account of costs as pre-condition to agreeing the extension. They are free to do so. But Jackson LJ warned against the imposition of onerous terms by the receiving party. Ultimately, if the request itself is reasonable it should be agreed. While a payment on account of costs may assist solicitor's cashflow, interest for the period at the judgment debt rate will in many cases be payable in the absence of a payment on account.

That sanction pre-dates the provisional assessment procedure in CPR 47.15, and it seems it would have no effect on the provisional assessment. The points of dispute are the only material from the paying party that the court will consider on provisional assessment in any event. The paying party may be in difficulty however if an oral hearing was sought under CPR 47.15(7) following the provisional assessment. If the case is not earmarked to settle it is advisable to seek relief from sanctions promptly.

There is no express sanction for serving replies to points of dispute later than the 21 days stated in CPR 47.13(2). There is a school of thought than an 'implied' sanction applies; i.e. the replies will not be considered if served later than 21 days after service of points of dispute. Either way, with no express sanction, the parties may agree to extend time almost indefinitely under CPR 2.11. No hearing date is likely to be jeopardised as the receiving party is unlikely to have requested one before he serves the intended replies.

Disallowance of interest for the period of delay is also the sanction when a request for an assessment in Form N258 is late. The time for requesting an assessment is ordinarily three months from the expiry of the time to commence detailed assessment proceedings; so, unless the court has ordered a variation of time, six months from the date of the event giving the right to detailed assessment. By agreement it may be extended by up to 28 days, but again receiving parties may choose to breach the deadline and sacrifice the interest.

Provisional assessment

Provisional assessment of a bill of costs is made on the papers and gives a rough guide to what the court might allow at a full hearing. A provisional assessment becomes a binding final assessment if it is not challenged within 21 days of receipt. Provisional assessment applies where the notice of commencement was served on or after 1 April 2013 and the costs claimed are no more than £75,000. Provisional assessment then applies in place of a detailed assessment hearing.

Disbursements only assessment

There is an exception to provisional assessment, which is not an option on Form N258 and is often overlooked by courts.

PD47 5.7 provides:

> *If the only dispute between the parties concerns disbursements, the bill of costs shall be limited to items (1) and (2) above [a title page and background information], a list of the disbursements in issue and brief written submissions in respect of those disbursements.*

PD47 13.5 says:

> *Unless the court otherwise orders, if the only dispute between the parties concerns disbursements, the hearing shall take place in the absence of the parties on the basis of the documents and the court will issue its decision in writing.*

This is a practice direction to CPR 47.14 which is titled 'Detailed assessment hearing', so this paper assessment is an alternative to the detailed assessment hearing. In practice courts still make a provisional assessment. The practical difference is that a challenge to a provisional assessment is by oral hearing, whereas a challenge to a detailed assessment hearing is by appeal.

The reasoning was set out in Jackson LJ's *Final Report*:

> *Certain disbursements in fast track cases will not be the subject of fixed costs. If the parties are unable to agree these disbursements, there should be a procedure whereby the disputed items can be referred to the court with submissions in writing, so that the costs judge or district judge can deal with the matter on the papers without a hearing. This should be a final decision (not a provisional assessment), although it would be subject to appeal in the usual way. The judge should have power to list the matter for oral argument, if an issue arises which merits oral argument.*

If a receiving party did want a disbursements only assessment, he should carefully explain the request in the covering letter to the court accompanying the N258 pack.

Filing a request for provisional assessment

The receiving party must request the provisional assessment. If the receiving party delays doing so, the paying party can apply for an unless order under CPR 47.14 which will force the receiving party to do so at risk of the costs being disallowed altogether.

The request must be filed at the 'appropriate office'. The provisions are in PD47 4.1. Generally it is the County Court hearing centre or District Registry that was dealing with the case. If it is a case in the High Court at the Royal Courts of Justice, the Court of Appeal or one of the following London County Court hearing centres, the request must be filed at the Senior Courts Costs Office. Those London County Court hearing centres are (per PD47 4.2(1)): Barnet, Brentford, Bromley, Central London, Clerkenwell and Shoreditch, Croydon, Edmonton, Ilford, Kingston, Mayors and City of London, Romford, Uxbridge, Wandsworth and Willesden.

Pursuant to PD47, the receiving party must file at court:

Typically –

- completed Form **N258**;
- copy of the notice of commencement in Form **N252**;
- the document giving the right to detailed assessment (i.e. **sealed order, notice of acceptance**);
- the **bill of costs** (for electronic bills, the SCCO requires a well-laid out hard copy and the electronic bill via CE-File, pursuant to PD47 5.1A and PD51O's electronic working pilot scheme, the main provisions of which are expected to become permanent after the pilot's expiry on 6 April 2021);
- a **spare copy** of the bill (for the judge to annotate), unless it is an electronic bill;

- copies of the **fee notes** of counsel and of any expert in respect of fees claimed in the bill, and written evidence as to any other disbursement which is claimed and which exceeds £500;
- completed **Precedent G** – the points of dispute and replies, ideally in one document – annotated to show items that have been agreed and their value, and items that remain in dispute and their value;
- the **offers** made (those marked 'without prejudice save as to costs' or made under Part 36 must be contained in a sealed envelope, marked 'Part 36 or similar offers', but not indicating which party or parties have made them);
- a **statement of costs** for the provisional assessment, drawn on the assumption that there will not be an oral hearing;
- a **statement of parties' details** signed by the receiving party or the legal representative giving the name, address for service, reference and telephone number and fax number, if any, of the receiving party and the paying party.

Occasionally in addition –

- where there is a dispute as to the receiving party's liability to pay costs to the legal representatives who acted for the receiving party, any agreement, letter or other written information provided by the legal representative to the client explaining how the legal representative's charges are to be calculated;
- if a costs management order has been made, a breakdown of the costs claimed for each phase of the proceedings if it is not in the electronic bill.

Rarely and in addition –

- copies of any other orders relating to the costs to be assessed;
- addition to the statement of parties of any other person who has served points of dispute or who has given to the receiving party notice in writing that that person has a

financial interest in the outcome of the assessment and wishes to be a party accordingly.

The annotations on Precedent G are often overlooked. Some judges have expressed confusion at seeing them because they are so uncommonly made. It can be difficult to place a value on all disputes and agreements, because it may depend on other disputed items. For instance, a value can only be placed on two hours of time if the hourly rate is agreed.

There is no requirement to serve these documents on the paying party. If however the receiving party wants the paying party to feel the additional pressure of escalating costs as a motivation to settle, it is sensible to send notification and a copy of at least the N258 to the paying party. Otherwise, the paying party will have no idea a provisional assessment has been requested until the court sends notice of the date or notice that it has been done.

The receiving party must also pay the court fee. This is sometimes called the 'lodgement fee'. The fee varies depending on the value of the bill, but does not differ for provisional assessments and detailed assessment hearings. The fees are set out in the Civil Proceedings Fees Order paragraph 5.2. They start at £369 for bills up to £15,000 and go up to £6,160 for bills over £500,000 at the time of writing. The fee can be recovered as part of the costs of assessment if the receiving party gets an order for his assessment costs. The risk that he might not means careful consideration should be given before incurring the fee. It is a lot to write off if the paying party's current offer is not beaten.

The receiving party's file of papers

For a detailed assessment hearing, PD47 13.11 says the receiving party must file the supporting papers for the bill between 14 and 7 days before the hearing. PD47 13.12 says those papers are:

> *(i) instructions and briefs to counsel arranged in chronological order together with all advices, opinions and drafts received and response to such instructions;*
> *(ii) reports and opinions of medical and other experts;*

(iii) any other relevant papers;
(iv) a full set of any relevant statements of case;
(v) correspondence, file notes and attendance notes.

PD47 14.2(2) says which of the practice directions to Part 47 apply to provisional assessment. PD47 13.11 does not apply. There is no mention of PD47 13.12. That means the court can still require the papers in support of the bill, but there is no automatic trigger to file them. Only the SCCO has indicated that it will give notice requiring the supporting papers. For provisional assessments in most other courts they are never filed.

In practice that means provisional assessment are conducted on trust, as the court cannot check against the file.

Defendant's statement of costs

There is no requirement in the rules for the paying party to file a statement of costs ahead of a provisional assessment.

PD47 14.3(c) requires the receiving party to file with the request for the provisional assessment 'a statement of the costs claimed in respect of the detailed assessment drawn on the assumption that there will not be an oral hearing following the provisional assessment'. There is no requirement to serve it, so unless it is sent voluntarily the paying party will not ordinarily see it.

A 'provisional assessment' is never referred to as a hearing in the CPR (although some parties and courts occasionally call it a 'provisional assessment hearing'). That is logical, since if no one is attending there is no one to be heard – at least not out loud. Therefore the requirement in PD44 9.5(b) to file a statement of costs 'not less than 24 hours before the time fixed for the hearing' does not apply.

Some courts have opted to make orders requiring both parties to file and serve statements of costs, which is sent out at the same time that the court gives notice of the date on which the provisional assessment will be made. The court's intention is to allow it to have all material before it to make the provisional assessment and assess both parties' statements of costs at the same time.

Absent that, if the defendant wins on the provisional assessment the practice has become that the defendant will file and serve a statement of costs once that has become apparent, after the arithmetic has been agreed. PD47 14.6 provides:

> *If a party wishes to be heard only as to the order made in respect of the costs of the initial provisional assessment, the court will invite each side to make written submissions and the matter will be finally determined without a hearing. The court will decide what if any order for costs to make in respect of this procedure.*

That appears to give scope for the court to revisit the costs of the assessment after the provisional assessment has been made.

<u>Dis-applying provisional assessment</u>

CPR 47.15(6) says:

> *The court may at any time decide that the matter is unsuitable for a provisional assessment and may give directions for the matter to be listed for hearing. The matter will then proceed under rule 47.14 without modification.*

That power tends to be exercised when the court makes its initial review of the papers filed to request the provisional assessment. If there are any technical points (unreasonable exit from the RTA or EL/PL Protocol are examples that have arisen in practice), that may persuade the court to give directions for a detailed assessment hearing. It usually arises of the court's own motion.

The parties could make representations to the court to seek such a direction, but as there is the right to an oral hearing following provisional assessment such representations are rarely successful. Parties should be wary of antagonising the court at this stage.

Timing

PD47 14.4(1) promises:

> *On receipt of the request for detailed assessment and the supporting papers, the court will use its best endeavours to undertake a provisional assessment within 6 weeks. No party will be permitted to attend the provisional assessment.*

Those best endeavours cannot be fulfilled by all court centres. Some provisional assessments take several months to be returned. The 'supporting papers' are described in the section below called 'What materials will the court consider?'

Different courts have different practices. Some will 'list' the provisional assessment, and send the parties notice of that listing. There is no requirement to do so but it is helpful to the parties. It may be the first indication the paying party gets that a provisional assessment has been requested. It may lead to a period of increased focus and ultimately a settlement, so the court can be informed that the provisional assessment no longer needs to be made.

Other courts place the request in box work and the provisional assessment is returned to the parties once completed. That may be the paying party's first notice that an assessment was even requested.

Settlement before the provisional assessment

If the costs are agreed before the provisional assessment is made, the court must be informed urgently, preferably by fax: PD47 13.8(2).

What materials will the court consider?

CPR 47.15(4) says:

> *The provisional assessment will be based on the information contained in the bill and supporting papers and the contentions set out in Precedent G (the points of dispute and any reply).*

That sounds delightfully simple. It's slightly unclear what is meant by 'supporting papers'; presumably it is all the paperwork supporting the N258, but elsewhere in PD47 the supporting papers means the receiving party's file of papers (in a specific order). A sensible approach is to treat it as both where the court has required the file of papers to be filed for the provisional assessment, or just the former otherwise.

The rule impliedly discourages but does not absolutely prohibit skeleton arguments. It also does not prohibit witness evidence, which may be required for some disputes. If it is, it may be a case better directed to continue to a detailed assessment hearing.

While it seems the court will admit fresh material for an oral hearing following provisional assessment (see below), it may be better to avoid the risk that it will not be admitted and file the material for the provisional assessment – even if the court ignores it.

What the court must return

CPR 47.15(7) provides:

> *When a provisional assessment has been carried out, the court will send a copy of the bill, as provisionally assessed, to each party with a notice stating that any party who wishes to challenge any aspect of the provisional assessment must, within 21 days of the receipt of the notice, file and serve on all other parties a written request for an oral hearing.*

PD47 14.4(2) says:

> *Once the provisional assessment has been carried out the court will return Precedent G (the points of dispute and any reply) with the court's decisions noted upon it.*

It is unhelpful that the rule and the practice direction refer to different materials. This may be an 'artefact' arising from the provisional assessment pilot scheme that ran before 2013.

To summarise, the court must send to each party:

- The provisionally assessed bill
- Notice of the right to challenge the provisional assessment
- Annotated Precedent G.

Of those documents, the annotated Precedent G is the most useful. It allows the parties to calculate the amount that has been allowed. Some courts, notably the SCCO, return only an annotated bill of costs rather than a completed Precedent G. It is very welcome when the court has worked out the arithmetic of the assessment, saving the parties a job, but not annotating the Precedent G can mean that there is no apparent decision on some of the disputes. If no annotated Precedent G is received and it not an SCCO case, it is worth checking with the court office whether it has been accidentally omitted.

Aside from some courts sending only one or other of the bill and Precedent G, there have been other problems in practice.

Some courts have sent only the notice but no other papers.

Some courts send the papers only to the receiving party, purportedly to save photocopying costs. In those circumstances, the paying party has to get a copy from the court or the receiving party. Aside from the delay, it causes problems under the rules. The timescales under the CPR 47.15(7) to challenge the provisional assessment and under PD47 14.4(2) to agree the arithmetic run from the date of receipt. Particularly with the parties agreeing the arithmetic, it can become unworkable if the parties have substantially different deadlines.

Some courts do not send the notice of the right to challenge the provisional assessment. As the time to challenge runs from the receipt of that notice, if it is not sent it is not clear if the time is running at all.

<u>What the parties must do</u>

Unless the court has done it already, the parties must work out and agree the arithmetic. Under PD47 14.4(2), that is within 14 days of receiving the Precedent G, but if the court has only sent an annotated bill the parties will work from that instead.

Although there is no requirement in the rules to inform the court of the agreement, for finality and perhaps to facilitate consequential orders (for instance, the court may not have decided liability for costs of the provisional assessment, or may wish to check the costs are proportionate) it may be helpful to do so.

Seeking clarification

Sometimes the provisional assessment is ambiguous and the parties are unable to agree the arithmetic. PD47 14.4(2) provides: 'If the parties are unable to agree the arithmetic, they must refer the dispute back to the court for a decision on the basis of written submissions.' That is different to seeking an oral hearing to challenge the decisions. It is about confirming what decisions have been made.

The request is usually made by letter, and may be made jointly by the parties, or they may send their own competing submissions.

It is also sensible to include a request that the court extends the time to request an oral hearing until 21 days after the clarification is received, pursuant to the power to extend time in CPR 3.1(2)(a). Otherwise, a disappointed party may find that he cannot challenge the decision. It is a risk to rely on the argument that the provisional assessment was not 'received' until the clarification was received.

The cap on costs of provisional assessment

CPR 47.15(5) sets a mandatory cap:

> *In proceedings which do not go beyond provisional assessment, the maximum amount the court will award to any party as costs of the assessment (other than the costs of drafting the bill of costs) is £1,500 together with any VAT thereon and any court fees paid by that party.*

This cap operates in conjunction with the rules on deciding which party pays the costs of the assessment in CPR 47.20. The cap applies whether the costs are allowed on the standard basis or the indemnity basis: *Lowin v W Portsmouth & Co Ltd* [2018] 1 WLR 1890.

The costs of drafting the bill of costs are included in the bill of costs and will be assessed when the bill is assessed.

The cap is not a fixed sum, and the court should consider whether a lesser sum is reasonable and proportionate. In most cases, it would be. As provisional assessment covers bills up to £75,000, one would expect those larger bills to reach the cap, whereas smaller bills would generate lesser costs.

In any legacy cases which still include a recoverable success fee, the success fee is included within the cap. CPR 48.1(1) provides: 'The provisions of CPR Parts 43 to 48 relating to funding arrangements, and the attendant provisions of the Costs Practice Direction, will apply in relation to a pre-commencement funding arrangement as they were in force immediately before 1 April 2013...' The cap in CPR 47.15(5) is for 'costs' and the definition of 'costs' in the pre-1 April 2013 CPR 43.2(1)(a) included 'any additional liability incurred under a funding arrangement'.

Claimants and defendants dispute whether the cap includes the costs of commencing costs-only proceedings. Defendants say that the cap covers costs of assessment in proceedings which do not go beyond provisional assessment, and that the costs of commencing costs-only proceedings are part of the costs of assessment, per *Crosbie v Munroe* [2003] 1 WLR 2033 at [34]. They argue that the order for costs of the costs-only proceedings is (usually) that they are 'in the assessment', so they are merged with the assessment costs. Also, as the only court fee in detailed assessment proceedings is the fee with the N258, why use the plural 'court fees' in CPR 47.15 unless to capture other fees such as the issue fee for costs-only proceedings? Claimants say the cap is strictly for the costs of the assessment, and that does not include the costs-only proceedings. The judgment of Sharp LJ in *Tasleem v Beverley* [2014] 1 WLR 3567 at [18] that '*The bringing of Part 8 costs-only proceedings is not the commencement of, or part of, the detailed assessment proceedings, albeit it is a necessary preliminary to that process if there are no underlying proceedings in existence*' supports that. *Tasleem* held that *Crosbie* was not authority that costs of assessment included costs of costs-only proceedings for the purposes of CPR 47.11, and it would follow that

Crosbie was not authority on CPR 47.15 either. Generally, the view that costs of the costs only proceedings are separately recoverable prevails.

They should however be modest. Costs of negotiating the amount of costs are incidental to the assessment. They are not costs of the costs-only proceedings simply because such negotiations may precede the commencement of the proceedings. Costs of the costs-only proceedings are limited to the claim form, court fee, filing and service, acknowledgement of service, court order and handling correspondence.

The argument may be academic in many cases. Claims that settled without Part 7 proceedings may attract fewer divisive costs issues, generate less work for the provisional assessment, and thus fall well within the £1,500 cap in any event.

It is also uncertain whether interim applications in the assessment, such as an application for an interim costs certificate, fall within the cap. By analogy, costs of interim applications in substantive proceedings can be costs of the proceedings, but it depends on the order for costs made on the interim application. An order for costs may stand apart; and order for costs in the assessment may place the costs under the cap.

Problems with provisional assessment

Provisional assessment is weighted heavily towards the receiving party. The receiving party files the papers and controls the way the case is presented. The main document is the bill of costs, prepared by the receiving party. The only document from the paying party is the points of dispute, which are mandatorily short and to the point. There is no such express restriction on replies, but merely that they are limited to points of principle and concessions. The receiving party has the first (bill) and last word (replies) in the run up to the provisional assessment.

By contrast if the case went to a detailed assessment hearing, on each point the paying party would open, the receiving party would reply, and the paying party would have a chance to make any additional rebuttal points. It is a more balanced approach.

The lack of specialist costs judges nationally and the brevity of the material means mistakes of law are often made. The classic mistake of those unfamiliar with costs is to assume that everything is in the court's discretion, when in fact the rules are often prescriptive and there are many binding senior courts decisions. Mistakes will inevitably happen.

Any breaches of assessment procedure, such as non-compliant bills, points of dispute and replies, are rarely noted and tackled by the court. That in itself can lead to an unfair advantage for a party.

Anecdotally, receiving parties do much better on provisional assessment than at detailed assessment hearings.

Oral hearings are available for redress, but there are hurdles to overcome.

Requesting an oral hearing

The time to request an oral hearing runs under CPR 47.15(7) from the date of the receipt by the party of the notice of the right to challenge the provisional assessment. Most courts set out that notice as part of a broader notice that the provisional assessment has taken place and giving consequential directions.

Every party has an unqualified right to seek an oral hearing, save for the strict time limit. The time to request an oral hearing is 21 days from receipt of the notice.

If no request is received in that time, the provisional assessment is then binding except in exceptional circumstances. There do not seem to be any reported decisions where there have been 'exceptional circumstances'. It is a very high threshold, and if a party has simply missed a deadline that is unlikely to be exceptional.

It would seem to be an abuse of process to attempt to appeal from the provisional assessment. In any event, if an oral hearing had not been requested in 21 days, an appeal would also be out of time.

The request for an oral hearing must be in writing and must be filed and served. A letter will suffice. It must state which items the party wishes the court to review, and give a time estimate for the oral hearing: CPR 47.15(8).

The absolute right to an oral hearing is not abrogated by agreeing the arithmetic of the provisional assessment. That has to be done in any event to set the baseline for deciding who gets the costs of the oral hearing (see below).

The court must give the parties at least 14 days' notice of the oral hearing: CPR 47.15(9).

Status of oral hearing: review or re-hearing?

There is debate about the nature of the oral hearing, and the scope of what the parties and the court can do. There is no doubt that the court can change its decision from the provisional assessment, if persuaded to do so. The debate is whether it is a 'review', in which the court will reconsider only the same material that was before it for the provisional assessment but with the added benefit of oral submissions; or a 're-hearing' in which the court will consider the point afresh, with oral submissions and potentially with further material, such as documents from the files or witness evidence. It could also be some composite of the two.

The rules are not decisive. On the one hand, as the assessment is 'provisional', nothing final can have been decided and it must be open to the court to re-hear the assessment. On the other hand, CPR 47.15(8)(a) uses the word 'review'. In comparison, appeals ordinarily take place by way of review, and there are limitations on introducing fresh material under the *Ladd v Marshall* principles.

There is no senior courts guidance so far, but there is some circuit level guidance. His Honour Judge Wood QC, the designated civil judge in Liverpool, has observed in appeals in *Ion v Ahmed* (1 September 2014, unreported) and *Mehmi v Pincher* (20 July 2015, unreported) that the power in PD47 13.13 is available on provisional assessment and oral hearings. That provision says:

> *The court may direct the receiving party to produce any document which in the opinion of the court is necessary to enable it to reach its decision. These documents will in the first instance be produced to the court, but the court may ask the receiving party to elect whether to disclose the particular document to the paying party in order to rely on the contents of the document, or whether to decline disclosure and instead rely on other evidence.*

He points out that because the power is available at any time during the assessment process, the court could ask for specific material for an oral hearing; and if a party chose to produce additional material, the court could within its discretion admit it.

In practice that may mean witness evidence or additional documents could be filed ahead of the hearing. A court may refuse to admit the material, so it is better where possible to file it in time for the provisional assessment, even if it is not considered until the oral hearing.

Coincidentally, there seems no reason why skeleton arguments cannot be filed and served ahead of an oral hearing, as they would be for any other hearing. Nothing suggests parties may not expand their submissions on the law beyond the initially succinct submissions in the bill, points of dispute or replies, as long as it is proportionate to do so.

<u>Oral hearing in practice</u>

An oral hearing is conducted very similarly to a detailed assessment hearing – see the section below. Although nothing in the CPR requires it, courts list the oral hearing before the same judge who made the provisional assessment wherever possible.

<u>Costs of the oral hearing</u>

CPR 47.15(10) creates a rebuttable presumption that the party who requested the oral hearing will pay the costs of and incidental to the hearing, unless:

(a) it achieves an adjustment in its own favour by 20% or more of the sum provisionally assessed; or
(b) the court otherwise orders.

The provision does not go so far as to say that if the party does get that 20% adjustment, the other party pays the costs. Understandably though that is the order sought in those circumstances.

The 20% of the sum provisionally assessed has generally been understood to be against the grand total allowed against the bill on provisional assessment, rather than against the items under review.

PD47 14.5 contributes: 'When considering whether to depart from the order indicated by rule 47.15(10) the court will take into account the conduct of the parties and any offers made.'

If the party does not get a 20% adjustment but beats his own offer, that would be a strong factor weighing in favour of the court making a different order.

Regarding the costs of the provisional assessment stage, remember that the cap in CPR 47.15(5) applies '*In proceedings which do not go beyond provisional assessment*'. Where there is an oral hearing, the cap is dis-applied. If the court has already assessed the costs of the provisional assessment stage, that would likely stand. The sum would not cease to be reasonable and proportionate because the proceedings had gone further. However, if the court has not yet assessed the costs, there is a chance that the successful party may get more than the cap. Parties should nevertheless be litigating mindful of the cap, and seeking to avoid incurring greater costs at the provisional assessment stage.

20% is a significant margin. The costs of an oral hearing may be similar to or more than 20% of the provisionally assessed sum. It means that mistakes in the assessment may go uncorrected because it would cost too much to do so. That seems that an unjust and unsatisfactory system.

Scope of appeals from oral hearings

In the SCCO, CPR 47.21 provides for an automatic right of appeal from the decision of an authorised court officer, namely the costs officers who sit in that court. Where a costs officer makes a provisional assessment and then some decisions are challenged at an oral hearing, the right of appeal relates only to the decisions on the oral hearing and not all points raised originally in the provisional assessment: Stewart J in *PME v The Scout Association* [2020] 1 WLR 1217.

Payments on account of costs and requests for an interim costs certificate

CPR 44.2(8) provides:

> *Where the court orders a party to pay costs subject to detailed assessment, it will order that party to pay a reasonable sum on account of costs, unless there is good reason not to do so.*

The rule is phrased in the present tense and was held by several district judges not to create an ongoing jurisdiction to order a payment on account of costs. That was in the face of an emerging cottage industry of making applications for interim payment in the context of provisional assessment with their £1,500 costs cap where there was no obvious reason why the receiving party had not sought a payment on account at the time of obtaining the order for detailed assessment.

However, the Court of Appeal held in *Global Assets Advisory Services Ltd v Grandlane Developments Ltd* [2020] 1 WLR 128 that following a Part 36 acceptance the court had jurisdiction to order a payment on account under CPR 44.2(8). The court observed the present tense in the rule but did not say anything turned on it. Therefore it would seem in any case a party could apply for a payment on account, whether the claim settled by Part 36 or otherwise.

A receiving party who omits to apply for a payment on account in a consent order settling his claim may be at risk on costs of later application for an interim payment; but that would depend also on the conduct of the paying party regarding an interim payment.

If the receiving party does not obtain an order for an interim payment under CPR 44.2(8), another opportunity and jurisdiction arises once a detailed assessment hearing has been requested. At that time or after, the receiving party may apply for an interim costs certificate under CPR 47.16. An interim costs certificate is effectively an order for a payment on account of costs. An application should be made under Part 23, setting out the amount sought and reasons.

Such applications are rare. Many paying parties prefer to avoid the 8% judgment debt rate for interest on costs, and thus volunteer payments on account. The paying party must always be given a reasonable opportunity to respond to a request for an interim payment before an application is made. The paying party often makes payments on account up to the value of its best offer.

If the court has to decide an amount to order as a payment on account, its approach is to conservatively estimate the likely sum the receiving party will get on assessment but that need not be an irreducible minimum: *Gollop v Pryke* (Warren J, Chancery Division, 29 November 2011, unreported).

Detailed assessment hearing

In claims to which provisional assessment does not apply, the receiving party will request a detailed assessment hearing. The request is virtually the same as filing a request for provisional assessment, save that a different box must be ticked on the N258 and a time estimate for the hearing must be given.

The court will send notice of the date of the detailed assessment to the parties. Depending on the time estimate given, the hearing may run over several days. The court must give at least 14 days' notice: PD47 13.6.

The court in its discretion can list a preliminary hearing to deal only with specific points. The advantage of doing that is the parties are often then able to agree the remaining points, and overall it saves court time and costs.

If the parties agree the costs once the detailed assessment hearing has been listed, they must notify the court urgently, preferably by fax: PD47 13.8(2).

The receiving party must file the supporting papers (see the section on 'The receiving party's file of papers' above) between 14 and 7 days before the hearing, ensuring it will arrive at court during that period. The receiving party's advocate should retain a copy of that file. It is helpful if it is paginated and tabbed, as it will make reference to the file during the hearing easier. A copy of the file is not normally provided to the paying party.

The detailed assessment hearing is not normally attended by the parties, although they may do so. Usually specialist costs advocates attend the hearing. There is a tendency to instruct counsel where the disputes are more technical in nature, or to instruct a costs specialist solicitor, fellow of CILEx or Costs Lawyer (fellow of the Association of Costs Lawyers) where the disputes are quantum based. That distinction is a rough guide only.

Sometimes the fee earner will attend as well as the advocate, particularly on the receiving party's side. The purpose of that attendance is to assist in explaining any part of the case to the judge. The contribution is unlikely to be substantial, but the fee earner's presence increases the receiving party's costs of assessment. There is a risk that the costs of the attendance will not be allowed.

Aim to arrive at court up to an hour before the hearing. That will allow time to complete security checks, check in with the usher and confer with the opposing advocate. It may be possible, subject to instructions, to reach agreement on some points. Well prepared advocates have a better understanding of the strengths and weaknesses of the case than the parties may have had up until that point.

Increasingly in the wake of the Covid-19 pandemic and ensuing lockdown, detailed assessments are being performed remotely by telephone or video call. Practical difficulties must be overcome, such as ensuring the court has a suitable electronic bundle (or bundles). The court will usually be provided with different papers to the paying party.

It remains to be seen if this practice will continue, but initial experiences show that it is viable and process will improve as court users become more familiar with it.

The court will only hear from the receiving party and the paying party and anyone else who has served points of dispute (but is not a paying party).

Part 47 does not set out how the hearing will be conducted, but in practice there is a consistent approach. It is the Precedent G – points of dispute – rather than the bill of costs that is the key document. Unlike other hearings, at which the claimant's advocate opens to begin the task of proving the claim, at a detailed assessment hearing the challenger begins.

Each point is dealt with one at a time. Sometimes, if the parties agree or the court chooses, the points of dispute are presented in a different order. The logic is that obtaining the court's decisions on key points may then enable the advocates to step outside and agree the rest.

The paying party presents the point, and expands on and amplifies the written point. There may be reference to key documents and key cases, with material being passed to the opposing advocate and the judge. The receiving party then replies. If there has been an optional reply to the point of dispute, bearing in mind the restrictions in PD47 12.1, the receiving party will expand on and amplify that reply. If there has been no written reply, no matter. That does not preclude the receiving party making submissions. An absence of a written reply merely indicates that the item is still in dispute. The receiving party too may hand to the opposing advocate and judge any material relied on. Privileged documents on which the receiving party may rely should have been filed already in the supporting papers, and in the course of submissions the receiving party may refer to that bundle. The paying party will not get to see that material unless the court decides to the put the receiving party to election to disclose certain documents under PD47 13.13, and the receiving party elects to do so. After the receiving party's submissions on the point, the paying party may then make final responses, and then the court will then make a decision on that point. The judge may apply the decision to the electronic bill on screen, and advocates may follow suit with their own copies on laptops. Everyone then moves on to the next point.

Only items specified in the points of dispute may be raised at the hearing, unless the court gives permission to raise others: CPR 47.14(6). 'Items' is generally used in Part 47 and PD47 to mean items in the bill of costs. It would also seem that there needs only to be a challenge to the item, and the paying party is not restricted in expanding or modifying the argument on that item as long as it has been challenged in the points of dispute. If the argument is radically different or the paying party challenges another item in the bill, the receiving party may say that permission is required, and the court will decide there and then whether to allow it.

Once decisions have been made on each point of dispute as required, the parties used then step out of the court room to agree the arithmetic. The parties then return before the judge to confirm the amount. Electronic bills may mean that is no longer required because recalculations are made on the fly. Any additional matters such as permission to appeal and costs of the assessment will be addressed. The costs of assessment will ordinarily be summarily assessed, with the court giving consideration to the parties' oral submissions. Interest on costs may be resolved then, or is often left for the parties to agree between themselves once the advocates are back at their offices.

The receiving party must take away any supporting hard copy papers that have been filed at the end of the hearing.

<u>Approach to proportionality on detailed assessment hearing</u>

In *West v Stockport NHS Foundation Trust* [2019] 1 WLR 6157 at [87]ff, the Court of Appeal gave guidance on applying the new proportionality test on assessment.

> *First, the judge should go through the bill line-by-line, assessing the reasonableness of each item of cost. If the judge considers it possible, appropriate and convenient when undertaking that exercise, he or she may also address the proportionality of any particular item at the same time. That is because, although reasonableness and proportionality are*

conceptually distinct, there can be an overlap between them, not least because reasonableness may be a necessary condition of proportionality: see Rogers [2007] 1 WLR 808, para 104. This will be a matter for the judge. It will apply, for example, when the judge considers an item to be clearly disproportionate, irrespective of the final figures.

At the conclusion of the line-by-line exercise, there will be a total figure which the judge considers to be reasonable (and which may, as indicated, also take into account at least some aspects of proportionality)…

The proportionality of that total figure must be assessed by reference to both rule 44.3(5) and rule 44.4(1). If that total figure is found to be proportionate, then no further assessment is required. If the judge regards the overall figure as disproportionate, then a further assessment is required. That should not be line-by-line, but should instead consider various categories of cost, such as disclosure or expert's reports, or specific periods where particular costs were incurred, or particular parts of the profit costs.

At that stage, however, any reductions for proportionality should exclude those elements of costs which are properly regarded as unavoidable, such as court fees…

The judge will undertake the proportionality assessment by looking at the different categories of costs (excluding the unavoidable items noted above) and considering, in respect of each such category, whether the costs incurred were disproportionate. If yes, then the judge will make such reduction as is appropriate. In that way, reductions for proportionality will be clear and transparent for both sides.

Once any further reductions have been made, the resulting figure will be the final amount of the costs assessment. There would be no further stage of standing back and, if necessary, undertaking a yet further review by reference to proportionality. That would introduce the risk of double-counting.

See the discussion of that approach to unavoidable items in Chapter 5, 'Reasonableness and proportionality'.

The court will be fettered further by the restrictions under CPR 3.18(b). See Chapter 6, Costs Budgeting. In *Harrison v University Hospitals Coventry and Warwickshire Hospital NHS Trust* [2017] 1 WLR 4456 at [52], David LJ said:

> *a costs judge on detailed assessment will be assessing incurred costs in the usual way and also will be considering budgeted costs (and not departing from such budgeted costs in the absence of "good reason") the costs judge ordinarily will still, as I see it, ultimately have to look at matters in the round and consider whether the resulting aggregate figure is proportionate, having regard to CPR r 44.3(2)(a)(5): a further potential safeguard, therefore, for the paying party.*

As budgeted costs are theoretically set at reasonable and proportionate amounts in a costs management order, any proportionality reduction would most likely bite only on incurred costs – unless the paying party succeeded in arguing that overall proportionality was a good reason to depart downwards from the budgeted costs.

Misconduct in detailed assessment proceedings

Anyone tempted to include anything doubtful in a bill of costs, knowing it is not properly recoverable, is well advised not to do so. All the more so now because *Bamrah v Gempride* [2019] 1 WLR 1545 has bared the teeth of CPR 44.11.

CPR 44.11 is headed 'Court's powers in relation to misconduct'. Under CPR 44.11(2), the court can disallow all or part of the costs being assessed, or order a party at fault or the legal representative to pay costs they caused another party to incur. The power can be invoked per CPR 44.11(1) where a party or the legal representative in a summary or detailed assessment fails to comply with a rule, practice direction or court order; or the court considers the conduct of the party or legal representative was unreasonable or improper.

Before *Bamrah*, those powers were not exercised frequently.

In *Bamrah*, the claimant had certified a bill of costs containing an hourly rate above that which was chargeable, and gave an untrue and misleading point of reply about the availability of BTE insurance. The claimant's solicitor had relied on her costs draftsman in these matters, but the Court of Appeal held that the solicitor remained ultimately responsible. The Court also held that dishonesty was not a requirement, only that the conduct was unreasonable and improper. Half of the claimant's costs were disallowed.

The crucial point of awareness was expressed by Hickinbottom LJ at [103]:

> *it seems to me to be an important matter of principle that solicitors on the record – and other authorised litigators and "legal representatives" for the purposes of the CPR – understand that they remain ultimately responsible for the acts and omissions of those to whom they delegate parts of the conduct of litigation, particularly where those to whom such work is delegated are not authorised. It is only in that way that the supervisory jurisdiction of the court can be effectively maintained. Although an order under CPR r 44.11 cannot be made against someone who is neither a party nor a legal representative, for the purposes of that rule the conduct of someone who is not an authorised litigator may be attributable to a legal representative on agency principles...*

Bamrah should have the effect of increasing a paying party's confidence in the signature to a bill of costs, on the basis that a receiving party will now be less likely to take the chance of including a claim unreasonably or improperly (or dishonestly) owing to the risk of facing a stringent sanction if found out. The reckless few may take the chance they will not be found out.

While the court in *Bamrah* held that dishonesty was not a necessary ingredient for CPR 44.11, it remains that cases of apparent dishonest are still the ones in which a CPR 44.11 application is most likely to be made. If a paying party does turn up compelling material to show that an item of costs has been claimed knowing that it was not recoverable, or there has been an untrue or misleading reply to a point of dispute, a CPR 44.11 application may be appropriate. As it is a serious issue, following proper form and making a Part 23 application on notice is recommended. Under PD44 11.1, '*the court must give the party or legal representative in question a reasonable opportunity to make written submissions or, if the legal representative so desires, to attend a hearing.'*

Liability for costs of assessment

The general principles for the liability for costs apply to all detailed assessments. Those within the scope of provisional assessment have extra criteria: the cap on costs for those cases going no further than provisional assessment, and the special rules for oral hearings.

CPR 47.20 sets the basic rule. There is a rebuttable presumption that the receiving party is entitled to the costs of the assessment unless an Act, rule or practice direction provides otherwise. No Acts are immediately relevant in personal injury claims. The rules in Part 36 may provide otherwise.

The court also has discretion to make a different order. The court shall have regard to all the circumstances, including the conduct of all parties, the amount by which the bill has been reduced, and whether it was reasonable to claim or dispute a particular item in the bill.

Relevant conduct may be the receiving party's failure to negotiate, and instead escalating through the assessment procedure; receiving parties withholding material that the court or paying party reasonably needs to consider; paying parties making unreasonably low offers unsupported by reasonable arguments; or failure to comply with the detailed assessment procedure.

CPR 47.20(4) confirms Part 36 applies with stated modification in detailed assessment proceedings, and such offers are covered in the section below called 'Part 36 costs offers'. Part 36 has automatic consequences in certain circumstances as to which party gets the costs of the assessment.

If the paying party has made another type of offer, such as a Calderbank or open offer, and that offer is not beaten, the court will usually make a different order for costs of the assessment. That may be costs from the date of the offer, with the receiving party recovering costs down to its date. The longer ago the offer was made, the more of the costs the paying party will recover. Brooke LJ said in *Crosbie v Munroe* [2003] 1 WLR 2033 at [35]:

> *If the costs judge or district judge considers that the receiving party ought to have accepted an offer made before the Part 8 proceedings commenced, then he is likely to conclude that the paying party should receive all his costs, including any costs involved in the subsequent Part 8 proceedings.*

Even if the paying party does not beat its own offer, the court still has discretion regarding the order if the bill is reduced substantially. Perhaps half or more would invoke that power.

Method of assessing costs of assessment

CPR 47.20(5) says the court will usually summarily assess the assessment costs at the conclusion of the detailed assessment proceedings. That works perfectly if the assessment concludes at a detailed assessment or an oral hearing. The court can also make a summary assessment on paper at a provisional assessment. But if the costs have been settled in advance of the hearing, a summary assessment may not be practical or procedurally possible. First, a Part 36 acceptance might create a deemed order for another detailed assessment. Second, there is the prohibition in PD44 9.7 that a court cannot make an order for summary assessment by a 'costs officer' (in the CPR's defined meaning of a district judge, costs judge or authorised court officer, rather than the officers with that title in the Senior Courts Costs Office), so a judge could not come on board just to assess the costs of the assessment. The reasoning is that a summary assessment should be made only by a judge who already knows the case. The practical solution often followed by the parties where costs cannot be agreed is to apply for an order for costs in principle, and then to seek a forthwith summary assessment at the hearing of the application, in accordance with PD47 9.1 and 9.2(b). It might be cheating, but it is more proportionate and quicker than a detailed assessment.

Making payment

Once costs are agreed, all that remains is to make payment. Payment will ordinarily be made to the solicitor on record for the receiving party. The solicitor has a known claim on the money; after all, if the client did not have a liability to pay the solicitor, the costs would not be recoverable under the indemnity principle.

If payment is made to the receiving party in person, for instance after he has terminated his retainer with his solicitors, the paying party runs the risk of having to pay the money again to the solicitors. The court will protect funds owed to a solicitor by a client if the paying party colludes with the receiving party to cheat the solicitor of payment, or, more likely, the paying party was on notice of the solicitor claim on the monies: *Khans Solicitors v Chifuntwe* [2014] 1 WLR 1185. The Supreme Court recognised the solicitors' rights over the fruits of litigation for payment of fees as the 'solicitor's equitable lien' in *Gavin Edmondson Solicitors Ltd v Haven Insurance Co Ltd* [2018] 1 WLR 2052.

ADR

When detailed assessment does not result in narrowing of the issues and a compromise being reached, there is no getting away from the fact that it can take a long time – months, years – to get a provisional assessment or detailed assessment hearing. Alternative Dispute Resolution in costs is increasingly popular. There are specialist services with an expert panel. Something akin to provisional assessment in which determinations are made on the papers is available for costs up to £100,000, binding or non-binding, and mediations are available for larger bills. Boosted by the Covid-19 lockdown, remote costs ADR is a more developed option now.

While a swifter resolution is attractive, many parties are still reticent to commit. In part it may be unfamiliarity, particularly among lawyers. In part it may be mistrust of the results, and reluctance to take the chance. It is easier to forlornly resign oneself to a judge's assessment. Receiving parties may think a non-specialist judge will be more generous than a specialist mediator.

Whatever the misgivings, it is well worth a try.

CHAPTER NINE
COSTS OFFERS, INTEREST AND QOCS

Costs offers

Several different types of offer can be made for costs. There are two purposes to making offers. First, to try to secure a settlement. Second, to protect oneself against having to pay the costs (or future costs) of an assessment.

Parties can make offers in any form they choose at any time they want, subject to certain specific requirements at specific stages of the assessment, and can make multiple offers.

Without Prejudice offers

An offer that is 'without prejudice' only, i.e. not followed by 'save as to costs', cannot be referred to at the end of assessment. It is private between the parties. Thus it offers no protection against assessment costs because the court cannot take it into account.

Without prejudice offers tend to be made by paying parties in the very early stages of negotiations where some information is missing and the offer is necessarily tentative. The offer will also usually request that information.

Telephone offers

The telephone is an important tool of costs negotiation. There is no more effective means of getting a resolution than discussion with the opponent's representative. Telephone offers will usually be 'global' offers, i.e. they include all costs and interest.

Parties should ordinarily make it clear at the outset of the call that it is a 'without prejudice' discussion, and record that in the attendance note.

Open offers

Any party can make an open offer, which is one that may be cited in court at any time.

Plus, PD47 8.3 requires that when points of dispute are served, they must be accompanied by an open letter stating what sum, if any, the paying party offers. That could be an offer for the precise amount to which the PODs reduce the bill. It could also be a round number. This requirement replaces the former requirement to make individual offers for each item challenged in points of dispute, and it makes sense if the offer correlates with the challenges in the points of dispute. If a paying party omits to send such an open letter, a receiving party should request it and in its continuing absence might apply for an 'unless' order, which might specify that unless the offer is made points of dispute will be struck out. The rules do not provide that the points of dispute are a nullity if the open offer is omitted or late, but the court may take the failure into account when dealing with costs of the assessment.

PD47 8.3 is not a compulsion to offer more than nil. Nil may be appropriate in some cases, depending on the points of dispute or the circumstances.

A paying party's representatives who might find themselves without instructions to make an offer should say no sum is offered in the open letter in order to comply with the practice direction, and improve on the position later on instructions with an actual offer.

The open letter is a formality. Paying parties may also make a protective offer at any time. The offer from the open letter is rarely accepted, as the receiving party knows it typically represent the paying party's best-case scenario.

The open offer is primarily for the benefit of the court. If the case goes to provisional assessment, an open offer will not go in a sealed envelope. It will allow the judge to see roughly what effect the PODs have on the bill.

The receiving party may use the open offer in support of an application for an interim costs certificate.

Calderbank offers

Named after the case of *Calderbank v Calderbank* [1976] Fam 93, these are offers that are made 'without prejudice save as to costs'. They are admissible at the end of the detailed assessment. They can be made as a global offer, but normally exclude interest, Part 8 costs-only costs and assessment costs.

Calderbank offers are especially useful to a party wishing to avoid the automatic costs consequences of a Part 36 offer. Part 36 can have a 'Russian doll' effect by opening up continuing rights to costs: if separate Part 36 offers were accepted for damages, then for costs of the claim, then for costs of the assessment, that would create three rights to detailed assessment.

Part 36 costs offers

With effect from 1 April 2013, offers for costs could be made pursuant to a specially modified version of Part 36.

CPR 36.5 provides that a Part 36 offer must:

- Be in writing;
- Make it clear that it is a Part 36 offer (i.e. be headed 'Part 36 offer');
- Specifies a period of not less than 21 days in which the offer may be accepted (called the 'relevant period');
- Specifies that the paying party will pay the receiving party's costs if the offer is accepted within the relevant period;
- State whether it relates to all or part of the claim;
- Specifies whether it takes into account any counter-claim.

CPR 36.16(1) provides that a Part 36 offer will be treated as 'without prejudice except as to costs'; but most letters state that also.

A Part 36 costs offer will usually be made for substantive costs, and the costs payable if the offer is accepted are the assessment costs.

However, where assessment costs themselves are in dispute, a Part 36 offer could be made for those. The additional costs payable if that offer was accepted would be the costs of arguing about the assessment costs. But, in most cases if there were a swift assessment there would be no such further costs.

Paying parties would be wise NOT to make Part 36 costs offers in unlitigated cases, unless the offer is very unlikely to be accepted and/or costs-only proceedings will be issued. The reason is that acceptance would create a right to additional costs for negotiating the amount, when otherwise none would exist. On that latter point, see *Jones v ALCOM* (HHJ Mitchell, Central London County Court, 11 November 2011, unreported).

Global offers – a party cannot make a global offer as a Part 36 offer. A costs inclusive offer is not a Part 36 offer (*Mitchell v James* [2002] EWCA Civ 997). A party wishing to make a global offer would have to make a telephone offer or a Calderbank offer.

Conditional offers – it is not possible to make a Part 36 offer subject to conditions, e.g. provision of missing information.

Making the Offer – a Part 36 offer has to be 'served': CPR 36.7. Serve on the representative on court record who can accept service. Parties should be cautious about emailing a Part 36 offer, because the rules on email service are arcane: PD6 paragraph 4. Sending the offer by email may be an error of procedure that risks robbing the offer of its consequences.

Late Offers – if a party wishes to make a Part 36 costs offer when there are fewer than 21 days until the start of the hearing or until the date set for provisional assessment, instead of saying 'If this offer is accepted within the next 21 days…', the offer should say 'If this offer is accepted before the start of the hearing on [date]…' or 'If this offer is accepted before the start of the provisional assessment on [date]…', as appropriate.

Acceptance – acceptance of a Part 36 offer must be served in writing. Follow the same approach as above for making an offer. A written acceptance should specify the date and the amount of the offer and state that it is it is accepted.

Open unless withdrawn – a Part 36 offer can be accepted at any time before the court assesses the costs unless the offeror has expressly withdrawn the offer in writing. A party could therefore try for a better deal in telephone negotiations, and if that fails then accept the Part 36 offer. A Part 36 offer cannot be accepted once a provisional assessment has been made: *Shepherd v Hughes* (HHJ Seys Llewellyn QC, County Court at Mold, 28 January 2015, unreported). This is a departure from the common law position, in which a rejection or a counter offer means the offer is no longer open for acceptance.

To illustrate, this is how the position differs from a Calderbank offer:

Calderbank position	Part 36 position
Paying party makes a Calderbank offer for £5,000.	Paying party makes a Part 36 offer for substantive costs of £5,000.
Receiving party counter offers £6,000.	Receiving party counter offers £6,000.
Paying party rejects the counter offer.	Paying party rejects the counter offer.
Receiving party cannot accept £5,000 unless paying party remakes that offer, as the counter offer was an implied rejection of the £5,000 meaning that it is no longer available.	Claimant can still accept £5,000.

Withdrawal – an offer can be withdrawn only if it has not been accepted and its relevant period has expired; if the relevant period has not expired, follow the procedure in CPR 36.10. To withdraw, serve notice in writing on the opposing party. State the date and amount of the offer and that it is withdrawn.

Sunset offers – the 2015 rule amendments allow Part 36 offers that expire automatically at the end of their relevant period. This is a useful tool to apply extra pressure to your opponent to decide quickly whether to accept. However, don't make it your only offer. Once withdrawn automatically, you can't rely on it at the end of the assessment. Perhaps use in later stages of negotiations, when you have already made an offer you can fall back on.

Multiple offers – each side may (intentionally or unintentionally) have multiple Part 36 offers open for acceptance at any one time.

Right to assessment costs – on acceptance of a Part 36 offer within its relevant period there is a right to additional costs. In litigated cases, acceptance of a Part 36 offer creates a deemed order for assessment costs. In pre-litigation cases, acceptance of a Part 36 offer creates an agreement to pay costs of the negotiations.

Acceptance outside the relevant period – if either party accepts a counter offer outside of the relevant period, there are no automatic costs consequences. There is no deemed order. Either the parties must agree costs terms by consent or the court will have to decide them on an application. The default position is that the offeree should have costs until the end of the relevant period, and the offeror gets costs thereafter: CPR 36.13(4)(b) and (5). Thus, the outcome depends on which party made the offer that has been accepted late.

Indemnity costs – indemnity costs do not apply automatically where a Part 36 offer is accepted after its relevant period: *Fitzpatrick Contractors v Tyco Fire* [2010] 2 Costs LR 115. Late acceptance is permitted by the CPR unless an offer is withdrawn. It would discourage constant review, re-evaluation and settlements if there were costs penalties for late acceptance. Indemnity costs apply only under CPR 36.17 when a party fails to beat an offer at trial (or at assessment, in the context of costs offers).

<u>Costs consequences for defendant beating own offer</u>

If the defendant beats its own Part 36 costs offer on assessment, the claimant will ordinarily have to pay the defendant's costs from the expiry of the winning offer's relevant period: CPR 36.17(3). Although the rule does not specify it, there is a corresponding presumption that the claimant gets costs down to the expiry of the relevant period. The court may set off one entitlement against the other.

Costs Consequences for claimant beating own offer

The Offers to Settle in Civil Proceedings Order 2013 (SI 2013/93) paved the way for enhancement awards to claimants who beat their own offers. The relevant rules are in CPR 36.17(4).

If the paying party does not accept the receiving party's Part 36 costs offer but then fails to beat it at assessment, then unless the court orders otherwise the claimant is entitled to:

- interest at up to 10% above base rate on the assessed costs;
- costs on the indemnity basis from the expiry of the winning offer's relevant period (but they will be still subject to the provisional assessment cap, where applicable, per *Lowin v W Portsmouth & Co Ltd* [2018] 1 WLR 1890);
- interest on the indemnity costs at up to 10% above base rate;
- 10% of the assessed sum (5% for any balance above £500,000) subject to a £75,000 cap, as long as there has been no prior order for this 10% sum.

It can be an expensive business for the paying party.

The High Court has confirmed that those provisions apply in detailed assessment proceedings, and while the court has discretion to find all or any of them would be unjust (under CPR 36.17(4), considering the factors in CPR 36.17(5)), there would have to be a clear reason why one was unjust and not others: *Cashman v Mid Essex Hospital Services NHS Trust* [2015] 3 Costs LO 411. It seems from that judgment that a significant reduction of the bill of costs would not make the awards unjust. It is now difficult to imagine circumstances where they may be unjust. Indeed, Stewart J has since held in *JLE (a child) v Warrington & Halton Hospitals NHS Foundation Trust* [2002] 1 WLR 934 it would be unusual for the circumstances to make some but not all of the orders unjust.

Note that the rule says the claimant is entitled to those enhancements, not his solicitors. While solicitors' retainers will almost certainly make provision for the client paying costs and interest to them, they do not generally make provision for the 10% additional amount being paid over. That money continues to belong to the receiving party personally, and the paying party would be entitled to pay it to him unless a copy of the retainer or a signed mandate were produced for it to be paid to the solicitors instead. It was common ground in *Cashman* that the 10% additional amount belonged to the claimant according to a report of the hearing, but it was not recorded in the judgment.

Costs Offers and Interest

PD47 19 provides:

> *Where an offer to settle is made, whether under Part 36 or otherwise, it should specify whether or not it is intended to be inclusive of the cost of preparation of the bill, interest and VAT. Unless the offer states otherwise it will be treated as being inclusive of these.*

It is best practice to specify whether or not the offer includes bill preparation, interest and VAT rather than rely on the default position. A Part 36 costs offer must include applicable interest to the end of the offer's relevant period. CPR 36.5 provides:

> *(4) A Part 36 offer which offers to pay or offers to accept a sum of money will be treated as inclusive of all interest until –*
>
> *(a) the date on which the [relevant period] expires.*

If the Part 36 costs offer is specifying the position on interest, that is what it must specify.

An offer which is expressed to exclude interest is not a Part 36 offer and cannot have Part 36 consequences: *King v City of London Corporation* [2020] 1 WLR 1517. Before the Jackson reforms in 2013 which extended Part 36 to detailed assessment, Part 47 provided for Calderbank offers under CPR 47.19. Those offers were generally made excluding interest, for ease of seeing straight away if they were successful after assessment. That may explain why interest exclusive purported

Part 36 offers arose in detailed assessments, where previously there had been no issue of interest exclusive offers under Part 36.

When working out if a Part 36 offer has been successful after an assessment, especially a paying party's Part 36 costs offer, interest to the end of the relevant period must be added to the assessed sum so that the grand total may be compared to the offer. See the instructions in the next section, and use the end of the relevant period as the last day for interest.

In claims worth less than £5,000, interest may not be applicable. See the next section on interest.

Interest on costs

Interest may apply to costs under s17 Judgments Act 1838 in the High Court and s74 County Courts Act 1984 in the County Court if there has been a judgment or order for costs.

Interest is not part of the definition of 'costs' in CPR 44.1(1). A right to interest is separate to a right to costs. If a judgment or order (including a deemed order) creates the right to costs, then there may also be a right to interest on those costs. To put it more simply, getting costs does not mean you definitely get interest on costs as well.

Fixed costs and interest

In Part 7 proceedings, if a Part 36 offer is accepted giving an entitlement to Section IIIA costs there is not also an automatic or deemed order for costs so there would be no right to interest on the fixed costs. The entitlement is not enough. Likewise, the entitlement to assessed costs under CPR 36.13(1) is not enough. Interest applies in those circumstances because a deemed order for detailed assessment on the standard basis is created by CPR 44.9(1). CPR 44.9(4) spells out that interest applies. There is no equivalent provision creating a deemed order for fixed costs under CPR 36.20. This is the problem that was considered by the House of Lords in *Legal Aid Board v Russell* [1991] 2 AC 317.

Calculating interest on costs

This is a summary of when interest applies, or not:

Any County Court claim in which the costs offer is £5,000 or less	No interest
Any claim where there are no proceedings	No interest
Any claim in which the costs offer is over £5,000, there are proceedings and an order for costs/assessment	Interest at the rate of 8% p.a.
Any claim in which CPR 36.17(4) consequences are ordered	Interest at the rate of 10% above base rate p.a. after the offer's relevant period, 8% p.a. before

If interest applies the next step is to work out the amount.

It is wrong to simply work out, say, 8% of the offer and add it on as interest. That 8% could only be accrued if the costs were outstanding for a whole year; it is the annual rate of interest. If interest builds up for less time, the amount of interest will be less.

Step 1: Work out the date from which interest on the costs runs. This will be the date of the order for costs (e.g. consent order, court order, or deemed order under a Part 36 acceptance (for which, see CPR 44.9(4) – and NB there is no deemed order when a Part 36 offer is accepted before proceedings have been started per CPR 44.9(2), and thus interest does not run from that date either)).

Step 2: Work out the date to which interest runs. If calculating interest to include in a Part 36 offer that date always be 21 days after the date of your Part 36 offer.

Step 3: Check if there have been any payments on account of costs ('POA').

- If a POA was made before the date from which interest runs, you only need to calculate interest on the remaining balance offered or allowed in addition to that POA.
- If a POA was made after the date from which interest runs, you will need to divide up the interest period. Note the date of the payment on account.

Step 4: Decide if interest stops on account of delays.

N252

- Interest runs for three months from the date of the order, unless the court has shortened or extended the time to commence detailed assessment proceedings. If the receiving party has not served an N252 by that date, interest stops running. Note deadline date if the N252 was late.
- Interest starts again when the receiving party serves an N252. Note the date of service of N252.

Assessment hearing

- Interest stops running again six months from the date of the order (unless the court varied the time) if the receiving party has not requested an assessment hearing by then. Note the date if interest stopped running.
- Interest starts again when the receiving party requests an assessment hearing. Note the date when the hearing was requested (or find out: ask the court).

Disregard the days for which the N252 or assessment request were late. The receiving party will get no interest for those days.

Step 5: Calculation

This looks more complicated than it is.
If there are no POAs, and no delay, simply work out interest using this formula:

Costs offer or assessed sum
× 8 ÷ 100 [to give you the yearly 8% figure]
÷ 365 [to give you the daily rate]
× number of days between the date from which interest runs and the end of the relevant period
[which is the period for which interest runs]
= the interest amount.

- If there was POA before the date from which interest runs, start the calculation with the balance of costs rather than the total of the offer.

- If there was a POA after the date from which interest runs, do the calculation twice. First, for the full amount of the offer for the number of days until the POA. Second, on the balance after the POA for the remaining number of days until the end of the relevant period.

- If there has been any period of delay, remove the number of days over which interest was not running.

You may need to apply any combination of those steps depending on the facts of your case.

Interest on assessment costs

Interest on assessment costs only runs from the date of a final, interim of default costs certificate: CPR 47.20(6). One of those is unlikely to have been issued by the time the parties come to deal with assessment costs. In most cases settled by negotiation or assessment, there will have been no such certificate and payment will be made before a final costs certificate is obtained (or needed). Therefore interest on assessment costs rarely arises. If it does, it should be calculated using the same principles as above.

Qualified One-Way Costs Shifting (QOCS)

'Costs shifting' means that one party to the litigation can recover its costs from another. 'One-way' means, in this context, that only the claimant can recover its costs from the defendant. The defendant cannot recover its costs from the claimant. 'Qualified' means that there are certain circumstances where the defendant can recover its costs.

At first glance QOCS appears unfair (and it may be unfair upon further consideration too). It helps to understand it in context. QOCS was a part of the Jackson reforms. The former regime of costs recovery in this jurisdiction allowed parties (who were predominantly claimants) to purchase insurance against paying their own and adverse costs and to enter into no win, no fee agreements with their solicitors which resulted in a claim for an uplift on costs (a success fee) if the claim was won. Such success fees and insurance premiums were recoverable from paying parties as part of the costs. That regime had flaws and was abolished. With effect from 1 April 2013, parties would pay the success fees and insurance premiums under such arrangements themselves. So that claimants could fund that, there were two other changes. General damages were increased by 10% (*Simmonds v Castle* [2012] EWCA Civ 1039 and [2012] EWCA Civ 1288) and QOCS was introduced.

Scope and operation

The way QOCS works is not by stopping an order for the defendant's costs being made, but by stopping the defendant enforcing payment. The court should proceed as it would have done before right up until the point where the defendant attempts to enforce payment, at which point enforcement should be dismissed unless an exception applies.

Broadly speaking, QOCS applies only to claims for damages for personal injuries or for fatalities. CPR 44.13(1) sets out the full scope.

The benefit of QOCS falls only to a party making a claim for damages for personal injuries: *Wagenaar v Weekend Travel Ltd (trading as Ski Weekend) (Serradj, third party)* [2015] 1 WLR 1968. That can include the claimant, a counterclaimant, or a party making a Part 20 claim: CPR 44.13(2). If the counterclaim or the Part 20 claim do not include damages for personal injury, the fact that the claimant has a claim for personal injury does not extend QOCS to the counterclaimant or Part 20 claimant.

QOCS does not apply where the claimant has entered into a pre-commencement funding arrangement, i.e. a conditional fee agreement or insurance premium pre-dating 1 April 2013 per CPR 44.17. That applies even where that pre-commencement funding arrangement was ended before the conclusion of the claim: *Catalano v Epley-Tyas Development Group* [2017] 4 Costs LR 769. That is the only exclusion; and QOCS thus applies retrospectively to a claim pre-dating 1 April 2013 without such a funding arrangement. See *Wagenaar*. There was a long tail of cases with pre-commencement funding arrangements so QOCS took a while to take hold.

QOCS does extend to an appeal in a claim for damages for personal injuries: *Parker v Butler* [2016] 3 Costs LR 435. It is also generally accepted that QOCS extends to detailed assessment, and an appeal from detailed assessment.

Exceptions

'Qualifications' or exceptions to the regime fall into two camps: those where the costs order can be enforced without the court's permission, and those where the court's permission is needed.

In the first camp, CPR 44.14(1) says than an order for costs against a claimant can be enforced up the value of orders for damages and interest in the claimant's favour. A claimant could come away empty handed because of that. It is especially relevant in detailed assessment proceedings (and appeals from detailed assessment). By then, the claimant will already have damages. If the claimant is ordered to pay any of the defendant's costs of the assessment, the defendant can enforce that order up to the value of any damages.

A note of caution: CPR 44.14(1) specifically says 'orders for damages and interest'. That is to read literally, and it narrows the application of the rule. Cases that settle by Tomlin order or Part 36 acceptance (unless perhaps judgment is entered after 14 days where the money has not been paid) do not involve 'orders for damages': *Cartwright v Venduct Engineering Ltd* [2018] 1 WLR 6137. The Civil Procedure Rules Committee has declined to amend the rule to accommodate sums under a Tomlin order but has apparently not considered a change for Part 36 offers.

Where damages and interest are ring-fenced by the mode of settlement, the Court of Appeal has twice held that defendant's costs can be set off against claimant's costs under CPR 44.12: *Howe v MIB (No 2)* [2020] Costs LR 297 and *Adelekun v Ho (No 2)* [2020] Costs LR 317. *Adelekun* is proceeding to the Supreme Court on that point.

Also in the first camp, CPR 44.15(1) provides that orders against a claimant can be enforced in full against the claimant when the proceedings have been struck out because:

- The claimant disclosed no reasonable grounds for bringing the claim; or
- The proceedings were an abuse of process; or
- Just disposal of the proceedings is likely to be obstructed by the claimant's conduct or a third party acting with the claimant's knowledge an on his behalf.

These reasons are similar to the court's powers to strike out a statement of case in CPR 3.4(2). In costs disputes, it is particularly relevant to the cases discussed in the section 'No proceedings and no agreement to pay costs', which are dismissed often on one of the first two grounds.

In the second camp, CPR 44.16(1) allows orders against a claimant to be enforced to the full value where the court gives its permission because the claimant was 'fundamentally dishonest'. That is a phrase that is readily understood, but hard to define. It is a matter for the court's judgment. CPR 44.16(2) sets out other similar exceptions for claims for the benefit of persons other than the claimant or a dependent within the meaning of s1(3) Fatal Accidents Act 1976, or where a claim is made for the claimant's benefit to which QOCS does not apply. Those may be the rarest exceptions.

If CPR 44.15 or 44.16 apply, they lift the cap on defendant's costs under CPR 45.29F, per sub-section (10) of that rule. The defendant could recover more than post portal costs in those circumstances.

CHAPTER TEN
COSTS APPEALS

This is a very brief summary of an expansive topic.

Costs appeals fall into two categories: appeals against the order for costs, and appeals against the assessment of costs.

Only a court decision can be appealed. Parties are stuck with anything they agree between themselves (except for consequential orders agreed after a judgment is given).

'Appeals against the order for costs' means appeals against court decisions about which party gets costs, or to what extent, or an order for fixed costs. It must be an order made by the court; there is no appeal against a deemed order for costs.

'Appeals against the assessment of costs' fall into two further categories: appeals against assessments made by authorised court officers; and appeals against assessments made by any other judge. The differences here are purely procedural and it is convenient to explain them first.

Part 47 appeals

Authorised court officers who assess costs currently sit only in the Senior Courts Costs Office, and have the title 'Costs Officer'. That can be a source of confusion. 'Costs Officer' is defined by CPR 41.1(1) as (i) a costs judge; (ii) a District Judge; or (iii) an authorised court officer. The title 'Costs Officer' has nothing to do with the CPR meaning of costs officer.

Permission to appeal an assessment by an authorised court officer is not required: CPR 47.21.

Per CPR 47.22, the appeal will go to a costs judge or a master in the SCCO, being the only place authorised court officers can be found.

An appeal from an authorised court officer is a **re-hearing**. Therefore it is not necessary to show that the SCCO Costs Officer was 'wrong', as the assessment is re-done. However, in practice it can help to show that the costs officer was indeed wrong as it may help persuade the costs judge to come to a different conclusion. The decisions most often appealed are on points of law, and there is often a right and a wrong answer.

It is not uncommon to appeal only certain parts of an SCCO Costs Officer's assessment. The appellant may think the assessment was wrong or unsatisfactory in only certain respects, and it is in the interests of the overriding objective to narrow the issues. Procedurally that does not appear to be a problem. Costs Judges have also remitted assessments to SCCO Costs Officers to finish off the assessment after deciding key points.

Part 52 appeals

Every other costs appeal, including those against costs orders and assessments by judges other than authorised court officers, is made under Part 52.

Permission to appeal is required. Permission can be obtained either from the judge who makes the order by a request at the end of the hearing, or by applying to the appeal court.

A Part 52 appeal is normally a **review** of the decision of the lower court: CPR 52.11(1). There is a restriction on admission of fresh evidence for appeals under CPR 52.11(2). In certain circumstances it can be done (see *Ladd v Marshall* [1954] 1 WLR 1489), but generally the appeal court will consider the same material that was before the lower court. Therefore, to win the appeal, the appellant must show that the decision of the lower court was wrong or procedurally irregular: CPR 52.11(3).

No stay

An appeal does not create an automatic stay on the decision of the lower court: CPR 52.7. Therefore if costs have been assessed or an order for a payment on account was made, payment must still be made within the 14 days under CPR 44.7 or such other time as the court specified unless and until the court grants a stay of execution. A request for a stay of execution can be included in the appellant's notice. As there is a risk the receiving party may enforce in the meantime it is common practice to satisfy the orders of the lower court. If an appeal is allowed, any money paid will be refundable. Payment might be withheld and a stay of execution might be sought in cases where there was a real concern about whether money would be refunded, e.g. financial difficulty of opponent (including their solicitors).

Time limit for appeals

All appeals must be made within 21 days. The start of that 21 period is the day on which the decision or the assessment was made. If the assessment was made over multiple days, the time begins from the last day – as long as it was not an assessment made by an authorised court officer: CPR 47.14(7) extends the time only for Part 52 appeals.

If an oral hearing following provisional assessment ends up being adjourned part heard, the time to appeal runs from the date of each decision and not the date of the last hearing. CPR 47.14(7) does not apply in provisional assessments, per PD47 14.2(1). If an oral hearing is adjourned part heard and there is any chance an appeal may be pursued, an advocate might sensibly cut in with a request for an extension of time to appeal.

What sort of things can be appealed?

The appeals with the best prospects raise points of law. They contend that the lower court was wrong on the law, such as misconstruing or misapplying a statute or rule, or construing a document wrongly in light of what the law says about construction. In such cases it is possible to say that the judge was outright 'wrong'.

Appeals against exercises of discretion are harder. Many awards in principle and assessments of costs are discretionary. The appellant has to show that the decision was outside the reasonable range of the judge's discretion. The fact that the appeal court might have made a different order from within that range is not enough. The trick is often to present an appeal against an exercise of discretion as an appeal on a point of law by identifying some way in which the judge misdirected himself on the law which led to a mistaken exercise of discretion.

Appeals against findings of fact and case management decisions in the assessment are very hard to win. A great deal of latitude is afforded to the view of the judge who heard and had the 'feel' of a case.

For further information on the legal principles, *Civil Procedure 2020*, known generally as the 'White Book' is a good source. See notes 47.24.2 and 52.1.8ff.

Starting an appeal

The party appealing must complete an appellant's notice in Form N161, which needs to be accompanied by grounds of appeal. Grounds of appeal 'must be set out on a separate sheet attached to the appellant's notice and must set out, in simple language, clearly and concisely, why the order of the lower court was wrong or unjust because of a serious procedural or other irregularity': PD52B 4.2(d).

The court fees for appeals are as follows:

	County Court	**High Court**	**Fee number in current Civil Proceedings Fees Order**
Appeal from small claims track	£120	n/a	2.3(a)
Appeal against an order for costs	£140	£240	2.3(b) and 2.2 respectively
Appeal against a summary assessment	£140	£240	2.3(b) and 2.2 respectively
Appeal against a detailed assessment or any decision made in detailed assessment proceedings	£231	£231	5.4

Skeleton arguments and transcripts

Skeleton arguments are optional in County Court and High Court appeals, but the appellant should consider whether a skeleton argument will assist the court, especially if the appeal raises points of law: PD52B 8.3. A skeleton argument can be filed later; it does not need to accompany the appellant's notice.

It is common to order a transcript of the hearing before the lower court. A form EX107 must be completed and sent to the court. For the Royal Court of Justice, it should be addressed to the Court Recording and Transcription Unit (rcj.cratu@hmcts.gsi.gov.uk). The transcript must be prepared by one of the six member companies of the approved court transcription panel. One should be nominated in EX107 and contacted to place the order before or at the same time the EX107 is filed. A list can be found in Form EX107GN.

Be aware that transcripts of judgments must be approved by the judge before they can be released to the parties. That process can take weeks or months. Be cautious when estimating when the transcript will become available.

Skeleton arguments are commonly prepared only once the transcript is available.

Where to file papers

Appeal papers must be filed at the appropriate appeal court. The appeal court depends on the lower court and the judge who heard the case. An appeal should be made to a judge or court of the next tier up.

If it was an assessment by an authorised court office in the SCCO, the appeal should be filed at the SCCO.

If it is a High Court case, the papers should be filed at the District Registry or in the appropriate division at the Royal Court of Justice, as the case may be. In London, the papers will be filed electronically on the CE-File platform.

If it is a County Court case, the appeal must be filed at the appeal centre listed in Table A at the end of PD52B. Beware of London County Court cases. Table A does not work for those. There are special provisions when the 'appropriate office' for the detailed assessment would be the County Court hearing centre at:

- Barnet,
- Brentford,
- Bromley,
- Central London,
- Clerkenwell and Shoreditch,
- Croydon,
- Edmonton,
- Ilford,
- Kingston,
- Mayor's and City of London,
- Romford,
- Uxbridge,
- Wandsworth,
- Willesden.

PD47 4.2(2)(a) requires that requests for detailed assessment in cases at those hearing centres are filed at the SCCO; and PD47 4.2(2)(c) says an appeal from such a case must be filed in the County Court at Central London.

Permission stage

In Part 52 appeals, the court will often give directions for the filing of a transcript of the lower court's judgment or for skeleton arguments and bundles. It will then make a decision about permission to appeal on the papers. The court will be deciding only whether the appeal has a real prospect of success or whether there is some other compelling reason to hear the appeal. Essentially, the appellant must get the appeal court interested in the point and show that there is something to it.

If permission to appeal if refused on the papers, within seven days of receiving the notice the appellant may request reconsideration at a hearing. The court will then list a short hearing. The approach on a hearing is usually to take the circuit judge through the best few points in an attempt to show an appeal has a real prospect of success.

The respondent's position

The appellant's notice and any other grounds should be served on the respondent, but nevertheless the respondent has a very limited role unless and until permission to appeal is granted. The respondent might file limited written submissions on whether the threshold for permission to appeal is met, but that is usually unnecessary and rarely done.

The respondent is not ordinarily entitled to costs at the permission to appeal stage: PD52B 8.1.

If permission is not needed or was granted by the lower court, the appeal starts as a full appeal and the respondent should start preparation as soon as the appeal is served.

A respondent who wants to cross appeal or who says the lower court's decision should be upheld for additional reasons that were not given in the judgment should file a respondent's notice. A court fee is payable that matches the fees for an appellant's notice.

A respondent should consider whether it will prepare a skeleton argument on the same basis as the appellant. In the absence of any order to the contrary, any respondent's skeleton argument must be filed, served and inserted in the bundles no later than 7 days before the appeal hearing: PD52B 6.6.

Appeal bundle

A bundle of the papers relevant to the appeal must be compiled. There is a specific running order: see PD52B 6.4. It must be filed within 35 days of filing the appellant's notice: PD52B 6.3, unless the court gives other directions (the County Court often does; the court does not want to be cluttered up with bundles sooner than they are needed). If permission is not needed or was granted by the lower court, the bundle must be served at the same time it is filed. Otherwise, it must be served within 14 days of permission to appeal being granted.

If a skeleton argument is appropriate but was not filed with the appellant's notice, the date of filing the bundle is often the last date for skeleton arguments. The court however may make a different order and require a skeleton argument and a transcript before the bundle is due.

Documents often need adding to the bundle after it has been filed and served. That is a bind. The best method is to send hole-punched and numbered pages with an amended index to the court and respondent so they can easily insert them. If page numbers need adding, the convention is to use decimal points to add them rather the renumber the whole bundle. For example, if extra pages need inserting after page 19, they might be numbered 19.1, 19.2, 19.3 etc. The transition to e-bundles will make the process of amendment of bundles less cumbersome, as a whole replacement bundle can be quickly filed and served.

Appeal hearing

Where permission is not needed or has been granted, the court may give directions for the appeal or may simply issue a notice of the appeal date.

The court may also list a rolled-up hearing for permission to appeal with the appeal to follow. Both parties attend and the court decides whether to grant or refuse permission and whether to allow or dismiss the appeal at the same time.

Appeals are likely to be conducted more strictly than an assessment hearing. The appellant presents the claim, the respondent replies, and the appellant may follow up shortly. Judgments may be given *ex tempore*, but are often reserved.

Appeal costs will be assessed if judgment is not reserved, so statements of costs in form N260 should be filed and served 24 hours in advance.

See PD52B for full details of County Court and High Court appeal procedure.

Second appeals

Second appeals on costs are possible where the court on the first appeal dismisses or allows the appeal (but not where permission to appeal was refused by the circuit judge; there is no appeal against a refusal of permission). The second appeals test must be satisfied; the appeal must raise an important point of principle or practice – and by definition, that must also be a point where the answer is not obvious. Only the Court of Appeal can grant permission for a second appeal. See CPR 52.7 and PD52C.

In rare cases, a 'leapfrog' may be granted, where a first appeal is assigned to the Court of Appeal thus skipping the circuit stage. There have been only a handful of such costs cases.

FURTHER READING

Inevitably this book cannot cover everything.

On matters of procedural law, *The White Book* is an excellent source for further information on topics such as additional liabilities, costs orders, costs budgeting, wasted costs and protective costs orders.

For more insight on the court's approach, see the Senior Courts Costs Office Guide:

https://www.gov.uk/government/publications/senior-courts-costs-office-guide
(accessed 26 July 2020).

Barrister Gordon Exall does a great service to the profession with his excellent and essential blog *Civil Litigation Brief*, keeping us up to date with developments and hot-off-the-press snippets of the important civil procedure cases:

https://www.civillitigationbrief.com
(accessed 31 July 2020).

GLOSSARY

CPR	Civil Procedure Rules
EL/PL Protocol	Pre-Action Protocol for Low Value Personal Injury (Employers' Liability and Public Liability) Claims
File/ filing	Send a document to the court.
Fixed costs	Costs prescribed by the *CPR* which are fixed in amount no matter the circumstances.
Fixed recoverable costs	Costs set out in the *CPR* which are calculated by a simple formula based on the amount of damages.
Jackson reforms	The interlocking package of costs reforms implemented on 1 April 2013 based on the recommendations of Lord Justice Jackson who had spent a year reviewing costs in civil litigation.
Portal	The online claims portal for bringing claims under the RTA Protocol or EL/PL Protocol.
Portal costs	The name used in this book for the *fixed costs* applicable to claims settling under the RTA or EL/PL Protocols which are set out in CPR 45 Section III.
Predictable costs	The scheme of fixed recoverable costs for road traffic accidents set out in CPR 45 Section II.
RTA Protocol	Pre-Action Protocol for Low Value Personal Injury Claims in Road Traffic Accidents
Section IIIA costs	The name used in this book for the *fixed recoverable costs* for claims that start under the RTA or EL/PL Protocols, but exit those Protocols before settlement, and which are set out in CPR 45 Section IIIA.

Serve	Send a document to another party by a method approved in CPR Part 6.
Success fee	A percentage of the profit costs charged as an additional cost by a solicitor under a CFA where he was won the claim for his client.

MORE BOOKS BY LAW BRIEF PUBLISHING

A selection of our other titles available now:-

'Covid-19, Homeworking and the Law – The Essential Guide to Employment and GDPR Issues' by Forbes Solicitors
'Covid-19, Force Majeure and Frustration of Contracts – The Essential Guide' by Keith Markham
'Covid-19 and Criminal Law – The Essential Guide' by Ramya Nagesh
'Covid-19 and Family Law in England and Wales – The Essential Guide' by Safda Mahmood
'Covid-19 and the Implications for Planning Law – The Essential Guide' by Bob Mc Geady & Meyric Lewis
'Covid-19, Residential Property, Equity Release and Enfranchisement – The Essential Guide' by Paul Sams and Louise Uphill
'Covid-19, Brexit and the Law of Commercial Leases – The Essential Guide' by Mark Shelton
'Covid-19 and the Law Relating to Food in the UK and Republic of Ireland – The Essential Guide' by Ian Thomas
'A Practical Guide to the General Data Protection Regulation (GDPR) – 2nd Edition' by Keith Markham
'Ellis on Credit Hire – Sixth Edition' by Aidan Ellis & Tim Kevan
'A Practical Guide to Working with Litigants in Person and McKenzie Friends in Family Cases' by Stuart Barlow
'Protecting Unregistered Brands: A Practical Guide to the Law of Passing Off' by Lorna Brazell
'A Practical Guide to Secondary Liability and Joint Enterprise Post-Jogee' by Joanne Cecil & James Mehigan

'A Practical Guide to the Pre-Action RTA Claims Protocol for Personal Injury Lawyers' by Antonia Ford

'A Practical Guide to Neighbour Disputes and the Law' by Alexander Walsh

'A Practical Guide to Forfeiture of Leases' by Mark Shelton

'A Practical Guide to Coercive Control for Legal Practitioners and Victims' by Rachel Horman

'A Practical Guide to Rights Over Airspace and Subsoil' by Daniel Gatty

'Tackling Disclosure in the Criminal Courts – A Practitioner's Guide' by Narita Bahra QC & Don Ramble

'A Practical Guide to the Law of Driverless Cars – Second Edition' by Alex Glassbrook, Emma Northey & Scarlett Milligan

'A Practical Guide to TOLATA Claims' by Greg Williams

'Artificial Intelligence – The Practical Legal Issues' by John Buyers

'A Practical Guide to the Law of Prescription in Scotland' by Andrew Foyle

'A Practical Guide to the Construction and Rectification of Wills and Trust Instruments' by Edward Hewitt

'A Practical Guide to the Law of Bullying and Harassment in the Workplace' by Philip Hyland

'How to Be a Freelance Solicitor: A Practical Guide to the SRA-Regulated Freelance Solicitor Model' by Paul Bennett

'A Practical Guide to Prison Injury Claims' by Malcolm Johnson

'A Practical Guide to the Small Claims Track' by Dominic Bright

'A Practical Guide to Advising Clients at the Police Station' by Colin Stephen McKeown-Beaumont

'A Practical Guide to Antisocial Behaviour Injunctions' by Iain Wightwick

'Practical Mediation: A Guide for Mediators, Advocates, Advisers, Lawyers, and Students in Civil, Commercial, Business, Property, Workplace, and Employment Cases' by Jonathan Dingle with John Sephton

'The Mini-Pupillage Workbook' by David Boyle

'A Practical Guide to Crofting Law' by Brian Inkster
'A Practical Guide to Spousal Maintenance' by Liz Cowell
'A Practical Guide to the Law of Domain Names and Cybersquatting' by Andrew Clemson
'A Practical Guide to the Law of Gender Pay Gap Reporting' by Harini Iyengar
'A Practical Guide to the Rights of Grandparents in Children Proceedings' by Stuart Barlow
'NHS Whistleblowing and the Law' by Joseph England
'Employment Law and the Gig Economy' by Nigel Mackay & Annie Powell
'A Practical Guide to Noise Induced Hearing Loss (NIHL) Claims' by Andrew Mckie, Ian Skeate, Gareth McAloon
'An Introduction to Beauty Negligence Claims – A Practical Guide for the Personal Injury Practitioner' by Greg Almond
'Intercompany Agreements for Transfer Pricing Compliance' by Paul Sutton
'Zen and the Art of Mediation' by Martin Plowman
'A Practical Guide to the SRA Principles, Individual and Law Firm Codes of Conduct 2019 – What Every Law Firm Needs to Know' by Paul Bennett
'A Practical Guide to Adoption for Family Lawyers' by Graham Pegg
'A Practical Guide to Industrial Disease Claims' by Andrew Mckie & Ian Skeate
'A Practical Guide to Redundancy' by Philip Hyland
'A Practical Guide to Vicarious Liability' by Mariel Irvine
'A Practical Guide to Applications for Landlord's Consent and Variation of Leases' by Mark Shelton
'A Practical Guide to Relief from Sanctions Post-Mitchell and Denton' by Peter Causton
'A Practical Guide to Equity Release for Advisors' by Paul Sams
'A Practical Guide to Unlawful Eviction and Harassment' by Stephanie Lovegrove
'A Practical Guide to the Law Relating to Food' by Ian Thomas

'A Practical Guide to Financial Services Claims' by Chris Hegarty
'The Law of Houses in Multiple Occupation: A Practical Guide to HMO Proceedings' by Julian Hunt
'A Practical Guide to Unlawful Eviction and Harassment' by Stephanie Lovegrove
'A Practical Guide to Solicitor and Client Costs' by Robin Dunne
'Occupiers, Highways and Defective Premises Claims: A Practical Guide Post-Jackson – 2nd Edition' by Andrew Mckie
'A Practical Guide to Financial Ombudsman Service Claims' by Adam Temple & Robert Scrivenor
'A Practical Guide to Advising Schools on Employment Law' by Jonathan Holden
'A Practical Guide to Running Housing Disrepair and Cavity Wall Claims: 2nd Edition' by Andrew Mckie & Ian Skeate
'A Practical Guide to Holiday Sickness Claims – 2nd Edition' by Andrew Mckie & Ian Skeate
'Arguments and Tactics for Personal Injury and Clinical Negligence Claims' by Dorian Williams
'A Practical Guide to QOCS and Fundamental Dishonesty' by James Bentley
'A Practical Guide to Drone Law' by Rufus Ballaster, Andrew Firman, Eleanor Clot
'A Practical Guide to Compliance for Personal Injury Firms Working With Claims Management Companies' by Paul Bennett
'A Practical Guide to the Landlord and Tenant Act 1954: Commercial Tenancies' by Richard Hayes & David Sawtell
'A Practical Guide to Dog Law for Owners and Others' by Andrea Pitt
'RTA Allegations of Fraud in a Post-Jackson Era: The Handbook – 2nd Edition' by Andrew Mckie
'RTA Personal Injury Claims: A Practical Guide Post-Jackson' by Andrew Mckie
'On Experts: CPR35 for Lawyers and Experts' by David Boyle
'An Introduction to Personal Injury Law' by David Boyle

‘A Practical Guide to Chronic Pain Claims’ by Pankaj Madan
‘A Practical Guide to Claims Arising from Fatal Accidents’ by James Patience
‘A Practical Guide to Subtle Brain Injury Claims’ by Pankaj Madan

These books and more are available to order online direct from the publisher at www.lawbriefpublishing.com, where you can also read free sample chapters. For any queries, contact us on 0844 587 2383 or mail@lawbriefpublishing.com.

Our books are also usually in stock at www.amazon.co.uk with free next day delivery for Prime members, and at good legal bookshops such as Wildy & Sons.

We are regularly launching new books in our series of practical day-to-day practitioners' guides. Visit our website and join our free newsletter to be kept informed and to receive special offers, free chapters, etc.

You can also follow us on Twitter at www.twitter.com/lawbriefpub.